The
Pontiac Uprising

The Pontiac Uprising
A Concise Account of the
Indian War of 1761

Thomas Guthrie Marquis

with

Pontiac—a Biographical Sketch
by Edson L. Whitney and Frances M. Perry

&

Ponteach—or
The Savages of America
a play by Robert Rogers

LEONAUR

The Pontiac Uprising: a Concise Account of the Indian War of 1761
by Thomas Guthrie Marquis
with
Pontiac—a Biographical Sketch
by Edson L. Whitney and Frances M. Perry
&
Ponteach—or The Savages of America
a play by Robert Rogers

First published in 1915 under the title
The War Chief of the Ottawas: a Chronicle of the Pontiac War

Published by Leonaur Ltd

Copyright in this form © 2010 Leonaur Ltd

ISBN: 978-1-84677-938-1 (hardcover)
ISBN: 978-1-84677-937-4 (softcover)

http://www.leonaur.com

Publisher's Notes

Contents

CHAPTER 1

The Times and the Men

There was rejoicing throughout the Thirteen Colonies, in the month of September 1760, when news arrived of the capitulation of Montreal. Bonfires flamed forth and prayers were offered up in the churches and meeting-houses in gratitude for deliverance from a foe that for over a hundred years had harried and had caused the Indians to harry the frontier settlements. The French armies were defeated by land; the French fleets were beaten at sea. The troops of the enemy had been removed from North America, and so powerless was France on the ocean that, even if success should crown her arms on the European continent, where the Seven Years' War was still raging, it would be impossible for her to transport a new force to America. The principal French forts in America were occupied by British troops. Louisbourg had been razed to the ground; the British flag waved over Quebec, Montreal, and Niagara, and was soon to be raised on all the lesser forts in the territory known as Canada. The Mississippi valley from the Illinois river southward alone remained to France. Vincennes on the Wabash and Fort Chartres on the Mississippi were the only posts in the hinterland occupied by French troops. These posts were under the government of Louisiana; but even these the American colonies were prepared to claim, basing the right on their 'sea to sea' charters.

The British in America had found the strip of land between the Alleghanies and the Atlantic far too narrow for a rapidly increasing population, but their advance westward had been barred by the French. Now, praise the Lord, the French were out of the way, and American traders and settlers could exploit the profitable fur-fields and the rich agricultural lands of the region beyond the mountains. True, the Indians were there, but these were not regarded as formidable foes. There was no longer any occasion to consider the Indians—so thought the colonists and the British officers in America. The red men had been a force to be reckoned with only because the French had supplied them with the sinews of war, but they might now be treated like other denizens of the forest— the bears, the wolves, and the wild cats. For this mistaken policy the British colonies were to pay a heavy price.

The French and the Indians, save for one exception, had been on terms of amity from the beginning. The reason for this was that the French had treated the Indians with studied kindness. The one exception was the Iroquois League or Six Nations. Champlain, in the first years of his residence at Quebec, had joined the Algonquins and Hurons in an attack on them, which they never forgot; and, in spite of the noble efforts of French missionaries and a lavish bestowal of gifts, the Iroquois thorn remained in the side of New France. But with the other Indian tribes the French worked hand in hand, with the Cross and the priest ever in advance of the trader's pack. French missionaries were the first white men to settle in the populous Huron country near Lake Simcoe. A missionary was the first European to catch a glimpse of Georgian Bay, and a missionary was probably the first of the French race to launch his canoe on the lordly Mississippi. As a father the priest watched over his wilderness flock; while the French traders fraternized with the red men, and often mated with dusky beauties. Many French traders, according to Sir William Johnson—a good authority, of whom we shall learn more later-were 'gentlemen in manners, character, and dress,' and they treated the natives kindly. At the great centres of trade—Montreal, Three Rivers, and Quebec—the chiefs were royally received with roll of drum and salute of guns. The governor himself —the 'Big Mountain,' as they called him—would extend to them a welcoming hand and take part in their feastings and councils. At the inland trading-posts the Indians were given goods for their winter hunts on credit and loaded with presents by the officials. To such an extent did the custom of giving presents prevail that it became a heavy tax on the treasury of France, insignificant, however, compared with the alternative of keeping in the hinterland an armed force. The Indians, too, had fought side by side with the French in many notable engagements. They had aided Montcalm, and had assisted in such triumphs as the defeat of Braddock. They were not only friends of the French; they were sword companions.

The British colonists could not, of course, entertain friendly feelings towards the tribes which sided with their enemies and often devastated their homes and murdered their people. But it must be admitted that, from the first, the British in America were far behind the French in Christian-like conduct towards the native races. The colonial traders generally despised the Indians and treated them as of commercial value only, as gatherers of pelts, and held their lives in little more esteem than the lives of the animals that yielded the pelts. The missionary zeal of New England, compared with that of New France, was exceedingly mild. Rum was a leading article of trade. The Indians were often cheated out of their furs; in some instances they were slain and their packs stolen. Sir William Johnson described the British traders as 'men of no zeal or capacity: men who even sacrifice the credit of the nation to the basest purposes.' There were exceptions, of course, in such men as Alexander Henry and Johnson himself, who, besides being a wise official and a successful military commander, was one of the leading traders.

9

No sooner was New France vanquished than the British began building new forts and blockhouses in the hinterland. By the hinterland is meant, of course, the regions beyond the zone of settlement; roughly, all west of Montreal and the Alleghanies. Since the French were no longer to be reckoned with, why were these forts needed? Evidently, the Indians thought, to keep the red children in subjection and to deprive them of their hunting-grounds! The gardens they saw in cultivation about the forts were to them the forerunners of general settlement. The French had been content with trade; the British appropriated lands for farming, and the coming of the white settler meant the disappearance of game. Indian chiefs saw in these forts and cultivated strips of land a desire to exterminate the red man and steal his territory; and they were not far wrong.

Outside influences, as well, were at work among the Indians. Soon after the French armies departed, the inhabitants along the St Lawrence had learned to welcome the change of government. They were left to cultivate their farms in peace. The tax-gatherer was no longer squeezing from them their last *sou* as in the days of Bigot; nor were their sons, whose labour was needed on the farms and in the workshops, forced to take up arms. They had peace and plenty, and were content. But in the hinterland it was different. At Detroit, Michilimackinac, and other forts were French trading communities, which, being far from the seat of war and government, were slow to realize that they were no longer subjects of the French king. Hostile themselves, these French traders naturally encouraged the Indians in an attitude of hostility to the incoming British. They said that a French fleet and army were on their way to Canada to recover the territory. Even if Canada were lost, Louisiana was still French, and, if only the British could be kept out of the west, the trade that had hitherto gone down the St Lawrence might now go by way of the Mississippi.

The commander-in-chief of the British forces in North America, Sir Jeffery Amherst, despised the red men. They were 'only fit to live with the inhabitants of the woods, being more nearly allied to the Brute than to the Human creation.' Other British officers had much the same attitude. Colonel Henry Bouquet, on a suggestion made to him by Amherst that blankets infected with small-pox might be distributed to good purpose among the savages, not only fell in with Amherst's views, but further proposed that dogs should be used to hunt them down. 'You will do well,' Amherst wrote to Bouquet, 'to try to inoculate the Indians by means of Blankets as well as to try every other method that can serve to extirpate this execrable race. I should be very glad if your scheme for hunting them down by dogs could take effect, but England is at too great a distance to think of that at present.' And Major Henry Gladwyn, who, as we shall see, gallantly held Detroit through months of trying siege, thought that the unrestricted sale of rum among the Indians would extirpate them more quickly than powder and shot, and at less cost.

There was, however, one British officer, at least, in America who did not hold such views towards the natives of the soil. Sir William Johnson, through his sympathy and generosity, had won the friendship of the Six Nations, the most courageous and the most cruel of the Indian tribes. It has been said by a recent writer that Johnson was 'as much Indian as white man.'[1] Nothing could be more misleading. Johnson was simply an enlightened Irishman of broad sympathies who could make himself at home in palace, hut, or wigwam. He was an astute diplomatist, capable of winning his point in controversy with the most learned and experienced legislators of the colonies, a successful military leader, a most successful trader; and there was probably no more progressive and scientific farmer in America. He had a cultivated mind; the orders he

1. Lucas's A History of Canada, 1763-1812, p. 58.

11

sent to London for books show that he was something of a scholar and in his leisure moments given to serious reading. His advice to the lords of trade regarding colonial affairs was that of a statesman. He fraternized with the Dutch settlers of his neighbourhood and with the Indians wherever he found them. At Detroit, in 1761, he entered into the spirit of the French settlers and joined with enthusiasm in their feasts and dances. He was one of those rare characters who can be all things to all men and yet keep an untarnished name. The Indians loved him as a firm friend, and his home was to them Liberty Hall. But for this man the Indian rising against British rule would have attained greater proportions. At the critical period he succeeded in keeping the Six Nations loyal, save for the Senecas. This was most important; for had the Six Nations joined in the war against the British, it is probable that not a fort west of Montreal would have remained standing. The line of communication between Albany and Oswego would have been cut, provisions and troops could not have been forwarded, and, inevitably, both Niagara and Detroit would have fallen.

But as it was, the Pontiac War proved serious enough. It extended as far north as Sault St. Marie and as far south as the borders of South Carolina and Georgia. Detroit was cut off for months; the Indians drove the British from all other points on the Great Lakes west of Lake Ontario; for a time they triumphantly pushed their war-parties, plundering and burning and murdering, from the Mississippi to the frontiers of New York. During the year 1763 more British lives were lost in America than in the memorable year of 1759, the year of the siege of Quebec and the world-famous battle of the Plains of Abraham.

CHAPTER 2

Pontiac and the Tribes of the Hinterland

Foremost among the Indian leaders was Pontiac, the over-chief of the Ottawa Confederacy. It has been customary to speak of this chief as possessed of 'princely grandeur' and as one 'honoured and revered by his subjects.' But it was not by a display of princely dignity or by inspiring awe and reverence that he influenced his bloodthirsty followers. His chief traits were treachery and cruelty, and his pre-eminence in these qualities commanded their respect. His conduct of the siege of Detroit, as we shall see, was marked by duplicity and diabolic savagery. He has often been extolled for his skill as a military leader, and there is a good deal in his siege of Detroit and in the murderous ingenuity of some of his raids to support this view. But his principal claim to distinction is due to his position as the head of a confederacy —whereas the other chiefs in the conflict were merely leaders of single tribes—and to the fact that he was situated at the very centre of the theatre of war. News from Detroit could be quickly heralded along the canoe routes and forest trails to the other tribes, and it thus happened that when Pontiac struck, the whole Indian country rose in arms. But the evidence clearly shows that, except against Detroit and the neighbouring blockhouses, he had no part in planning the attacks. The war as a whole was a leaderless war.

Let us now look for a moment at the Indians who took part in the war. Immediately under the influence of Pontiac were three tribes—the Ottawas, the Chippewas, and the Potawatomis. These had their hunting-grounds chiefly in the Michigan peninsula, and formed what was known as the Ottawa Confederacy or the Confederacy of the Three Fires. It was at the best a loose confederacy, with nothing of the organized strength of the Six Nations. The Indians in it were of a low type—sunk in savagery and superstition. A leader such as Pontiac naturally appealed to them. They existed by hunting and fishing—feasting to-day and famishing to-morrow—and were easily roused by the hope of plunder. The weakly manned forts containing the white man's provisions, ammunition, and traders' supplies were an attractive lure to such savages. Within the confederacy, however, there were some who did not rally round Pontiac. The Ottawas of the northern part of Michigan, under the influence of their priest, remained friendly to the British. Including the Ottawas and Chippewas of the Ottawa and Lake Superior, the confederates numbered many thousands; yet at no time was Pontiac able to command from among them more than one thousand warriors.

In close alliance with the Confederacy of the Three Fires were the tribes dwelling to the west of Lake Michigan—the Menominees, the Winnebagoes, and the Sacs and Foxes. These tribes could put into the field about twelve hundred warriors; but none of them took part in the war save in one instance, when the Sacs, moved by the hope of plunder, assisted the Chippewas in the capture of Fort Michilimackinac.

The Wyandots living on the Detroit river were a remnant of the ancient Hurons of the famous mission near Lake Simcoe. For more than a century they had been bound to the French by ties of amity. They were courageous, intelligent, and in every way on a higher plane of life than the tribes of the Ottawa Confederacy. Their two hundred and fifty braves were to be Pontiac's most important allies in the siege of Detroit.

South of the Michigan peninsula, about the head-waters of the rivers Maumee and Wabash, dwelt the Miamis, numbering probably about fifteen hundred. Influenced by French traders and by Pontiac's emissaries, they took to the war-path, and the British were thus cut off from the trade-route between Lake Erie and the Ohio.

The tribes just mentioned were all that came under the direct influence of Pontiac. Farther south were other nations who were to figure in the impending struggle. The Wyandots of Sandusky Bay, at the south-west corner of Lake Erie, had about two hundred warriors, and were in alliance with the Senecas and Delawares. Living near Detroit, they were able to assist in Pontiac's siege. Directly south of these, along the Scioto, dwelt the Shawnees—the tribe which later gave birth to the great Tecumseh—with three hundred warriors. East of the Shawnees, between the Muskingum and the Ohio, were the Delawares. At one time this tribe had lived on both sides of the Delaware river in Pennsylvania and New York, and also in parts of New Jersey and Delaware. They called themselves *Leni-Lenape*, real men; but were, nevertheless, conquered by the Iroquois, who 'made women' of them, depriving them of the right to declare war or sell land without permission. Later, through an alliance with the French, they won back their old independence. But they lay in the path of white settlement, and were ousted from one hunting-ground after another, until finally they had to seek homes beyond the Alleghanies. The British had robbed the Delawares of their ancient lands, and the Delawares hated with an undying hatred the race that had injured them. They mustered six hundred warriors.

Almost directly south of Fort Niagara, by the upper waters of the Genesee and Alleghany rivers, lay the homes of the Senecas, one of the Six Nations. This tribe looked upon the British settlers in the Niagara region as squatters on their territory. It was the Senecas, not Pontiac, who began the plot for the destruction of the British in the hinterland, and in the war which followed more than a thousand Seneca warriors took part. Happily, as has been mentioned, Sir William Johnson was able to keep the other tribes of the Six Nations loyal to the British; but the 'Door-keepers of the Long House,' as the Senecas were called, stood aloof and hostile.

The motives of the Indians in the rising of 1763 may, therefore, be summarized as follows: amity with the French, hostility towards the British, hope of plunder, and fear of aggression. The first three were the controlling motives of Pontiac's Indians about Detroit. They called it the 'Beaver War.' To them it was a war on behalf of the French traders, who loaded them with gifts, and against the British, who drove them away empty-handed. But the Senecas and the Delawares, with their allies of the Ohio valley, regarded it as a war for their lands. Already the Indians had been forced out of their hunting-grounds in the valleys of the Juniata and the Susquehanna. The Ohio valley would be the next to go, unless the Indians went on the war-path. The chiefs there had good reason for alarm. Not so Pontiac at Detroit, because no settlers were invading his hunting-grounds. And it was for this lack of a strong motive that Pontiac's campaign, as will hereafter appear, broke down before the end of the war; that even his own confederates deserted him; and that, while the Senecas and Delawares were still holding out, he was wandering through the Indian country in a vain endeavour to rally his scattered warriors.

CHAPTER 3

The Gathering Storm

When Montreal capitulated, and the whole of Canada passed into British hands, it was the duty of Sir Jeffery Amherst, the commander-in-chief, to arrange for the defence of the country that had been wrested from France. General Gage was left in command at Montreal, Colonel Burton at Three Rivers, and General Murray at Quebec. Amherst himself departed for New York in October, and never again visited Canada. Meanwhile provision had been made, though quite inadequate, to garrison the long chain of forts[1] that had been established by the French in the vaguely defined Indian territory to the west. The fortunes of war had already given the British command of the eastern end of this chain. Fort Levis, on what is now Chimney Island, a few miles east of Ogdensburg, had been captured. Fort Frontenac had been destroyed by Bradstreet, and was left without a garrison. British troops were in charge of Fort Oswego, which had been built in 1759. Niagara, the strongest fort on the Great Lakes, had been taken by Sir William Johnson. Near

---

1. Except for these forts or trading-posts, the entire region west of Montreal was at this time practically an unbroken wilderness. There were on the north shore of the St Lawrence a few scattered settlements, on Ile Perrot and at Vaudreuil, and on the south shore at the Cedars and Chateauguay; but anything like continuity of settlement westward ceased with the island of Montreal.

it were two lesser forts, one at the foot of the rapids, where Lewiston now stands, and the other, Fort Schlosser, on the same side of the river, above the falls. Forts Presquisle, Le Boeuf, and Venango, on the trade-route between Lake Erie and Fort Pitt, and Fort Pitt itself, were also occupied. But all west of Fort Pitt was to the British unknown country. Sandusky, at the south-west end of Lake Erie; Detroit, guarding the passage between Lakes Erie and St Clair; Miami and Ouiatanon, on the trade-route between Lake Erie and the Wabash; Michilimackinac, at the entrance to Lake Michigan; Green Bay (La Baye), at the southern end of Green Bay; St Joseph, on Lake Michigan; Sault Ste Marie, at the entrance to Lake Superior—all were still commanded by French officers, as they had been under New France.

The task of raising the British flag over these forts was entrusted to Major Robert Rogers of New England, who commanded Rogers's Rangers, a famous body of Indian-fighters. On September 13, 1760, with two hundred Rangers in fifteen whale-boats, Rogers set out from Montreal. On November 7 the contingent without mishap reached a river named by Rogers the Chogage, evidently the Cuyahoga, on the south shore of Lake Erie. Here the troops landed, probably on the site of the present city of Cleveland; and Rogers was visited by a party of Ottawa Indians, whom he told of the conquest of Canada and of the retirement of the French armies from the country. He added that his force had been sent by the commander-in-chief to take over for their father, the king of England, the western posts still held by French soldiers. He then offered them a peace-belt, which they accepted, and requested them to go with him to Detroit to take part in the capitulation and 'see the truth' of what he had said. They promised to give him an answer next morning. The *calumet* was smoked by the Indians and the officers in turn; but a careful guard was kept, as Rogers was suspicious of the Indians. In the morning, however, they returned with a favourable reply, and the younger warriors of the band agreed to accompany their new friends. Owing to stormy weather nearly a week passed—the Indians keeping the camp supplied with venison and turkey, for which Rogers paid them liberally—before the party, on November 12, moved forward towards Detroit.

Detroit was at this time under the command of the Sieur de Beletre, or Bellestre. This officer had been in charge of the post since 1758 and had heard nothing of the surrender of Montreal. Rogers, to pave the way; sent one of his men in advance with a letter to Beletre notifying him that the western posts now belonged to King George and informing him that he was approaching with a letter from the Marquis de Vaudreuil and a copy of the capitulation. Beletre was irritated; the French armies had been defeated and he was about to lose his post. He at first refused to believe the tidings; and it appears that he endeavoured to rouse the inhabitants and Indians about Detroit to resist the approaching British, for on November 20 several Wyandot sachems met the advancing party and told Rogers that four hundred warriors were in ambush at the entrance to the Detroit river to obstruct his advance. The Wyandots wished to know the truth regarding the conquest of Canada, and on being convinced that it was no fabrication, they took their departure 'in good temper.' On the 23rd Indian messengers, among whom was an Ottawa chief,[2] arrived at the British camp, at the western end of Lake Erie, reporting that Beletre intended to fight and that he had arrested the officer who bore Rogers's message. Beletre's chief reason for doubting the truth of Rogers's statement appears to have been that no French officers

---

2. In Rogers's journal of this trip no mention is made of Pontiac's name. In A Concise Account of North America, published in 1765, with Rogers's name on the title-page, a detailed account of a meeting with Pontiac at the Cuyahoga is given, but this book seems to be of doubtful authenticity. It was, however, accepted by Parkman.

had accompanied the British contingent from Montreal.

When the troops entered the Detroit river Rogers sent Captain Donald Campbell to the fort with a copy of the capitulation of Montreal and Vaudreuil's letter instructing Beletre to hand over his fort to the British. These documents were convincing, and Beletre[3] consented, though with no good grace; and on November 29 Rogers formally took possession of Detroit. It was an impressive ceremony. Some seven hundred Indians were assembled in the vicinity of Fort Detroit, and, ever ready to take sides with the winning party, appeared about the stockade painted and plumed in honour of the occasion. When the lilies of France were lowered and the cross of St George was thrown to the breeze, the barbarous horde uttered wild cries of delight. A new and rich people had come to their hunting-grounds, and they had visions of unlimited presents of clothing, ammunition, and rum. After the fort was taken over the militia were called together and disarmed and made to take the oath of allegiance to the British king.

Captain Campbell was installed in command of the fort, and Beletre and the other prisoners of war were sent to Philadelphia. Two officers were dispatched with twenty men to bring the French troops from Forts Miami and Ouiatanon. A few soldiers were stationed at Fort Miami to keep the officers at Detroit informed of any interesting events in that neighbourhood. Provisions being scarce at Detroit, Rogers sent the majority of his force to Niagara; and on December 10 set out for Michilimackinac with an officer and thirty-seven men. But he was driven back by stormy weather and ice, and forced, for the present year, to give up the attempt to garrison the posts on Lakes Huron and Michigan. Leaving everything

---

3. Although Beletre received Rogers and his men in no friendly spirit, he seems soon to have become reconciled to British rule for in 1763 he was appointed to the first Legislative Council of Canada, and until the time of his death in May 1793 he was a highly respected citizen of Quebec.

in peace at Detroit, Rogers went to Fort Pitt, and for nine months the forts in the country of the Ottawa Confederacy were to be left to their own resources.

Meanwhile the Indians were getting into a state of unrest. The presents, on which they depended so much for existence, were not forthcoming, and rumours of trouble were in the air. Senecas, Shawnees, and Delawares were sending warbelts east and west and north and south. A plot was on foot to seize Pitt, Niagara, and Detroit. Seneca ambassadors had visited the Wyandots in the vicinity of Detroit, urging them to fall on the garrison. After an investigation, Captain Campbell reported to Amherst that an Indian rising was imminent, and revealed a plot, originated by the Senecas, which was identical with that afterwards matured in 1763 and attributed to Pontiac's initiative. Campbell warned the commandants of the other forts of the danger; and the Indians, seeing that their plans were discovered, assumed a peaceful attitude.

Still, the situation was critical; and, to allay the hostility of the natives and gain their confidence, Amherst dispatched Sir William Johnson to Detroit with instructions 'to settle and establish a firm and lasting treaty' between the British and the Ottawa Confederacy and other nations inhabiting the Indian territory, to regulate the fur trade at the posts, and to settle the price of clothes and provisions. He was likewise to collect information as exhaustive as possible regarding the Indians, their manners and customs, and their abodes. He was to find out whether the French had any shipping on Lakes Huron, Michigan, and Superior, what were the best posts for trade, and the price paid by the French for pelts. He was also to learn, if possible, how far the boundaries of Canada extended towards the Mississippi, and the number of French posts, settlements, and inhabitants along that river.

Sir William left his home at Fort Johnson on the Mohawk river early in July 1761. Scarcely had he begun his journey when he was warned that it was dangerous to proceed, as the nations in the west were unfriendly and would surely fall upon his party. But Johnson was confident that his presence among them would put a stop to 'any such wicked design.' As he advanced up Lake Ontario the alarming reports continued. The Senecas, who had already stolen horses from the whites and taken prisoners, had been sending ambassadors abroad, endeavouring to induce the other nations to attack the British. Johnson learned, too, that the Indians were being cheated in trade by British traders; that at several posts they had been roughly handled, very often without cause; that their women were taken from them by violence; and that they were hindered from hunting and fishing on their own grounds near the posts, even what they did catch or kill being taken from them. He heard, too, that Seneca and Ottawa warriors had been murdered by whites near Forts Pitt and Venango. At Niagara he was visited by Seneca chiefs, who complained that one of their warriors had been wounded near by and that four horses had been stolen from them. Johnson evidently believed the story, for he gave them 'two casks of rum, some paint and money to make up their loss,' and they left him well satisfied. On Lake Erie, stories of the hostility of the Indians multiplied. They were ready to revolt; even before leaving Niagara, Johnson had it on good authority that the Indians 'were certainly determined to rise and fall on the English,' and that 'several thousands of the Ottawas and other nations' had agreed to join the dissatisfied member 'of the Six Nations in this scheme or plot.' But Johnson kept on his way, confident that he could allay dissatisfaction and win all the nations to friendship.

When Sir William reached Detroit on September 3 he was welcomed by musketry volleys from the Indians and by cannon from the fort. His reputation as the great superintendent of Indian Affairs, the friend of the red man, had gone before him, and he was joyously received, and at once given quarters in the house of the former commandant of

Detroit, Beletre. On the day following his arrival the Wyandots and other Indians, with their priest, Father Pierre Potier (called Pottie by Johnson), waited on him. He treated them royally, and gave them pipes and tobacco and a barbecue of a large ox roasted whole. He found the French inhabitants most friendly, especially Pierre Chesne, better known as La Butte, the interpreter of the Wyandots, and St Martin, the interpreter of the Ottawas. The ladies of the settlement called on him, and were regaled 'with cakes, wine and cordial. He was hospitably entertained by the officers and settlers, and in return gave several balls, at which, it appears, he danced with 'Mademoiselle Curie—a fine girl.' This vivacious lady evidently made an impression on the susceptible Irishman; for after the second ball—'there never was so brilliant an affair' at Detroit before—he records in his private diary: 'Promised to write Mademoiselle Curie my sentiments.'

While at Niagara on his journey westward Johnson had been joined by Major Henry Gladwyn, to whom Amherst had assigned the duty of garrisoning the western forts and taking over in person the command of Fort Detroit. Gladwyn had left Niagara a day or two in advance of Johnson, but on the way to his new command he had been seized with severe fever and ague and totally incapacitated for duty. On Johnson fell the task of making arrangements for the still unoccupied posts. He did the work with his customary promptitude and thoroughness, and by September 10 had dispatched men of Gage's Light Infantry and of the Royal Americans from Detroit for Michilimackinac, Green Bay, and St Joseph.

The chiefs of the various tribes had flocked to Detroit to confer with Sir William. He won them all by his honeyed words and liberal distribution of presents; he was told that his 'presents had made the sun and sky bright and clear, the earth smooth and level, the roads all pleasant'; and they begged that he 'would continue in the same friendly disposition towards them and they would be a happy people.' His work completed, Johnson set out, September 19, on his homeward journey, leaving behind him the promise of peace in the Indian territory.[4] For the time being Johnson's visit to Detroit had a salutary effect, and the year 1761 terminated with only slight signs of unrest among the Indians; but in the spring of 1762 the air was again heavy with threatening storm. The Indians of the Ohio valley were once more sending out their war-belts and bloody hatchets. In several instances Englishmen were murdered and scalped and horses were stolen. The Shawnees and Delawares held British prisoners whom they refused to surrender. By Amherst's orders presents were withheld. Until they surrendered all prisoners and showed a proper spirit towards the British he would suppress all gifts, in the belief that 'a due observance of this alone will soon produce more than can ever be expected from bribing them.' The reply of the Shawnees and Delawares to his orders was stealing horses and terrorizing traders. Sir William Johnson and his assistant in office, George Croghan, warned Amherst of the danger he was running in rousing the hatred of the savages. Croghan in a letter to Bouquet said: 'I do not approve of General Amherst's plan of distressing them too much, as in my opinion they will not consider consequences if too much distressed, tho' Sir Jeffery thinks they will.' Although warnings were pouring in upon him, Amherst was of the opinion that there was 'no necessity for any more at the several posts than are just enough to keep up the communication, there being nothing to fear from the Indians in our present circumstances.' To Sir William Johnson he wrote that it was 'not in the power of the Indians to effect anything of consequence.'

In the spring of 1763 the war-cloud was about to burst; but in remote New York the commander-in-chief failed to grasp the situation, and turned a deaf ear to those who

---

4. It is remarkable that Johnson in his private diary or in his official correspondence makes no mention of Pontiac. The Ottawa chief apparently played no conspicuous part in the plots of 1761 and 1762.

warned him that an Indian war with all its horrors was inevitable. These vague rumours, as Amherst regarded them, of an imminent general rising of the western tribes, took more definite form as the spring advanced. Towards the end of March Lieutenant Edward Jenkins, the commandant of Fort Ouiatanon, learned that the French traders had been telling the Indians that the British would 'all be prisoners in a short time.' But what caused most alarm was information from Fort Miami of a plot for the capture of the forts and the slaughter of the garrisons. A war-belt was received by the Indians residing near the fort, and with it came the request that they should hold themselves in readiness to attack the British. Robert Holmes, the commandant of Fort Miami, managed to secure the 'bloody belt' and sent it to Gladwyn, Gladwyn's illness in 1761 proved so severe that he had to take a journey to England to recuperate; but he was back in Detroit as commandant in August 1762. who in turn sent it to Amherst.

News had now reached the Ohio tribes of the Treaty of Paris, but the terms of this treaty had only increased their unrest. On April 30, 1763, Croghan wrote to Amherst that the Indians were 'uneasy since so much of North America was ceded to Great Britain,' holding that the British had no right in their country. 'The Peace,' added Croghan, 'and hearing so much of this country being given up has thrown them into confusion and prevented them bringing in their prisoners this spring as they promised.' Amherst's reply was: 'Whatever idle notions they may entertain in regard to the cessions made by the French crown can be of very little consequence.' On April 20 Gladwyn, though slow to see danger, wrote to Amherst: 'They (the Indians) say we mean to make slaves of them by taking so many posts in the country, and that they had better attempt something now to recover their liberty than wait till we are better established.' Even when word that the Indians were actually on the war-path reached

Amherst, he still refused to believe it a serious matter, and delayed making preparations to meet the situation. It was, according to him, a 'rash attempt of that turbulent tribe the Senecas'; and, again, he was 'persuaded this alarm will end in nothing more than a rash attempt of what the Senecas have been threatening.' Eight British forts in the west were captured and the frontiers of the colonies bathed in blood before he realized that 'the affair of the Indians was more general than they apprehended.'

The Indians were only waiting for a sudden, bold blow at some one of the British posts, and on the instant they would be on the war-path from the shores of Lake Superior to the borders of the southernmost colonies of Great Britain. The blow was soon to be struck. Pontiac's war-belts had been sent broadcast, and the nations who recognized him as over-chief were ready to follow him to the slaughter. Detroit was the strongest position to the west of Niagara; it contained an abundance of stores, and would be a rich prize. As Pontiac yearly visited this place during the trading season, he knew the locality well and was familiar with the settlers, the majority of whom were far from being friendly to the British. Against Detroit he would lead the warriors, under the pretence of winning back the country for the French.

In the spring of 1763, instead of going direct to his usual camping-place, an island in Lake St Clair, Pontiac pitched his wigwam on the bank of the river Ecorces, ten miles south of Detroit, and here awaited the tribes whom he had summoned to a council to be held 'on the 15th of the moon'—the 27th of April. And at the appointed time nearly five hundred warriors—Ottawas, Potawatomis, Chippewas, and Wyandots—with their squaws and papooses, had gathered at the meeting-place, petty tribal jealousies and differences being laid aside in their common hatred of 'the dogs dressed in red,' the British soldiers.

When the council assembled Pontiac addressed them

with fiery words. The Ottawa chief was at this time about fifty years old. He was a man of average height, of darker hue than is usual among Indians, lithe as a panther, his muscles hardened by forest life and years of warfare against Indian enemies and the British. Like the rush of a mountain torrent the words fell from his lips. His speech was one stream of denunciation of the British. In trade they had cheated the Indians, robbing them of their furs, overcharging them for the necessaries of life, and heaping insults and blows upon the red men, who from the French had known only kindness. The time had come to strike. As he spoke he flashed a red and purple *wampum* belt before the gaze of the excited braves. This, he declared, he had received from their father the king of France, who commanded his red children to fight the British. Holding out the belt, he recounted with wild words and vehement gestures the victories gained in the past by the Indians over the British, and as he spoke the blood of his listeners pulsed through their veins with battle ardour. To their hatred and sense of being wronged he had appealed, and he saw that every warrior present was with him; but his strongest appeal was to their superstition. In spite of the fact that French missionaries had been among them for a century, they were still pagan, and it was essential to the success of his project that they should believe that the Master of Life favoured their cause. He told them the story of a Wolf (Delaware) Indian who had journeyed to heaven and talked with the Master of Life, receiving instructions to tell all the Indians that they were to 'drive out' and 'make war upon' the 'dogs clothed in red who will do you nothing but harm.' When he had finished, such chiefs as Ninevois of the Chippewas and Takay of the Wyandots—'the bad Hurons,' as the writer of the 'Pontiac Manuscript' describes them to distinguish them from Father Potier's flock—spoke in similar terms. Every warrior present shouted his readiness to go to war, and before the council broke up it was agreed that in four days Pontiac 'should go to the fort with his young men for a peace dance' in order to get information regarding the strength of the place. The blow must be struck before the spring boats arrived from the Niagara with supplies and additional troops. The council at an end, the different tribes scattered to their several summer villages, seemingly peaceful Indians who had gathered together for trade.

CHAPTER 4

The Siege of Detroit

At the time of the Pontiac outbreak there were in the vicinity of Fort Detroit between one thousand and two thousand white inhabitants. Yet the place was little more than a wilderness post. The settlers were cut off from civilization and learned news of the great world outside only in the spring, when the traders' boats came with supplies. They were out of touch with Montreal and Quebec, and it was difficult for them to realize that they were subjects of the hated king of England. They had not lost their confidence that the armies of France would yet be victorious and sweep the British from the Great Lakes, and in this opinion they were strengthened by traders from the Mississippi, who came among them. But the change of rulers had made little difference in their lives. The majority of them were employed by traders, and the better class contentedly cultivated their narrow farms and traded with the Indians who periodically visited them.

The settlement was widely scattered, extending along the east shore of the Detroit river for about eight miles from Lake St Clair, and along the west shore for about six miles, four above and two below the fort. On either side of the river the fertile fields and the long row of whitewashed, low-built houses, with their gardens and orchards of apple and pear trees, fenced about with rounded pickets, presented a picture of peace and plenty. The summers of the inhabitants were enlivened by the visits of the Indians and the traders; and in winter they light-heartedly whiled away the tedious hours with gossip and dance and feast, like the habitants along the Richelieu and the St Lawrence.

The militia of the settlement, as we have seen, had been deprived of their arms at the taking over of Detroit by Robert Rogers; and for the most part the settlers maintained a stolid attitude towards their conquerors, from whom they suffered no hardship and whose rule was not galling. The British had nothing to fear from them. But the Indians were a force to be reckoned with. There were three Indian villages in the vicinity—the Wyandot, on the east side of the river, opposite the fort; the Ottawa, five miles above, opposite Ile au Cochon (Belle Isle); and the Potawatomi about two miles below the fort on the west shore. The Ottawas here could muster 200 warriors, the Potawatomis about 150, and the Wyandots 250, while near at hand were the Chippewas, 320 strong. Pontiac, although head chief of the Ottawas, did not live in the village, but had his *wigwam* on Ile a la Peche, at the outlet of Lake St Clair, a spot where whitefish abounded. Here he dwelt with his squaws and papooses, not in 'grandeur,' but in squalid savagery. Between the Indians and the French there existed a most friendly relationship; many of the habitants, indeed, having Indian wives.

Near the centre of the settlement, on the west bank of the river, about twenty miles from Lake Erie, stood Fort Detroit, a miniature town. It was in the form of a parallelogram and was surrounded by a palisade twenty-five feet high. According to a letter of an officer, the walls had an extent of over one thousand paces. At each corner was a bastion and over each gate a blockhouse. Within the walls were about one hundred houses, the little Catholic church of Ste Anne's, a council-house, officers' quarters, and a range of barracks. Save for one or two exceptions the buildings were of wood, thatched with bark or straw, and stood close together. The streets were exceedingly narrow; but immediately within the palisade a wide road extended round the entire village. The spiritual welfare of the French and Indian Catholics in the garrison was looked after by Father Potier, a Jesuit, whose mission was in the Wyandot village, and by Father Bocquet, a Recollet, who lived within the fort; Major Henry Gladwyn was in command. He had a hundred and twenty soldiers, and two armed schooners, the Gladwyn and the Beaver, were in the river near by.

On the first day of May 1763, Pontiac came to the main gate of the fort asking to be allowed to enter, as he and the warriors with him, forty in all, desired to show their love for the British by dancing the *calumet* or peace dance. Gladwyn had not the slightest suspicion of evil intent, and readily admitted them. The savages selected a spot in front of the officers' houses; and thirty of them went through their grotesque movements, shouting and dancing to the music of the Indian drum, and all the while waving their *calumets* in token of friendship. While the dancers were thus engaged, the remaining ten of the party were busily employed in surveying the fort—noting the number of men and the strength of the palisades. The dance lasted about an hour. Presents were then distributed to the Indians, and all took their departure.

Pontiac now summoned the Indians about Detroit to another council. On this occasion the chiefs and warriors assembled in the council-house in the Potawatomi village south of the fort. When all were gathered together Pontiac rose and, as at the council at the river Ecorces, in a torrent of words and with vehement gestures, denounced the British. He declared that under the new occupancy of the forts in the Indian country the red men were neglected and their wants were no longer supplied as they had been in the days of the French; that exorbitant prices were charged by the traders for goods; that when the Indians were departing for their winter camps to hunt for furs they were no longer able to obtain ammunition and clothing on credit; and, finally, that the British desired the death of the Indians, and it was therefore necessary as an act of self-preservation to destroy them. He once more displayed the war-belt that he pretended to have received from the king of France. This belt told him to strike in his own interest and in the interest of the French. He closed his speech by saying that he had sent belts to the Chippewas of Saginaw and the Ottawas of Michilimackinac and of the river La Tranche (the Thames). Seeing that his words were greeted with grunts and shouts of approval and that the assembled warriors were with him to a man, Pontiac revealed a plan he had formed to seize the fort and slaughter the garrison. He and some fifty chiefs and warriors would wait on Gladwyn on the pretence of discussing matters of importance. Each one would carry beneath his blanket a gun, with the barrel cut short to permit of concealment. Warriors and even women were to enter the fort as if on a friendly visit and take up positions of advantage in the streets, in readiness to strike with tomahawks, knives, and guns, all which they were to have concealed beneath their blankets. At the council Pontiac was to address Gladwyn and, in pretended friendship, hand him a *wampum* belt. If it were wise to strike, he would on presenting the belt hold its reverse side towards Gladwyn. This was to be the signal for attack. Instantly blankets were to be thrown aside and the officers were to be shot down. At the sound of firing in the council-room the Indians in the streets were to fall on the garrison and every British soldier was to be slain, care being taken that no Frenchman suffered. The plan, by its treachery, and by its possibilities of slaughter and plunder, appealed to the savages; and they dispersed to make preparations for the morning of the 7th, the day chosen for carrying out the murderous scheme.

The plot was difficult to conceal. The aid of French black-smiths had to be sought to shorten the guns. Moreover, the British garrison had some friends among the Indians. Scarcely had the plot been matured when it was discussed among the

32

French, and on the day before the intended massacre it was revealed to Gladwyn. His informant is not certainly known. A Chippewa maiden, an old squaw, several Frenchmen, and an Ottawa named Mahiganne have been mentioned. It is possible that Gladwyn had it from a number of sources, but most likely from Mahiganne. The 'Pontiac Manuscript,' probably the work of Robert Navarre, the keeper of the notarial records of the settlement, distinctly states that Mahiganne revealed the details of the plot with the request that Gladwyn should not divulge his name; for, should Pontiac learn, the informer would surely be put to death. This would account for the fact that Gladwyn, even in his report of the affair to Amherst, gives no hint as to the person who told him.

Gladwyn at once made preparations to receive Pontiac and his chiefs. On the night of the 6th instructions were given to the soldiers and the traders within the fort to make preparations to resist an attack, and the guards were doubled. As the sentries peered out into the darkness occasional yells and whoops and the beating of drums reached their ears, telling of the war-dance that was being performed in the Indian villages to hearten the warriors for the slaughter.

Gladwyn determined to act boldly. On the morning of the 7th all the traders' stores were closed and every man capable of bearing weapons was under arms; but the gates were left open as usual, and shortly after daylight Indians and squaws by twos and threes began to gather in the fort as if to trade. At ten in the morning a line of chiefs with Pontiac at their head filed along the road leading to the river gate. All were painted and plumed and each one was wrapped in a brightly coloured blanket. When they entered the fort they were astonished to see the warlike preparations, but stoically concealed their surprise. Arrived in the council-chamber, the chiefs noticed the sentinels standing at arms, the commandant and his officers seated, their faces stern and set, pistols in their belts and swords by their sides. So perturbed were the chiefs by all this warlike display that it was some time before they would take their seats on the mats prepared for them. At length they recovered their composure, and Pontiac broke the silence by asking why so many of the young men were standing in the streets with their guns. Answer was made through the interpreter La Butte that it was for exercise and discipline. Pontiac then addressed Gladwyn, vehemently protesting friendship. All the time he was speaking Gladwyn bent on him a scrutinizing gaze, and as the chief was about to present the *wampum* belt, a signal was given and the drums crashed out a charge. Every doubt was removed from Pontiac's mind—his plot was discovered. His nervous hand lowered the belt; but he recovered himself immediately and presented it in the ordinary way. Gladwyn replied to his speech sternly, but kindly, saying that he would have the protection and friendship of the British so long as he merited it. A few presents were then distributed among the Indians, and the council ended. The chiefs, with their blankets still tightly wrapped about them, filed out of the council-room and scattered to their villages, followed by the disappointed rabble of fully three hundred Indians, who had assembled in the fort.

On the morrow, Pontiac, accompanied by three chiefs, again appeared at the fort, bringing with him a pipe of peace. When this had been smoked by the officers and chiefs, he presented it to Captain Campbell, as a further mark of friendship. The next day he was once more at the gates seeking entrance. But he found them closed: Gladwyn felt that the time had come to take no chances. This morning a rabble of Potawatomis, Ottawas, Wyandots, and Chippewas thronged the common just out of musket range. On Pontiac's request for a conference with Gladwyn he was sternly told that he might enter alone. The answer angered him, and he strode back to his followers. Now, with yells and war-whoops, parties of the savages bounded away on a murderous mission. Half a mile behind the fort an English woman, Mrs Turnbull, and her two sons cultivated a small farm. All three were straightway slain. A party of Ottawas leapt into their canoes and paddled swiftly to Ile au Cochon, where lived a former sergeant, James Fisher. Fisher was seized, killed, and scalped, his young wife brutally murdered, and their two little children carried into captivity. On this same day news was brought to the fort that Sir Robert Davers and Captain Robertson had been murdered three days before on Lake St Clair by, Chippewas who were on their way from Saginaw to join Pontiac's forces. Thus began the Pontiac War in the vicinity of Detroit. For several months the garrison was to know little rest.

That night at the Ottawa village arose the hideous din of the war-dance, and while the warriors worked themselves into a frenzy the squaws were busy breaking camp. Before daylight the village was moved to the opposite side of the river, and the wigwams were pitched near the mouth of Parent's Creek, about a mile and a half above the fort. On the morning of the 10th the siege began in earnest. Shortly after daybreak the yells of a horde of savages could be heard north and south and west. But few of the enemy could be seen, as they had excellent shelter behind barns, outhouses, and fences. For six hours they kept up a continuous fire on the garrison, but wounded only five men. The fort vigorously returned the fire, and none of the enemy dared attempt to rush the palisades. A cluster of buildings in the rear sheltered a particularly ferocious set of savages. A three-pounder—the only effective artillery in the fort—was trained on this position; spikes were bound together with wire, heated red-hot, and fired at the buildings. These were soon a mass of flames, and the savages concealed behind them fled for their lives.

Presently the Indians grew tired of this useless warfare and withdrew to their villages. Gladwyn, thinking that he might bring Pontiac to terms, sent La Butte to ask the cause of the attack and to say that the British were ready to redress any wrongs from which the Indians might be suffering. La Butte was accompanied by Jean Baptiste Chapoton, a captain of the militia and a man of some importance in the fort, and Jacques Godfroy, a trader and likewise an officer of militia. It may be noted that Godfroy's wife was the daughter of a Miami chief. The ambassadors were received in a friendly manner by Pontiac, who seemed ready to cease hostilities. La Butte returned to the fort with some of the chiefs to report progress; but when he went again to Pontiac he found that the Ottawa chief had made no definite promise. It seems probable, judging from their later actions, that Chapoton and Godfroy had betrayed Gladwyn and urged Pontiac to force the British out of the country. Pontiac now requested that Captain Donald Campbell, who had been in charge of Detroit before Gladwyn took over the command, should come to his village to discuss terms. Campbell was confident that he could pacify the Indians, and, accompanied by Lieutenant George McDougall, he set out along the river road for the Ottawas' encampment at Parent's Creek. As the two officers crossed the bridge at the mouth of the creek, they were met by a savage crowd—men, women, and children—armed with sticks and clubs. The mob rushed at them with yells and threatening gestures, and were about to fall on the officers when Pontiac appeared and restored order. A council was held, but as Campbell could get no satisfaction he suggested returning to the fort. Thereupon Pontiac remarked: 'My father will sleep to-night in the lodges of his red children.' Campbell and McDougall were given good quarters in the house of Jean Baptiste Meloche. For nearly two months they were to be kept close prisoners.

So far only part of the Wyandots had joined Pontiac: Father Potier had been trying to keep his flock neutral. But on the 11th Pontiac crossed to the Wyandot village, and threatened it with destruction if the warriors did not take up the tomahawk. On this compulsion they consented, no doubt glad of an excuse to be rid of the discipline of their priest.

Another attack on the fort was made, this time by about six

hundred Indians; but it was as futile as the one of the earlier day. Pontiac now tried negotiation. He summoned Gladwyn to surrender, promising that the British should be allowed to depart unmolested on their vessels. The officers, knowing that their communications with the east were cut, that food was scarce, that a vigorous assault could not fail to carry the fort, urged Gladwyn to accept the offer, but he sternly refused. He would not abandon Detroit while one pound of food and one pound of powder were left in the fort. Moreover, the treacherous conduct of Pontiac convinced him that the troops and traders as they left the fort would be plundered and slaughtered. He rejected Pontiac's demands, and advised him to disperse his people and save his ammunition for hunting.

At this critical moment Detroit was undoubtedly saved by a French Canadian. But for Jacques Baby, the grim spectre Starvation would have stalked through the little fortress. Baby was a prosperous trader and merchant who, with his wife Susanne Reaume, lived on the east shore of the river, almost opposite the fort. He had a farm of one thousand acres, two hundred of which were under cultivation. His trading establishment was a low-built log structure eighty feet long by twenty wide. He owned thirty slaves—twenty men and ten women. He seems to have treated them kindly; at any rate, they loyally did his will. Baby agreed to get provisions into the fort by stealth; and on a dark night, about a week after the siege commenced, Gladwyn had a lantern displayed on a plank fixed at the water's edge. Baby had six canoes in readiness; in each were stowed two quarters of beef, three hogs, and six bags of meal. All night long these canoes plied across the half-mile stretch of water and by daylight sufficient food to last the garrison for several weeks had been delivered.

From day to day the Indians kept up a desultory firing, while Gladwyn took precautions against a long siege. Food was taken from the houses of the inhabitants and placed in a common storehouse. Timber was torn from the walls and

37

used in the construction of portable bastions, which were erected outside the fort. There being danger that the roofs of the houses would be ignited by means of fire-arrows, the French inhabitants of the fort were made to draw water and store it in vessels at convenient points. Houses, fences, and orchards in the neighbourhood were destroyed and levelled, so that skulking warriors could not find shelter. The front of the fort was comparatively safe from attack, for the schooners guarded the river gate, and the Indians had a wholesome dread of these floating fortresses.

About the middle of the month the *Gladwyn* sailed down the Detroit to meet a convoy that was expected with provisions and ammunition from Fort Schlosser. At the entrance to Lake Erie, as the vessel lay becalmed in the river, she was suddenly beset by a swarm of savages in canoes; and Pontiac's prisoner, Captain Campbell, appeared in the foremost canoe, the savages thinking that the British would not fire on them for fear of killing him. Happily, a breeze sprang up and the schooner escaped to the open lake. There was no sign of the convoy; and the *Gladwyn* sailed for the Niagara, to carry to the officers there tidings of the Indian rising in the west.

On May 30 the watchful sentries at Detroit saw a line of *bateaux* flying the British flag rounding a point on the east shore of the river. This was the expected convoy from Fort Schlosser, and the cannon boomed forth a welcome. But the rejoicings of the garrison were soon stilled. Instead of British cheers, wild war-whoops resounded from the *bateaux*. The Indians had captured the convoy and were forcing their captives to row. In the foremost boat were four soldiers and three savages. Nearing the fortress one of the soldiers conceived the daring plan of overpowering the Indian guard and escaping to the *Beaver*, which lay anchored in front of the fort. Seizing the nearest savage he attempted to throw him into the river; but the Indian succeeded in stabbing him, and both fell overboard and were drowned. The other savages, dreading capture, leapt out of the boat and swam ashore. The *bateau* with the three soldiers in it reached the *Beaver*, and the provisions and ammunition it contained were taken to the fort. The Indians in the remaining *bateaux*, warned by the fate of the leading vessel, landed on the east shore; and, marching their prisoners overland past the fort, they took them across the river to Pontiac's camp, where most of them were put to death with fiendish cruelty.

The soldiers who escaped to the *Beaver* told the story of the ill-fated convoy. On May 13 Lieutenant Abraham Cuyler, totally ignorant of the outbreak of hostilities at Detroit, had left Fort Schlosser with ninety-six men in ten *bateaux*. They had journeyed in leisurely fashion along the northern shore of Lake Erie, and by the 28th had reached Point Pelee, about thirty miles from the Detroit river. Here a landing was made, and while tents were being pitched a band of painted savages suddenly darted out of the forest and attacked a man and a boy who were gathering wood. The man escaped, but the boy was tomahawked and scalped. Cuyler drew up his men in front of the boats, and a sharp musketry fire followed between the Indians, who were sheltered by a thick wood, and the white men on the exposed shore. The raiders were Wyandots from Detroit, the most courageous and intelligent savages in the region. Seeing that Cuyler's men were panic-stricken, they broke from their cover, with unusual boldness for Indians, and made a mad charge. The soldiers, completely unnerved by the savage yells and hurtling tomahawks, threw down their arms and dashed in confusion to the boats. Five they succeeded in pushing off, and into these they tumbled without weapons of defence. Cuyler himself was left behind wounded; but he waded out, and was taken aboard under a brisk fire from the shore. The Indians then launched two of the abandoned boats, rushed in pursuit of the fleeing soldiers, speedily captured three of the boats, and brought them ashore in triumph. The two others, in one of which was Cuyler, hoisted sail and escaped. The Indians, as we have seen, brought the captured boats and their prisoners to Detroit. Cuyler had directed his course to Sandusky, but finding the blockhouse there burnt to the ground, he had rowed eastward to Presqu'isle, and then hastened to Niagara to report the disaster.

The siege of Detroit went on. Towards the middle of June, Jacques Baby brought word to the commandant that the *Gladwyn* was returning from the Niagara with supplies and men, and that the Indians were making preparations to capture her. A few miles below Detroit lay Fighting Island; between it and the east shore, Turkey Island. Here the savages had erected a breastwork, so carefully concealed that it would be difficult even for the keenest eyes to detect its presence. The vessel would have to pass within easy range of this barricade; and it was the plan of the Indians to dart out in their canoes as the schooner worked up-stream, seize her, and slay her crew. On learning this news *Gladwyn* ordered cannon to be fired to notify the captain that the fort still held out, and sent a messenger to meet the vessel with word of the plot. It happened that the *Gladwyn* was well manned and prepared for battle. On board was Cuyler with twenty-two survivors of the ill-starred convoy, besides twenty-eight men of Captain Hopkins's company. To deceive the Indians as to the number of men, all the crew and soldiers, save ten or twelve, were concealed in the hold; to invite attack, the vessel advanced boldly up-stream, and at nightfall cast anchor in the narrow channel in front of Turkey Island. About midnight the Indians stealthily boarded their canoes and cautiously, but confidently, swept towards her with muffled paddles. The *Gladwyn* was ready for them. Not a sound broke the silence of the night as the Indians approached the schooner; when suddenly the clang of a hammer against the mast echoed over the calm waters, the signal to the soldiers in the hold. The Indians were almost on their prey; but before they had time to utter the war-whoop, the soldiers had

40

come up and had attacked the savages with bullets and cannon shot. Shrieks of death arose amid the din of the firing and the splash of swimmers hurriedly making for the shore from the sinking canoes. In a moment fourteen Indians were killed and as many more wounded. From behind the barricade the survivors began a harmless musketry fire against the schooner, which simply weighed anchor and drifted down-stream to safety. A day or two later she cleared Turkey Island and reached the fort, pouring a shattering broadside into the Wyandot village as she passed it. Besides the troops, the *Gladwyn* had on board a precious cargo of a hundred and fifty barrels of provisions and some ammunition. She had not run the blockade unscathed, for in passing Turkey Island one sergeant and four men had been wounded. There was rejoicing in the fort when the reinforcement marched in. This additional strength in men and provisions, it was expected, would enable the garrison to hold out for at least another month, within which time soldiers would arrive in sufficient force to drive the Indians away.

In the meantime Pontiac was becoming alarmed. He had expected an easy victory, and was not prepared for a protracted siege. He had drawn on the French settlers for supplies; his warriors had slain cattle and taken provisions without the consent of the owners. Leaders in the settlement now waited on Pontiac, making complaint. He professed to be fighting for French rule, and expressed sorrow at the action of his young men, promising that in future the French should be paid. Acting, no doubt, on the suggestion of some of his French allies, he made a list of the inhabitants, drew on each for a definite quantity of supplies, and had these deposited at Meloche's house near his camp on Parent's Creek. A commissary was appointed to distribute the provisions as required. In payment he issued letters of credit, signed with his *totem*, the otter. It is said that all of them were afterwards redeemed; but this is almost past belief in the face of what actually happened.

41

From the beginning of the siege Pontiac had hoped that the French traders and settlers would join him to force the surrender of the fort. The arrival of the reinforcement under Cuyler made him despair of winning without their assistance, and early in July he sent his Indians to the leading inhabitants along the river, ordering them to a council, at which he hoped by persuasion or threats to make them take up arms. This council was attended by such settlers as Robert Navarre, Zacharie Sicotte, Louis Campau, Antoine Cuillerier, Francois Meloche, all men of standing and influence. In his address to them Pontiac declared: 'If you are French, accept this war-belt for yourselves, or your young men, and join us; if you are English, we declare war upon you.'

The *Gladwyn* had brought news of the Peace of Paris between France and England. Many of the settlers had been hoping that success would crown the French arms in Europe and that Canada would be restored. Some of those at the council said that these articles of peace were a mere ruse on the part of Gladwyn to gain time. Robert Navarre, who had published the articles of peace to the French and Indians, and several others were friendly to the British, but the majority of those present were unfriendly. Sicotte told Pontiac that, while the heads of families could not take up arms, there were three hundred young men about Detroit who would willingly join him. These words were probably intended to humour the chief; but there were those who took the belt and commenced recruiting among their fellows. The settlers who joined Pontiac were nearly all half-breeds or men mated with Indian wives. Others, such as Pierre Reaume and Louis Campau, believing their lives to be in danger on account of their loyalty to the new rulers, sought shelter in the fort.

By July 4 the Indians, under the direction of French allies, had strongly entrenched themselves and had begun a vigorous attack. But a force of about sixty men marched out from the fort and drove them from the position. In the retreat two

Indians were killed, and one of the pursuing soldiers, who had been a prisoner among the Indians and had learned the ways of savage warfare, scalped one of the fallen braves. The victim proved to be a nephew of the chief of the Saginaw Chippewas, who now claimed life for life, and demanded that Captain Campbell should be given up to him. According to the 'Pontiac Manuscript' Pontiac acquiesced, and the Saginaw chief killed Campbell 'with a blow of his tomahawk, and after cast him into the river.' Campbell's fellow-prisoner McDougall, along with two others, had escaped to the fort some days before.

The investment continued, although the attacks became less frequent. The schooners manoeuvring in the river poured broadsides into the Indian villages, battering down the flimsy wigwams. Pontiac moved his camp from the mouth of Parent's Creek to a position nearer Lake St Clair, out of range of their guns, and turned his thoughts to contrive some means of destroying the troublesome vessels. He had learned from the French of the attempt with fire-ships against the British fleet at Quebec, and made trial of a similar artifice. *Bateaux* were joined together, loaded with inflammable material, ignited, and sent on their mission but these 'fire-ships' floated harmlessly past the schooners and burnt themselves out. Then for a week the Indians worked on the construction of a gigantic fire-raft, but nothing came of this ambitious scheme.

It soon appeared that Pontiac was beginning to lose his hold on the Indians. About the middle of July ambassadors from the Wyandots and Potawatomis came to the fort with an offer of peace, protesting, after the Indian manner, love and friendship for the British. After much parleying they surrendered their prisoners and plunder; but, soon after, a temptation irresistible to their treacherous natures offered itself, and they were again on the war-path.

Amherst at New York had at last been aroused to the danger; and Captain James Dalyell had set out from Fort

Schlosser with twenty-two barges, carrying nearly three hundred men, with cannon and supplies, for the relief of Detroit. The expedition skirted the southern shore of Lake Erie until it reached Sandusky. The Wyandot villages here were found deserted. After destroying them Dalyell shaped his course for the Detroit river. Fortune favoured the expedition. Pontiac was either ignorant of its approach or unable to mature a plan to check its advance. Through the darkness and fog of the night of July 28 the barges cautiously crept up-stream, and when the morning sun of the 29th lifted the mists from the river they were in full view of the fort. Relief at last! The weary watching of months was soon to end. The band of the fort was assembled, and the martial airs of England floated on the morning breeze. Now it was that the Wyandots and Potawatomis, although so lately swearing friendship to the British, thought the opportunity too good to be lost. In passing their villages the barges were assailed by a musketry fire, which killed two and wounded thirteen of Dalyell's men. But the soldiers, with muskets and swivels, replied to the attack, and put the Indians to flight. Then the barges drew up before the fort to the welcome of the anxious watchers of Detroit.

The reinforcement was composed of men of the 55th and 8th regiments, and of twenty Rangers under Major Robert Rogers. Like their commander, Dalyell, many of them were experienced in Indian fighting and were eager to be at Pontiac and his warriors. Dalyell thought that Pontiac might be taken by surprise, and urged on Gladwyn the advisability of an immediate advance. To this Gladwyn was averse; but Dalyell was insistent, and won his point. By the following night all was in readiness. At two o'clock in the morning of the 31st the river gate was thrown open and about two hundred and fifty men filed out.

Heavy clouds hid both moon and stars, and the air was oppressively hot. The soldiers marched along the dusty road, guided by Baby and St Martin, who had volunteered for the work. Not a sound save their own dull tramp broke the silence. On their right gleamed the calm river, and keeping pace with them were two large *bateaux* armed with swivels. Presently, as the troops passed the farm-houses, drowsy watch-dogs caught the sound of marching feet and barked furiously. Pontiac's camp, however, was still far away; this barking would not alarm the Indians. But the soldiers did not know that they had been betrayed by a spy of Pontiac's within the fort, nor did they suspect that snake-like eyes were even then watching their advance.

At length Parent's Creek was reached, where a narrow wooden bridge spanned the stream a few yards from its mouth. The advance-guard were half-way over the bridge, and the main body crowding after them, when, from a black ridge in front, the crackle of musketry arose, and half the advance-guard fell. The narrow stream ran red with their blood, and ever after this night it was known as Bloody Run. On the high ground to the north of the creek a barricade of cordwood had been erected, and behind this and behind barns and houses and fences, and in the corn-fields and orchards, Indians were firing and yelling like demons. The troops recoiled, but Dalyell rallied them; again they crowded to the bridge. There was another volley and another pause. With reckless bravery the soldiers pressed across the narrow way and rushed to the spot where the musket-flashes were seen. They won the height, but not an Indian was there. The musket-flashes continued and war-whoops sounded from new shelters. The *bateaux* drew up alongside the bridge, and the dead and wounded were taken on board to be carried to the fort. It was useless to attempt to drive the shifty savages from their lairs, and so the retreat was sounded. Captain Grant, in charge of the rear company, led his men back across the bridge while Dalyell covered the retreat; and now the fight took on a new aspect. As the soldiers retreated along the road leading to the fort, a destructive fire poured upon them from houses and barns, from behind fences, and from a newly dug cellar. With the river on their left, and with the enemy before and behind as well as on their sight, they were in danger of being annihilated. Grant ordered his men to fix bayonets: a dash was made where the savages were thickest, and they were scattered. As the fire was renewed panic seized the troops. But Dalyell came up from the rear, and with shouts and threats and flat of sword restored order. Day was breaking; but a thick fog hung over the scene, under cover of which the Indians continued the attack. The house of Jacques Campau, a trader, sheltered a number of Indians who were doing most destructive work. Rogers and a party of his Rangers attacked the house, and, pounding in the doors, drove out their assailants. From Campau's house Rogers covered the retreat of Grant's company, but was himself in turn besieged. By this time the armed *bateaux*, which had borne the dead and wounded to the fort, had returned, and, opening fire with their swivels on the Indians attacking Rogers, drove them off; the Rangers joined Grant's company, and all retreated for the fort. The shattered remnant of Dalyell's confident forces arrived at Fort Detroit at eight in the morning, after six hours of marching and desperate battle, exhausted and crestfallen. Dalyell had been slain— an irreparable loss. The casualty list was twenty killed and forty-two wounded. The Indians had suffered but slightly. However, they gained but little permanent advantage from the victory, as the fort had still about three hundred effective men, with ample provisions and ammunition, and could defy assault and withstand a protracted siege.

In this fight Chippewas and Ottawas took the leading part. The Wyandots had, however, at the sound of firing crossed the river, and the Potawatomis also had joined in the combat, in spite of the truce so recently made with Gladwyn. At the battle of Bloody Run at least eight hundred warriors were engaged in the endeavour to cut off Dalyell's men. There was rejoicing in the Indian villages, and more British scalps adorned the warriors' wigwams. Runners were sent out to the surrounding nations with news of the victory, and many recruits were added to Pontiac's forces.

CHAPTER 5

The Fall of the Lesser Forts

While Fort Detroit was withstanding Pontiac's hordes, the smaller forts and block-houses scattered throughout the hinterland were faring badly. On the southern shore of Lake Erie, almost directly south of the Detroit river, stood Fort Sandusky—a rude blockhouse surrounded by a stockade. Here were about a dozen men, commanded by Ensign Christopher Paully. The blockhouse could easily have been taken by assault; but such was not the method of the band of Wyandots in the neighbourhood. They preferred treachery, and, under the guise of friendship, determined to destroy the garrison with no risk to themselves.

On the morning of May 16 Paully was informed that seven Indians wished to confer with him. Four of these were members of the Wyandot tribe, and three belonged to Pontiac's band of Ottawas. The Wyandots were known to Paully, and as he had no news of the situation at Detroit, and no suspicion of danger to himself, he readily admitted them to his quarters. The Indians produced a *calumet* and handed it to Paully in token of friendship. As the pipe passed from lip to lip a warrior appeared at the door of the room and raised his arm. It was the signal for attack. Immediately Paully was seized by the Indians, two of whom had placed themselves on either side of him. At the same moment a war-whoop rang out and firing began; and as Paully was rushed across the parade-ground he saw the bodies of several of his men, who had been treacherously slain. The sentry had been tomahawked as he stood at arms at the gate; and the sergeant of the little company was killed while working in the garden of the garrison outside the stockade.

When night fell Paully and two or three others, all that remained of the garrison, were placed in canoes, and these were headed for Detroit. As the prisoners looked back over the calm waters of Sandusky Bay, they saw the blockhouse burst into flames. Paully and his men were landed at the Ottawa camp, where a horde of howling Indians, including women and children, beat them and compelled them to dance and sing for the entertainment of the rabble. Preparations were made to torture Paully to death at the stake; but an old squaw, who had recently lost her husband, was attracted by the handsome, dark-skinned young ensign, and adopted him in place of her deceased warrior. Paully's hair was cut close; he was dipped into the stream to wash the white blood from his veins; and finally he was dressed and painted as became an Ottawa brave.

News of the destruction of Fort Sandusky was brought to Gladwyn by a trader named La Brosse, a resident of Detroit, and a few days later a letter was received from Paully himself. For nearly two months Paully had to act the part of an Ottawa warrior. But early in July—Pontiac being in a state of great rage against the British—his squaw placed him in a farmhouse for safe keeping. In the confusion arising out of the attack on Fort Detroit on the 4th of the month, and the murder of Captain Campbell, he managed to escape, by the aid, it is said, of an Indian maiden. He was pursued to within musket-shot of the walls of Detroit. When he entered the fort, so much did he resemble an Indian that at first he was not recognized.

The next fort to fall into the hands of the Indians was St Joseph, on the east shore of Lake Michigan, at the mouth of the St Joseph river. This was the most inaccessible of the posts on the Great Lakes. The garrison here lived lonely lives. Around them were thick forests and swamps, and in front the desolate waters of the sea-like lake. The Indians about St Joseph had long been under the influence of the French. This place had been visited by La Salle; and here in 1688 the Jesuit Allouez had established a mission. In 1763 the post was held by Ensign Francis Schlosser and fourteen men. For months the little garrison had been without news from the east, when, on May 25, a party of Potawatomis from about Detroit arrived on a pretended visit to their relations living in the village at St Joseph, and asked permission to call on Schlosser. But before a meeting could be arranged, a French trader entered the fort and warned the commandant that the Potawatomis intended to destroy the garrison.

Schlosser at once ordered his sergeant to arm his men, and went among the French settlers seeking their aid. Even while he was addressing them a shrill death-cry rang out—the sentry at the gate had fallen a victim to the tomahawk of a savage. In an instant a howling mob of Potawatomis under their chief Washee were within the stockade. Eleven of the garrison were straightway put to death, and the fort was plundered. Schlosser and the three remaining members of his little band were taken to Detroit by some Foxes who were present with the Potawatomis. On June 10 Schlosser had the good fortune to be exchanged for two chiefs who were prisoners in Fort Detroit.

The Indians did not destroy Fort St Joseph, but left it in charge of the French under Louis Chevalier. Chevalier saved the lives of several British traders, and in every way behaved so admirably that at the close of the Indian war he was given a position of importance under the British, which position he held until the outbreak of the Revolutionary War.

We have seen that when Major Robert Rogers visited Detroit in 1760, one of the French forts first occupied was

Miami, situated on the Maumee river, at the commence-
ment of the portage to the Wabash, near the spot where Fort
Wayne was afterwards built. At the time of the outbreak of
the Pontiac War this fort was held by Ensign Robert Holmes
and twelve men. Holmes knew that his position was critical.
In 1762 he had reported that the Senecas, Shawnees, and
Delawares were plotting to exterminate the British in the
Indian country, and he was not surprised when, towards the
end of May 1763, he was told by a French trader that Detroit was besieged by the Ottawa Confederacy. But though
Holmes was on the alert, and kept his men under arms,
he was nevertheless to meet death and his fort was to be
captured by treachery. In his desolate wilderness home the
young ensign seems to have lost his heart to a handsome
young squaw living in the vicinity of the fort. On May 27
she visited him and begged him to accompany her on a
mission of mercy—to help to save the life of a sick Indian
woman. Having acted as physician to the Indians on former
occasions, Holmes thought the request a natural one. The
young squaw led him to the Indian village, pointed out the
wigwam where the woman was supposed to be, and then left
him. As he was about to enter the *wigwam* two musket-shots
rang out, and he fell dead. Three soldiers, who were outside
the fort, rushed for the gate, but they were tomahawked
before they could reach it. The gate was immediately closed,
and the nine soldiers within the fort made ready for resistance. With the Indians were two Frenchmen, Jacques Godfroy, whom we have met before as the ambassador to Pontiac
in the opening days of the siege of Detroit, and one Miny
Chesne; (this is the only recorded instance, except at Detroit, in which any French took part with the Indians in the
capture of a fort. And both Godfroy and Miny Chesne had
married Indian women) and they had an English prisoner,
a trader named John Welsh, who had been captured and
plundered at the mouth of the Maumee while on his way

51

to Detroit. The Frenchmen called on the garrison to surrender, pointing out how useless it would be to resist and how dreadful would be their fate if they were to slay any Indians. Without a leader, and surrounded as they were by a large band of savages, the men of the garrison saw that resistance would be of no avail. The gates were thrown open; the soldiers marched forth, and were immediately seized and bound; and the fort was looted. With Welsh the captives were taken to the Ottawa village at Detroit, where they arrived on June 4, and where Welsh and several of the soldiers were tortured to death.

A few miles south of the present city of Lafayette, on the south-east side of the Wabash, at the mouth of Wea Creek, stood the little wooden fort of Ouiatanon. It was connected with Fort Miami by a footpath through the forest. It was the most westerly of the British forts in the Ohio country, and might be said to be on the borderland of the territory along the Mississippi, which was still under the government of Louisiana. There was a considerable French settlement, and near by was the principal village of the Weas, a sub-tribe of the Miami nation. The fort was guarded by the usual dozen of men, under the command of Lieutenant Edward Jenkins. In March Jenkins had been warned that an Indian rising was imminent and that soon all the British in the hinterland would be prisoners. The French and Indians in this region were under the influence of the Mississippi officers and traders, who were, in Jenkins's words, 'eternally telling lies to the Indians,' leading them to believe that a great army would soon arrive to recover the forts. Towards the end of May ambassadors arrived at Ouiatanon, either from the Delawares or from Pontiac, bringing war-belts and instructions to the Weas to seize the fort. This, as usual, was achieved by treachery. Jenkins was invited to one of their cabins for a conference. Totally unaware of the Pontiac conspiracy, or of the fall of St Joseph, Sandusky, or Miami, he accepted the invitation. While passing out of the fort he was seized and bound, and, when taken to the cabin, he saw there several of his soldiers, prisoners like himself. The remaining members of the garrison surrendered, knowing how useless it would be to resist, and under the threat that if one Indian were killed all the British would be put to death. It had been the original intention of the Indians to seize the fort and slaughter the garrison, but, less blood-thirsty than Pontiac's immediate followers, they were won to mercy by two traders, Maisonville and Lorain, who gave them presents on the condition that the garrison should be made prisoners instead of being slain. Jenkins and his men were to have been sent to the Mississippi, but their removal was delayed, and they were quartered on the French inhabitants, and kindly treated by both French and Indians until restored to freedom.

The capture of Forts Miami and Ouiatanon gave the Indians complete control of the route between the western end of Lake Erie and the rivers Ohio and Mississippi. The French traders, who had undoubtedly been instrumental in goading the Indians to hostilities, had now the trade of the Wabash and lower Ohio, and of the tributaries of both, in their own hands. No British trader could venture into the region with impunity; the few who attempted it were plundered and murdered.

The scene of hostilities now shifts to the north. Next to Detroit the most important fort on the Great Lakes west of Niagara was Michilimackinac, situated on the southern shore of the strait connecting Lakes Huron and Michigan. The officer there had supervision of the lesser forts at Sault Ste Marie, Green Bay, and St Joseph. At this time Sault Ste Marie was not occupied by troops. In the preceding winter Lieutenant Jamette had arrived to take command; but fire had broken out in his quarters and destroyed the post, and he and his men had gone back to Michilimackinac, where they still were when the Pontiac War broke out. There were two important Indian tribes in the vicinity of Michilimackinac, the Chippewas and the Ottawas. The Chippewas had populous villages on the island of Mackinaw and at Thunder Bay on Lake Huron. They had as their hunting-grounds the eastern half of the peninsula which is now the state of Michigan. The Ottawas claimed as their territory the western half of the peninsula, and their chief village was L'Arbre Croche, where the venerable Jesuit priest, Father du Jaunay, had long conducted his mission.

The Indians about Michilimackinac had never taken kindly to the new occupants of the forts in their territory. When the trader Alexander Henry arrived there in 1761, he had found them decidedly hostile. On his journey up the Ottawa he had been warned of the reception in store for him. At Michilimackinac he was waited on by a party of Chippewas headed by their chief, Minavavna, a remarkably sagacious Indian, known to the French as *Le Grand Sauteur*, whose village was situated at Thunder Bay. This chief addressed Henry in most eloquent words, declaring that the Chippewas were the children of the French king, who was asleep, but who would shortly awaken and destroy his enemies. The king of England, he said, had entered into no treaty with the Chippewas and had sent them no presents: they were therefore still at war with him, and until he made such concessions they must look upon the French king as their chief. 'But,' he continued, 'you come unarmed: sleep peacefully!' The pipe of peace was then passed to Henry. After smoking it he bestowed on the Indians some gifts, and they filed out of his presence. Almost immediately on the departure of the Chippewas came some two hundred Ottawas demanding of Henry, and of several other British traders who were also there, ammunition, clothing, and other necessaries for their winter hunt, on credit until spring. The traders refused, and, when threatened by the Indians, they and their employees, some thirty in all, barricaded themselves in a house, and prepared to resist the demands by force of arms. Fortunately, at this critical moment word arrived of a strong British contingent that was approaching from Detroit to take over the fort, and the Ottawas hurriedly left for their villages.

For nearly two years the garrison at Michilimackinac lived in peace. In the spring of 1763 they were resting in a false security. Captain George Etherington, who was in command, heard that the Indians were on the war-path and that the fort was threatened; but he treated the report lightly. It is noteworthy, too, that Henry, who was in daily contact with the French settlers and Indians, and had his agents scattered throughout the Indian country, saw no cause for alarm. But it happened that towards the end of May news reached the Indians at Michilimackinac of the situation at Detroit, and with the news came a war-belt signifying that they were to destroy the British garrison. A crowd of Indians, chiefly Chippewas and Sacs, presently assembled at the post. This was a usual thing in spring, and would cause no suspicion. The savages, however, had planned to attack the fort on June 4, the birthday of George III. The British were to celebrate the day by sports and feasting, and the Chippewas and Sacs asked to be allowed to entertain the officers with a game of lacrosse. Etherington expressed pleasure at the suggestion, and told the chiefs who waited on him that he would back his friends the Chippewas against their Sac opponents. On the morning of the 4th posts were set up on the wide plain behind the fort, and tribe was soon opposed to tribe. The warriors appeared on the field with moccasined feet, and otherwise naked save for breech-cloths. Hither and thither the ball was batted, thrown, and carried. Player pursued player, tripping, slashing, shouldering each other, and shouting in their excitement as command of the ball passed with the fortunes of the game from Chippewa to Sac and from Sac to Chippewa. Etherington and Lieutenant Leslie were standing near the gate, interested spectators of the game; and all about, and scattered throughout the fort, were squaws with stoical faces, each holding tight about her a gaudily coloured blanket. The game was at its height, when a player threw the ball to a spot near the gate of the fort. There was a wild rush for it; and, as the gate was reached, lacrosse sticks were cast aside, the squaws threw open their blankets, and the players seized the tomahawks and knives held out in readiness to them. The shouts of play were changed to war-whoops. Instantly Etherington and Leslie were seized and hurried to a near-by wood. Into the fort the horde dashed. Here stood more squaws with weapons; and before the garrison had time to seize their arms, Lieutenant Jamette and fifteen soldiers were slain and scalped, and the rest made prisoners, while the French inhabitants stood by, viewing the tragedy with apparent indifference.

Etherington, Leslie, and the soldiers were held close prisoners. A day or two after the capture of the fort a Chippewa chief, Le Grand Sable, who had not been present at the massacre, returned from his wintering-ground. He entered a hut where a number of British soldiers were bound hand and foot, and brutally murdered five of them. The Ottawas, it will be noted, had taken no part in the capture of Michilimackinac. In fact, owing to the good offices of their priest, they acted towards the British as friends in need. A party of them from L'Arbre Croche presently arrived on the scene and prevented further massacre. Etherington and Leslie were taken from the hands of the Chippewas and removed to L'Arbre Croche. From this place Etherington sent a message to Green Bay, ordering the commandant to abandon the fort there. He then wrote to Gladwyn at Detroit, giving an account of what had happened and asking aid. This message was carried to Detroit by Father du Jaunay, who made the journey in company with seven Ottawas and eight Chippewas commanded by Kinonchanek, a son of Minavavna. But, as we know, Gladwyn was himself in need of assistance, and could give none. The prisoners at L'Arbre Croche, however, were well treated, and finally taken to Montreal by way of the Ottawa river, under an escort of friendly Indians.

On the southern shore of Lake Erie, where the city of Erie now stands, was the fortified post of Presqu'isle, a stockaded fort with several substantial houses. It was considered a strong position, and its commandant, Ensign John Christie, had confidence that he could hold out against any number of Indians that might beset him. The news brought by Cuyler when he visited Presqu'isle, after the disaster at Point Pelee, put Christie on his guard. Presqu'isle had a blockhouse of unusual strength, but it was of wood, and inflammable. To guard against fire, there was left at the top of the building an opening through which water could be poured in any direction. The blockhouse stood on a tongue of land—on the one side a creek, on the other the lake. The most serious weakness of the position was that the banks of the creek and the lake rose in ridges to a considerable height, commanding the blockhouse and affording a convenient shelter for an attacking party within musket range.

Christie had twenty-four men, and believed that he had nothing to fear, when, on June 15, some two hundred Wyandots arrived in the vicinity. These Indians were soon on the ridges, assailing the blockhouse. Arrows tipped with burning tow and balls of blazing pitch rained upon the roof, and the utmost exertions of the garrison were needed to extinguish the fires. Soon the supply of water began to fail. There was a well near by on the parade-ground, but this open space was subject to such a hot fire that no man would venture to cross it. A well was dug in the blockhouse, and the resistance continued. All day the attack was kept up, and during the night there was intermittent firing from the ridges. Another day passed, and at night came a lull in the siege. A demand was made to surrender. An English soldier who had been adopted by the savages, and was aiding them in the attack, cried out that the destruction of the fort was inevitable, that in the morning it would be fired at the top and bottom, and that unless the garrison yielded they would all be burnt to death. Christie asked till morning to consider; and, when morning came, he agreed to yield up the fort on condition that the garrison should be allowed to march to the next post. But as his men filed out they were seized and bound, then cast into canoes and taken to Detroit. Their lives, however, were spared; and early in July, when the Wyandots made with Gladwyn the peace which they afterwards broke, Christie and a number of his men were the first prisoners given up.

A few miles inland, south of Presqu'isle, on the trade-route leading to Fort Pitt, was a rude blockhouse known as Le Boeuf. This post was at the end of the portage from Lake Erie, on Alleghany Creek, where the canoe navigation of the Ohio valley began. Here were stationed Ensign George Price and thirteen men. On June 18 a band of Indians arrived before Le Boeuf and attacked it with muskets and fire-arrows. The building was soon in flames. As the walls smoked and crackled the savages danced in wild glee before the gate, intending to shoot down the defenders as they came out. But there was a window at the rear of the blockhouse, through which the garrison escaped to the neighbouring forest. When night fell the party became separated. Some of them reached Fort Venango two days later, only to find it in ruins. Price and seven men laboriously toiled through the forest to Fort Pitt, where they arrived on June 26. Ultimately, all save two of the garrison of Fort Le Boeuf reached safety.

The circumstances attending the destruction of Fort Venango on June 20 are but vaguely known. This fort, situated near the site of the present city of Franklin, had long been a centre of Indian trade. In the days o the French occupation it was known as Fort Machault. After the French abandoned the place in the summer of 1760 a new fort had been erected and named Venango. In 1763 there was a small garrison here under Lieutenant Gordon. For a time all that was known of its fate was reported by the fugitives from Le Boeuf and a soldier named Gray, who had escaped from Presqu'isle. These fugitives had found Venango completely destroyed, and, in the ruins, the blackened bones of the garrison. It was afterwards learned that the attacking Indians were Senecas, and that they had tortured the commandant to death over a slow fire, after compelling him to write down the reason for the attack. It was threefold: (1) the British charged exorbitant prices for powder, shot, and clothing; (2) when Indians were ill-treated by British soldiers they could obtain no redress; (3) contrary to the wishes of the Indians, forts were being built in their country, and these could mean but one thing—the determination of the invaders to deprive them of their hunting-grounds.

With the fall of Presqu'isle, Le Boeuf, and Venango, the trade-route between Lake Erie and Fort Pitt was closed. Save for Detroit, Niagara, and Pitt, not a British fort remained in the great hinterland; and the soldiers at these three strong positions could leave the shelter of the palisades only at the risk of their lives. Meanwhile, the frontiers of the British settlements, as well as the forts, were being raided. Homes were burnt and the inmates massacred. Traders were plundered and slain. From the eastern slopes of the Alleghanies to the Mississippi no British life was safe.

CHAPTER 6

The Relief of Fort Pitt

On the tongue of land at the confluence of the Monongahela and Aheghany rivers stood Fort Pitt, on the site of the old French fort Duquesne. It was remote from any centre of population, but was favourably situated for defence, and so strongly garrisoned that those in charge of it had little to fear from any attempts of the Indians to capture it. Floods had recently destroyed part of the ramparts, but these had been repaired and a parapet of logs raised above them.

Captain Simeon Ecuyer, a Swiss soldier in the service of Great Britain and an officer of keen intelligence and tried courage, was in charge of Fort Pitt. He knew the Indians. He had quickly realized that danger threatened his wilderness post, and had left nothing undone to make it secure. On the fourth day of May, Ecuyer had written to Colonel Henry Bouquet, who was stationed at Philadelphia, saying that he had received word from Gladwyn that he 'was surrounded by rascals.' Ecuyer did not treat this alarm lightly. He not only repaired the ramparts and made them stronger, but also erected palisades within them to surround the dwellings. Everything near the fort that could give shelter to a lurking foe was levelled to the ground. There were in Fort Pitt at this time about a hundred women and their children—families of settlers who had come to the fertile Ohio valley to take up homes. These were provided with shelter in houses made shot-proof.

Small-pox had broken out in the garrison, and a hospital was prepared under the drawbridge, where the patients in time of siege would be in no danger from musket-balls or arrows. But the best defence of Fort Pitt was the capacity of Ecuyer— brave, humorous, foresighted; a host in himself—giving courage to his men and making even the women and children think lightly of the power of the Indians.

It was nearly three weeks after the siege of Detroit had begun that the savages appeared in force about Fort Pitt. On May 27 a large band of Indians came down the Alleghany bearing packs of furs, in payment for which they demanded guns, knives, tomahawks, powder, and shot, and would take nothing else. Soon after their departure word was brought to Ecuyer of the murder of some traders and settlers not far from the fort. From that time until the beginning of August it was hazardous for any one to venture outside the walls; but for nearly a month no attack was to be made on the fort itself. However, as news of the capture of the other forts reached the garrison, and as nearly all the messengers sent to the east were either slain or forced to return, it was evident that, in delaying the attack on Fort Pitt, the Indians were merely gathering strength for a supreme effort against the strongest position in the Indian territory.

On June 22 a large body of Indians assembled in the forest about the fort, and, creeping stealthily within range of its walls, opened fire from every side. It was the garrison's first experience of attack; some of the soldiers proved a trifle overbold, and two of them were killed. The firing, however, lasted but a short time. Ecuyer selected a spot where the smoke of the muskets was thickest, and threw shells from his howitzers into the midst of the warriors, scattering them in hurried flight. On the following day a party came within speaking distance, and their leader, Turtle's Heart, a Delaware chief, informed Ecuyer that all the western and northern forts had been cut off, and that a host of warriors were coming to destroy Fort Pitt and its garrison. He begged Ecuyer to withdraw the inmates of the fort while there was yet time. He would see to it that they were protected on their way to the eastern settlements. He added that when the Ottawas and their allies arrived, all hope for the lives of the inhabitants of Fort Pitt would be at an end. All this Turtle's Heart told Ecuyer out of 'love for the British.' The British officer, with fine humour, thanked him for his consideration for the garrison, but told him that he could hold out against all the Indians in the woods. He could be as generous as Turtle's Heart, and so warned him that the British were coming to relieve Fort Pitt with six thousand men; that an army of three thousand was ascending the Great Lakes to punish the Ottawa Confederacy; and that still another force of three thousand had gone to the frontiers of Virginia. 'Therefore,' he said, 'take pity on your women and children, and get out of the way as soon as possible. We have told you this in confidence, out of our great solicitude, lest any of you should be hurt; and,' he added, 'we hope that you will not tell the other Indians, lest they should escape from our vengeance.' The howitzers and the story of the approaching hosts had their effect, and the Indians vanished into the surrounding forest. For another month Fort Pitt had comparative peace, and the garrison patiently but watchfully awaited a relieving force which Amherst was sending. In the meantime news came of the destruction of Presqu'isle, Le Boeuf, and Venango; and the fate of the garrisons, particularly at the last post, warned the inhabitants of Fort Pitt what they might expect if they should fall into the hands of the Indians.

On July 26 some Indian ambassadors, among them Turtle's Heart, came to the post with a flag of truce. They were loud in their protestations of friendship, and once more solicitous for the safety of the garrison. The Ottawas, they said, were coming in a vast horde, to 'seize and eat up everything' that came in their way. The garrison's only hope of escape would be to vacate the fort speedily and 'go home to their wives and children.' Ecuyer replied that he would never abandon his position 'as long as a white man lives in America.' He despised the Ottawas, he said, and was 'very much surprised at our brothers the Delawares for proposing to us to leave this place and go home. This is our home.' His humour was once more in evidence in the warning he gave the Indians against repeating their attack on the fort: 'I will throw bomb-shells, which will burst and blow you to atoms, and fire cannon among you, loaded with a whole bagful of bullets. Therefore take care, for I don't want to hurt you.'

The Indians now gave up all hope of capturing Fort Pitt by deception, and prepared to take it by assault. That very night they stole within range, dug shelter-pits in the banks of the Alleghany and Monongahela, and at daybreak began a vigorous attack on the garrison. Musket-balls came whistling over the ramparts and smote every point where a soldier showed himself. The shrieking balls and the wild war-whoops of the assailants greatly alarmed the women and children; but never for a moment was the fort in real danger or did Ecuyer or his men fear disaster. So carefully had the commandant seen to his defences, that, although hundreds of missiles fell within the confines of the fort, only one man was killed and only seven were wounded. Ecuyer himself was among the wounded: one of two arrows that fell within the fort had, to use his own words, 'the insolence to make free' with his 'left leg.' From July 27 to August 1 this horde of Delawares, Shawnees, Wyandots, and Mingoes kept up the attack. Then, without apparent cause, as suddenly as they had arrived, they all disappeared. To the garrison the relief from constant vigil, anxious days, and sleepless nights was most welcome.

The reason for this sudden relief was that the red men had learned of a rich prize for them, now approaching Fort Pitt. Bouquet, with a party of soldiers, was among the defiles of the Alleghanies. The fort could wait; the Indians would endeavour to annihilate Bouquet's force as they had annihilated Braddock's army in the same region eight years before; and if successful, they could then at their leisure return to Fort Pitt and starve it out or take it by assault.

In June, when Amherst had finally come to the conclusion that he had a real war on his hands—and had, as we have seen, dispatched Dalyell to Detroit—he had, at the same time, sent orders to Colonel Bouquet to get ready a force for the relief of Fort Pitt. Bouquet, like Ecuyer, was a Swiss soldier, and the best man in America for this particular task. After seven years' experience in border warfare he was as skilled in woodcraft as the Indians themselves. He had now to lead a force over the road, two hundred odd miles long, which connected Fort Pitt with Carlisle, his point of departure in Pennsylvania; but every foot of the road was known to him. In 1758, when serving under General Forbes, he had directed the construction of this road, and knew the strength of every fort and block-house on the way; even the rivers and creeks and morasses and defiles were familiar to him. Best of all, he had a courage and a military knowledge that inspired confidence in his men and officers. Cool, calculating, foreseeing, dauntlessly brave—there was not in the New World at this time a better soldier than this heroic Swiss.

Amherst was in a bad way for troops. The only available forces for the relief of Fort Pitt were 242 men of the 42nd Highlanders—the famous Black Watch—with 133 of the 77th (Montgomery's) Highlanders, and some Royal Americans. These, with a few volunteers, made up a contingent 550 strong. It was a force all too small for the task before it, and the majority of the soldiers had but recently arrived from the West Indies and were in wretched health.

Bouquet had sent instructions to Carlisle to have supplies ready for him and sufficient wagons assembled there for the expedition, but when he reached the place at the end of June he found that nothing had been done. The frontier was in a state of paralysis from panic. Over the entire stretch of country from Fort Pitt the Indians were on the war-path. Every day brought tragic stories of the murder of settlers and the destruction of their homes. There was no safety outside the precincts of the feeble forts that dotted the Indian territory. Bouquet had hoped for help from the settlers and government of Pennsylvania; but the settlers thought only of immediate safety, and the government was criminally negligent in leaving the frontier of the state unprotected, and would vote neither men nor money for defence. But they must be saved in spite of themselves. By energetic efforts, in eighteen days after his arrival at Carlisle, Bouquet was ready for the march. He began his campaign with a wise precaution. The last important fort on the road to Pitt was Ligonier, about one hundred and fifty miles from Carlisle. It would be necessary to use this post as a base; but it was beset by Indians and in danger of being captured. Lieutenant Archibald Blane in charge of it was making a gallant defence against a horde of savages. Bouquet, while waiting at Carlisle, engaged guides and sent in advance thirty Highlanders, carefully selected men, to strengthen the garrison under Blane. These, by keeping off the main trail and using every precaution, succeeded in reaching the fort without mishap.

Bouquet led his force westward. Sixty of his soldiers were so ill that they were unable to march and had to be carried in wagons. It was intended that the sick should take the place of the men now in Forts Bedford and Ligonier, and thus help to guard the rear. The road was found to be in frightful condition. The spring freshets had cut it up; deep gullies crossed the path; and the bridges over the streams had been in most cases washed away. As the little army advanced, panic-stricken settlers by the way told stories of the destruction of homes and the slaughter of friends. Fort Bedford, where Captain Lewis Ourry was in command, was reached on the 25th. Here three days were spent, and thirty more guides were secured to serve as an advance-guard of scouts and give warning of the presence of enemies. Bouquet had tried his Highlanders at this work; but they were unfamiliar with the forest, and, as they invariably got lost, were of no value as scouts. Leaving his invalided officers and men at Bedford, Bouquet, with horses rested and men refreshed, pressed forward and arrived at Ligonier on August 2. Preparations had now to be made for the final dash to Fort Pitt, fifty odd miles away, over a path that was beset by savages, who also occupied all the important passes. It would be impossible to get through without a battle—a wilderness battle—and the thought of the Braddock disaster was in the minds of all. But Bouquet was not a Braddock, and he was experienced in Indian warfare. To attempt to pass ambuscades with a long train of cumbersome wagons would be to invite disaster; so he discarded his wagons and heavier stores, and having made ready three hundred and forty pack-horses loaded with flour, he decided to set out from Ligonier on the 4th of August. It was planned to reach Bushy Creek—'Bushy Run,' as Bouquet called it—on the following day, and there rest and refresh horses and men. In the night a dash would be made through the dangerous defile at Turtle Creek; and, if the high broken country at this point could be passed without mishap, the rest of the way could be easily won.

At daylight the troops were up and off. It was an oppressively hot August morning, and no breath of wind stirred the forest. Over the rough road trudged the long line of sweltering men. In advance were the scouts; then followed several light companies of the Black Watch; then the main body of the little army; and in the rear came the toiling pack-horses. Until noon the soldiers marched, panting and tortured by mosquitoes, but buoyed up by the hope that at Bushy Run they would be able to quench their burning thirst and rest until nightfall. By one o'clock in the afternoon they had covered seventeen miles and were within a mile and a half of their objective point. Suddenly in their front they heard the sharp reports of muskets; the firing grew in intensity: the advance-guard was evidently in contact with a considerable body of Indians. Two light companies were rushed forward to their support, and with fixed bayonets cleared the path. This, however, was but a temporary success. The Indians merely changed their position and appeared on the flanks in increased numbers. From the shelter of trees the foe were creating havoc among the exposed troops, and a general charge was necessary. Highlanders and Royal Americans, acting under the directing eye of Bouquet, again drove the Indians back with the bayonet. Scarcely had this been accomplished when a fusillade was heard in the rear. The convoy was attacked, and it was necessary to fall back to its support. Until nightfall, around a bit of elevated ground—called Edge Hill by Bouquet—on which the convoy was drawn up, the battle was waged. About the pack-horses and stores the soldiers valiantly fought for seven hours against their invisible foe. At length darkness fell, and the exhausted troops could take stock of their losses and snatch a brief, broken rest. In this day of battle two officers were killed and four wounded, and sixty of the rank and file were killed or wounded.

Flour-bags were piled in a circle, and within this the wounded were placed. Throughout the night a careful watch was kept; but the enemy made no attack during the darkness, merely firing an occasional shot and from time to time uttering defiant yells. They were confident that Bouquet's force would be an easy prey, and waited for daylight to renew the battle.

The soldiers had played a heroic part. Though unused to forest warfare, they had been cool as veterans in Indian fighting, and not a man had fired a shot without orders. But the bravest of them looked to the morning with dread. They had barely been able to hold their own on this day, and by morning the Indians would undoubtedly be greatly strengthened. The cries and moans of the wounded vividly reminded them of what had already happened. Besides, they were worn out with marching and fighting; worse than physical fatigue and more trying than the enemy's bullets was torturing thirst; and not a drop of water could be obtained at the place where they were hemmed in.

By the flickering light of a candle Bouquet penned one of the noblest letters ever written by a soldier in time of battle. He could hardly hope for success, and defeat meant the most horrible of deaths; but he had no craven spirit, and his report to Amherst was that of a true soldier—a man 'whose business it is to die.' After giving a detailed account of the occurrences leading up to this attack and a calm statement of the events of the day, and paying a tribute to his officers, whose conduct, he said, 'is much above my praise,' he added: 'Whatever our fate may be, I thought it necessary to give Your Excellency this information... I fear unsurmountable difficulties in protecting and transporting our provisions, being already so much weakened by the loss in this day of men and horses.' Sending a messenger back with this dispatch, he set himself to plan for the morrow.

At daybreak from the surrounding wood the terrifying war-cries of the Indians fell on the ears of the troops. Slowly the shrill yells came nearer; the Indians were endeavouring to strike terror into the hearts of their foes before renewing the fight, knowing that troops in dread of death are already half beaten. When within five hundred yards of the centre of the camp the Indians began firing. The troops replied with great steadiness. This continued until ten in the morning. The wounded within the barricade lay listening to the sounds of battle, ever increasing in volume, and the fate of Braddock's men rose before them. It seemed certain that their sufferings must end in death—and what a death! The pack-horses, tethered at a little distance from the barricade, offered an easy target, against which the Indians soon directed their fire, and the piteous cries of the wounded animals added to the tumult of the battle. Some of the horses, maddened by wounds, broke their fastenings and galloped into the forest. But the kilted Highlanders and the red-coated Royal Americans gallantly fought on. Their ranks were being thinned; the fatiguing work of the previous day was telling on them; their throats were parched and their tongues swollen for want of water. Bouquet surveyed the field. He saw his men weakening under the terrible strain, and realized that something must be done promptly. The Indians were each moment becoming bolder, pressing ever nearer and nearer.

Then he conceived one of the most brilliant movements known in Indian warfare. He ordered two companies, which were in the most exposed part of the field, to fall back as though retreating within the circle that defended the hill. At the same time the troops on the right and left opened their files, and, as if to cover the retreat, occupied the space vacated in a thinly extended line. The strategy worked even better than Bouquet had expected. The yelling Indians, eager for slaughter and believing that the entire command was at their mercy, rushed pell-mell from their shelter, firing sharp volleys into the protecting files. These were forced back, and the savages dashed forward for the barricade which sheltered the wounded. Meanwhile the two companies had taken position on the right, and from a sheltering hill that concealed them from the enemy they poured an effective fire into the savages. The astonished Indians replied, but with little effect, and before they could reload the Highlanders were on them with the bayonet. The red men then saw that they had fallen into a trap, and turned to flee. But suddenly on their left two more companies rose from ambush and sent a storm of bullets into the retreating savages, while the Highlanders and Royal Americans dashed after them with fixed bayonets. The Indians at other parts of the circle, seeing their comrades in flight, scattered into the forest. The defiant war-cries ceased and the muskets were silent. The victory was complete: Bouquet had beaten the Indians in their own woods and at their own game. About sixty of the enemy lay dead and as many more wounded. In the two days of battle the British had fifty killed, sixty wounded, and five missing. It was a heavy price; but this victory broke the back of the Indian war.

Many horses had been killed or had strayed away, and it was impossible to transport all the stores to Fort Pitt. What could not be carried with the force was destroyed, and the victors moved on to Bushy Creek, at a slow pace on account of the wounded. No sooner had they pitched their tents at the creek than some of the enemy again appeared; the Highlanders, however, without waiting for the word of command, scattered them with the bayonet. On the following day the march began for Fort Pitt. Three days later, on August 10, the garrison of that fort heard the skirl of the bagpipes and the beat of the drum, and saw through the forest the plaids and plumes of the Highlanders and the red coats of the Royal Americans. The gate was thrown open, and the victors of Edge Hill marched in to the welcome of the men and women who for several months had had no news from their friends in the east.

Bouquet had been instructed to invade the Ohio country and teach the Shawnees and Delawares a lesson. But his men were worn out, half of them were unfit for service, and so deficient was he in horses and supplies that this task had to be abandoned for the present year.

Pennsylvania and Virginia rejoiced. This triumph meant much to them. Their borders would now be safe, but for occasional scalping parties. Amherst was delighted, and took to himself much of the credit of Bouquet's victory. He congratulated the noble Swiss officer on his victory over 'a band of savages that would have been very formidable against any troops but such as you had with you.' But it was not the troops that won the battle; it was Bouquet. In the hands of a Braddock, a Loudoun, an Abercromby, these war-worn veterans would have met a fate such as befell Braddock's troops. But Bouquet animated every man with his own spirit; he knew how to fight Indians; and at the critical moment—'the fatal five minutes between victory and defeat'—he proved himself the equal of any soldier who ever battled against the red men in North America.

CHAPTER 7

Detroit Once More

While Fort Pitt was holding out against the Ohio Indians and Bouquet was forcing his way through the defiles of the Alleghanies to its relief, Fort Detroit was still in a state of siege. The defeat of Dalyell's force at Bloody Run had given the Indians a greater degree of confidence. They had not dared, however, to make a general assault, but had merely kept the garrison aware of their presence by desultory and irritating attacks.

Nothing of importance took place until September 3. On this day the little *Gladwyn*, which had gone to the Niagara with dispatches, entered the Detroit river on her return trip. She was in charge of Captain Horst, who was assisted by Jacobs as mate, and a crew of ten men. There were likewise on board six Iroquois Indians. It was a calm morning; and as the vessel lay with idly flapping sails waiting for a wind, the Iroquois asked permission to stretch their limbs on shore. Horst foolishly granted their request, and as soon as they had made a landing they disappeared into the forest, and no doubt hurried to Pontiac's warriors to let them know how weakly manned was the schooner. The weather continued calm, and by nightfall the *Gladwyn* was still nine miles below the fort. As darkness fell on that moonless night the captain, alarmed at the flight of the Iroquois, posted a careful guard and had his cannon at bow and stern made ready to resist attack. So dark was the night that it was impossible to discern objects at any distance. Along the black shore Indians were gathering, and soon a fleet of canoes containing over three hundred warriors was slowly and silently moving towards the becalmed *Gladwyn*. So noiseless was their approach that they were within a few yards of the vessel before a watchful sentry, the boatswain, discerned them. At his warning cry the crew leapt to their quarters. The bow gun thundered out, and its flash gave the little band on the boat a momentary glimpse of a horde of painted enemies. There was no time to reload the gun. The canoes were all about the schooner, and yelling warriors were clambering over the stern and bow and swarming on the deck. The crew discharged their muskets into the savages, and then seized spears and hatchets and rushed madly at them, striking and stabbing —determined at least to sell their lives dearly. For a moment the Indians in the black darkness shrank back from the fierce attack. But already Horst was killed and several of the crew were down with mortal wounds. The vessel seemed lost when Jacobs—a dare-devil seaman—now in command, ordered his men to blow up the vessel. A Wyandot brave with some knowledge of English caught the words and shouted a warning to his comrades. In an instant every warrior was over the side of the vessel, paddling or swimming to get to safety. When morning broke not an Indian was to be seen, and the little *Gladwyn* sailed in triumph to Fort Detroit. So greatly was the gallantry of her crew appreciated that Amherst had a special medal struck and given to each of the survivors.

Meanwhile, at Niagara, supplies were being conveyed over the portage between the lower landing (now Lewiston) and Fort Schlosser, in readiness for transport to the western posts. The Senecas claimed the territory about Niagara, and the invasion of their land had greatly irritated them. They particularly resented the act of certain squatters who, without their consent, had settled along the Niagara portage. Fort Niagara was too strong to be taken by assault; but the Senecas hoped, by biding their time, to strike a deadly blow against parties conveying goods over the portage. The opportunity came on September 14. On this day a sergeant and twenty-eight men were engaged in escorting down to the landing a wagon-train and pack-horses which had gone up to Fort Schlosser the day before loaded with supplies. The journey up the river had been successfully made, and the party were returning, off their guard and without the slightest thought of danger. But their every movement had been watched by Indian scouts; and, at the Devil's Hole, a short distance below the falls, five hundred warriors lay in ambush. Slowly the returning provision-train wound its way along the bank of the Niagara. On the right were high cliffs, thickly wooded; on the left a precipice, whose base was fretted by the furious river. In the ears of the soldiers and drivers sounded the thunderous roar of the mighty cataract. As men and horses threaded their way past the Devil's Hole savage yells burst from the thick wood on their right, and simultaneously a fusillade from a hundred muskets. The terrified horses sprang over the cliffs, dragging wagons and drivers with them. When the smoke cleared and the savages rushed forward, not a living member of the escort nor a driver was to be seen. The leader of the escort, Philip Stedman, had grasped the critical character of the situation at the first outcry, and, putting spurs to his horse, had dashed into the bushes. A warrior had seized his rein; but Stedman had struck him down and galloped free for Fort Schlosser. A drummer-boy, in terror of his life, had leapt over the cliff. By good fortune his drum-strap caught on the branch of a dense tree; here he remained suspended until the Indians left the spot, when he extricated himself. One of the teamsters also escaped. He was wounded, but managed to roll into the bushes, and found concealment in the thick undergrowth. The terrific musketry fire was heard at the lower landing, where a body of troops of the 60th and 80th regiments were encamped. The soldiers hastily armed themselves and in great disorder rushed to the aid of the convoy. But the Indians were not now at the Devil's Hole. The murderous work completed there, they had taken up a position in a thick wood half a mile farther down, where they silently waited. They had chosen well their place of concealment; and the soldiers in their excitement walked into the trap set for them. Suddenly the ominous war-cries broke out, and before the troops could turn to face the foe a storm of bullets had swept their left flank. Then the warriors dashed from their ambush, tomahawking the living and scalping both dead and dying. In a few minutes five officers and seventy-six of the rank and file were killed and eight wounded, and out of a force of over one hundred men only twenty escaped unhurt. The news of this second disaster brought Major Wilkins up from Fort Niagara, with every available man, to chastise the Indians. But when Wilkins and his men arrived at the gruesome scene of the massacre not a red man was to be found. The Indians had disappeared into the forest, after having stripped their victims even of clothing. With a heavy heart the troops marched back to Niagara, mourning the loss of many gallant comrades. This was the greatest disaster, in loss of life, of the Pontiac War; but, like the defeat of Dalyell, it had little effect on the progress of the campaign. The Indians did not follow it up; with scalps and plunder they returned to their villages to exult in wild orgies over the victory.

Detroit was still besieged; but the Indians were beginning to weaken, and for the most part had given up hope of forcing the garrison to surrender. They had been depending almost wholly on the settlement for sustenance, and provisions were running low. Ammunition, too, was well-nigh exhausted. They had replenished their supply during the summer by the captures they had made, by the plundering of traders, and by purchase or gift from the French of the Mississippi. Now they had little hope of capturing more supply-boats; the traders were holding aloof; and, since the arrival of definite news of the surrender to Great Britain by France of the region east of the Mississippi, supplies from the French had been stopped. If the Indians were to escape starvation they must scatter to their hunting-grounds. There was another reason why many of the chiefs deemed it wise to leave the vicinity of Detroit. They had learned that Major Wilkins was on his way from Niagara with a strong force and a fleet of *bateaux* loaded with ammunition and supplies. So, early in October, the Potawatomis, Wyandots, and Chippewas held a council and concluded to bury the hatchet and make peace with Gladwyn. On the 12th of the month a delegation from these tribes came to the fort bearing a pipe of peace. Gladwyn knew from experience how little they were to be trusted, but he gave them a seemingly cordial welcome. A chief named Wapocomoguth acted as spokesman, and stated that the tribes represented regretted 'their bad conduct' and were ready to enter into a treaty of peace. Gladwyn replied that it was not in his power to grant peace to Indians who without cause had attacked the troops of their father the king of England; only the commander-in-chief could do that; but he consented to a cessation of hostilities. He did this the more willingly as the fort was short of food, and the truce would give him a chance to lay in a fresh stock of provisions.

As the autumn frosts were colouring the maples with brilliant hues, the Potawatomis, Wyandots, and Chippewas set out for fields where game was plentiful; but for a time Pontiac with his Ottawas remained, threatening the garrison, and still strong in his determination to continue the siege. During the summer he had sent ambassadors to Fort Chartres on the Mississippi asking aid in fighting what he asserted to be the battle of the French traders. Towards the end of July the messengers had returned with word from Neyon de Villiers, the commandant of Fort Chartres, saying that he must await more definite news as to whether peace had been concluded between France and England. Pontiac still hoped; and, after his allies had deserted, he waited at his camp above Detroit for further word from Neyon. On the last day of October Louis Cesair Dequindre arrived at Detroit from Fort Chartres, with the crushing answer that Neyon de Villiers could give him no aid. England and France were at peace, and Neyon advised the Ottawas—no doubt with reluctance, and only because of the demand of Amherst—to bury the hatchet and give up the useless contest. To continue the struggle for the present would be vain. Pontiac, though enraged by the desertion of his allies, and by what seemed to him the cowardly conduct of the French, determined at once to accept the situation, sue for peace, and lay plans for future action. So far he had been fighting ostensibly for the restoration of French rule. In future, whatever scheme he might devise, his struggle must be solely in the interests of the red man. Next day he sent a letter to Gladwyn begging that the past might be forgotten. His young men, he said, had buried their hatchets, and he declared himself ready not only to make peace, but also to 'send to all the nations concerned in the war' telling them to cease hostilities. No trust could Gladwyn put in Pontiac's words; yet he assumed a friendly bearing towards the treacherous conspirator, who for nearly six months had given him no rest. Gladwyn's views of the situation at this time are well shown in a report he made to Amherst. The Indians, he said, had lost many of their best warriors, and would not be likely again to show a united front. It was in this report that he made the suggestion, unique in warfare, of destroying the Indians by the free sale of rum to them. 'If your Excellency,' he wrote, 'still intends to punish them further for their barbarities, it may easily be done without any expense to the Crown, by permitting a free sale of rum, which will destroy them more effectually than fire and sword.' He thought that the French had been the real plotters of the Indian war: 'I don't imagine there will be any danger of their [the Indians] breaking out again, provided some examples are made of our good friends, the French, who set them on.'

Pontiac and his band of savages paddled southward for the Maumee, and spent the winter among the Indians along its upper waters. Again he broke his plighted word and plotted a new confederacy, greater than the Three Fires, and sent messengers with *wampum* belts and red hatchets to all the tribes as far south as the mouth of the Mississippi and as far north as the Red River. But his glory had departed. He could call; but the warriors would not come when he summoned them.

Fort Detroit was freed from hostile Indians, and the soldiers could go to rest without expecting to hear the call to arms. But before the year closed it was to be the witness of still another tragedy. Two or three weeks after the massacre at the Devil's Hole, Major Wilkins with some six hundred troops started from Fort Schlosser with a fleet of *bateaux* for Detroit. No care seems to have been taken to send out scouts to learn if the forest bordering the river above the falls was free from Indians, and, as the *bateaux* were slowly making their way against the swift stream towards Lake Erie, they were savagely attacked from the western bank by Indians in such force that Wilkins was compelled to retreat to Fort Schlosser. It was not until November that another attempt was made to send troops and provisions to Detroit. Early in this month Wilkins once more set out from Fort Schlosser, this time with forty-six bateaux heavily laden with troops, provisions, and ammunition. While they were in Lake Erie there arose one of the sudden storms so prevalent on the Great Lakes in autumn. Instead of creeping along the shore, the *bateaux* were in mid-lake, and before a landing could be made the gale was on them in all its fury. There was a wild race for land; but the choppy, turbulent sea beat upon the boats, of which some were swamped and the crews plunged into the chilly waters. They were opposite a forbidding shore, called by Wilkins Long Beach, but there was no time to look for a harbour. An attempt was made to land, with disastrous results. In all sixteen boats were sunk; three officers, four sergeants, and sixty-three privates were drowned. The thirty *bateaux* brought ashore were in a sinking condition; half the provisions were lost and the remainder water-soaked. The journey to Detroit was out of the question. The few provisions saved would not last the remnant of Wilkins's own soldiers for a month, and the ammunition was almost entirely lost. Even if they succeeded in arriving safely at Detroit, they would only be an added burden to Gladwyn; and so, sick at heart from failure and the loss of comrades, the survivors beat their way back to the Niagara.

A week or two later a messenger arrived at Fort Detroit bearing news of the disaster. The scarcity of provisions at Detroit was such that Gladwyn decided to reduce his garrison. Keeping about two hundred men in the fort, he sent the rest to Niagara. Then the force remaining at Detroit braced themselves to endure a hard, lonely winter. Theirs was not a pleasant lot. Never was garrison duty enjoyable during winter in the northern parts of North America, but in previous winters at Detroit the friendly intercourse between the soldiers and the settlers had made the season not unbearable. Now, so many of the French had been sympathizers with the besieging Indians, and, indeed, active in aiding them, that the old relations could not be resumed. So, during this winter of 1763-64, the garrison for the most part held aloof from the French settlers, and performed their weary round of military duties, longing for spring and the sight of a relieving force.

CHAPTER 8

Winding Up the Indian War

Amherst was weary of America. Early in the summer of 1763 he had asked to be relieved of his command; but it was not until October that General Thomas Gage, then in charge of the government of Montreal, was appointed to succeed him, and not until November 17, the day after Gage arrived in New York, that Amherst sailed for England.

The new commander-in-chief was not as great a general as Amherst. It is doubtful if he could have planned and brought to a successful conclusion such campaigns as the siege of Louisbourg and the threefold march of 1760 on Montreal, which have given his predecessor a high place in the military history of North America. But Gage was better suited for winding up the Indian war. He knew the value of the officers familiar with the Indian tribes, and was ready to act on their advice. Amherst had not done this, and his best officers were now anxious to resign. George Croghan had resigned as assistant superintendent of Indian Affairs, but was later induced by Gage to remain in office. Gladwyn was 'heartily wearied' of his command and hoped to 'be relieved soon'; Blane and Ourry were tired of their posts; and the brave Ecuyer was writing in despair: 'For God's sake, let me go and raise cabbages.' Bouquet; too, although determined to see the war to a conclusion, was not satisfied with the situation.

Meanwhile, Sir William Johnson was not idle among the tribes of the Six Nations. The failure of Pontiac to reduce Fort Detroit and the victory of Bouquet at Edge Hill had convinced the Iroquois that ultimately the British would triumph, and, eager to be on the winning side, they consented to take the field against the Shawnees and Delawares. In the middle of February 1764, through Johnson's influence and by his aid, two hundred Tuscaroras and Oneidas, under a half-breed, Captain Montour, marched westward. Near the main branch of the Susquehanna they surprised forty Delawares, on a scalping expedition against the British settlements, and made prisoners of the entire party. A few weeks later a number of Mohawks led by Joseph Brant (Thayendanegea) put another band of Delawares to rout, killing their chief and taking three prisoners. These attacks of the Iroquois disheartened the Shawnees and Delawares and greatly alarmed the Senecas, who, trembling lest their own country should be laid waste, sent a deputation of four hundred of their chief men to Johnson Hall—Sir William Johnson's residence on the Mohawk—to sue for peace. It was agreed that the Senecas should at once stop all hostilities, never again take up arms against the British, deliver up all prisoners at Johnson Hall, cede to His Majesty the Niagara carrying-place, allow the free passage of troops through their country, renounce all intercourse with the Delawares and Shawnees, and assist the British in punishing them. Thus, early in 1764, through the energy and diplomacy of Sir William Johnson, the powerful Senecas were brought to terms.

With the opening of spring preparations began in earnest for a twofold invasion of the Indian country. One army was to proceed to Detroit by way of Niagara and the Lakes, and another from Fort Pitt was to take the field against the Delawares and the Shawnees. To Colonel John Bradstreet, who in 1758 had won distinction by his capture of Fort Frontenac, was assigned the command of the contingent that was to go to Detroit. Bradstreet was to punish the Wyandots of San-dusky, and likewise the members of the Ottawa Confederacy if he should find them hostile. He was also to relieve Gladwyn and re-garrison the forts captured by the Indians in 1763. Bradstreet left Albany in June with a large force of colonial troops and regulars, including three hundred French Canadi-ans from the St Lawrence, whom Gage had thought it wise to have enlisted, in order to impress upon the Indians that they need no longer expect assistance from the French in their wars against the British.

To prepare the way for Bradstreet's arrival Sir William Johnson had gone in advance to Niagara, where he had called together ambassadors from all the tribes, not only from those that had taken part in the war, but from all with-in his jurisdiction. He had found a vast concourse of Indi-ans awaiting him. The *wigwams* of over a thousand warriors dotted the low-lying land at the mouth of the river. In a few days the number had grown to two thousand —repre-sentatives of nations as far east as Nova Scotia, as far west as the Mississippi, and as far north as Hudson Bay. Pontiac was absent, nor were there any Delaware, Shawnee, or Seneca ambassadors present. These were absent through dread; but later the Senecas sent deputies to ratify the treaty made with Johnson in April. When Bradstreet and his troops arrived negotiations were in full swing. For nearly a month councils were held, and at length all the chiefs present had entered into an alliance with the British. This accomplished, John-son, on August 6, left Niagara for his home, while Bradstreet continued his journey towards Detroit.

Bradstreet halted at Presqu'isle. Here he was visited by pretended deputies from the Shawnees and Delawares, who ostensibly sought peace. He made a conditional treaty with them and agreed to meet them twenty-five days later at Sandusky, where they were to bring their British prisoners. From Presqu'isle he wrote to Bouquet at Fort Pitt, saying that it would be unnecessary to advance into the Delaware country, as the Delawares were now at peace. He also reported his success, as he considered it, to Gage, but Gage was not impressed: he disavowed the treaty and instructed Bouquet to continue his preparations. Continuing his journey, Bradstreet rested at Sandusky, where more Delawares waited on him and agreed to make peace. It was at this juncture that he sent Captain Thomas Morris on his ill-starred mission to the tribes of the Mississippi.[1]

Bradstreet was at Detroit by August 26, and at last the worn-out garrison of the fort could rest after fifteen months of exacting duties. Calling the Indians to a council, Bradstreet entered into treaties with a number of chiefs, and pardoned several French settlers who had taken an active part with the Indians in the siege of Detroit. He then sent troops to occupy Michilimackinac; Green Bay, and Sault Ste Marie; and sailed for Sandusky to meet the Delawares and Shawnees, who had promised to bring in their prisoners. But none awaited him: the Indians had deliberately deceived him and were playing for time while they continued their attacks on the border settlers. Here he received a letter from Gage ordering him to disregard the treaty he had made with the Delawares and to join Bouquet at Fort Pitt, an order which Bradstreet did not obey, making the excuse that the low state of the water in the rivers made impossible an advance to Fort Pitt. On October 18 he left Sandusky for Niagara, having accomplished noth-

---

1. Morris and his companions got no farther than the rapids of the Maumee, where they were seized, stripped of clothing, and threatened with death. Pontiac was now among the Miamis, still striving to get together a following to continue the war. The prisoners were taken to Pontiac's camp. But the Ottawa chief did not deem it wise to murder a British officer on this occasion, and Morris was released and forced to retrace his steps. He arrived at Detroit after the middle of September, only to find that Bradstreet had already departed. The story will be found in more detail in Parkman's Conspiracy of Pontiac.

ing except occupation of the forts. Having already blundered hopelessly in dealing with the Indians, he was to blunder still further. On his way down Lake Erie he encamped one night, when storm threatened, on an exposed shore, and a gale from the north-east broke upon his camp and destroyed half his boats. Two hundred and eighty of his soldiers had to march overland to Niagara. Many of them perished; others, starved, exhausted, frost-bitten, came staggering in by twos and threes till near the end of December. The expedition was a fiasco. It blasted Bradstreet's reputation, and made the British name for a time contemptible among the Indians.

The other expedition from Fort Pitt has a different history. All through the summer Bouquet had been recruiting troops for the invasion of the Delaware country. The soldiers were slow in arriving, and it was not until the end of September that all was ready. Early in October Bouquet marched out of Fort Pitt with one thousand provincials and five hundred regulars. Crossing the Alleghany, he made his way in a north-westerly direction until Beaver Creek was reached, and then turned westward into the unbroken forest. The Indians of the Muskingum valley felt secure in their wilderness fastness. No white soldiers had ever penetrated to their country. To reach their villages dense woods had to be penetrated, treacherous marshes crossed, and numerous streams bridged or forded. But by the middle of October Bouquet had led his army, without the loss of a man, into the heart of the Muskingum valley, and pitched his camp near an Indian village named Tuscarawa, from which the inhabitants had fled at his approach. The Delawares and Shawnees were terrified: the victor of Edge Hill was among them with an army strong enough to crush to atoms any war-party they could muster. They sent deputies to Bouquet. These at first assumed a haughty mien; but Bouquet sternly rebuked them and ordered them to meet him at the forks of the Muskingum, forty miles distant to the south-west, and to bring in all their prisoners. By the beginning of November the troops were at the appointed place, where they encamped. Bouquet then sent messengers to all the tribes telling them to bring thither all the captives without delay. Every white man, woman, and child in their hands, French or British, must be delivered up. After some hesitation the Indians made haste to obey. About two hundred captives were brought, and chiefs were left as hostages for the safe delivery of others still in the hands of distant tribes. So far Bouquet had been stern and unbending; he had reminded the Indians of their murder of settlers and of their black treachery regarding the garrisons, and hinted that except for the kindness of their British father they would be utterly destroyed. He now unbent and offered them a generous treaty, which was to be drawn up and arranged later by Sir William Johnson. Bouquet then retraced his steps to Fort Pitt, and arrived there on November 28 with his long train of released captives. He had won a victory over the Indians greater than his triumph at Edge Hill, and all the greater in that it was achieved without striking a blow.

There was still, however, important work to be done before any guarantee of permanent peace in the hinterland was possible. On the eastern bank of the Mississippi, within the country ceded to England by the Treaty of Paris, was an important settlement over which the French flag still flew, and to which no British troops or traders had penetrated. It was a hotbed of conspiracy. Even while Bouquet was making peace with the tribes between the Ohio and Lake Erie, Pontiac and his agents were trying to make trouble for the British among the Indians of the Mississippi.

French settlement on the Mississippi began at the village of Kaskaskia, eighty-four miles north of the mouth of the Ohio. Six miles still farther north was Fort Chartres, a strongly built stone fort capable of accommodating three hundred men. From here, at some distance from the river, ran a road to Cahokia, a village situated nearly opposite the site of the present city of St Louis. The intervening country was settled by prosperous traders and planters who, including their four hundred negro slaves, numbered not less than two thousand. But when it was learned that all the territory east of the great river had been ceded to Britain, the settlers began to migrate to the opposite bank. The French here were hostile to the incoming British, and feared lest they might now lose the profitable trade with New Orleans. It was this region that Gage was determined to occupy.

Already an effort had been made to reach Fort Chartres. In February 1764 Major Arthur Loftus had set out from New Orleans with four hundred men; but, when about two hundred and forty miles north of his starting-point, his two leading boats were fired upon by Indians. Six men were killed and four wounded. To advance would mean the destruction of his entire company. Loftus returned to New Orleans, blaming the French officials for not supporting his enterprise, and indeed hinting that they were responsible for the attack. Some weeks later Captain Philip Pittman arrived at New Orleans with the intention of ascending the river; but reports of the enmity of the Indians to the British made him abandon the undertaking. So at the beginning of 1765 the French flag still flew over Fort Chartres; and Saint-Ange, who had succeeded Neyon de Villiers as commandant of the fort, was praying that the British might soon arrive to relieve him from a position where he was being daily importuned by Pontiac or his emissaries for aid against what they called the common foe.

But, if the route to Fort Chartres by way of New Orleans was too dangerous, Bouquet had cleared the Ohio of enemies, and the country which Gage sought to occupy was now accessible by way of that river. As a preliminary step, George Croghan was sent in advance with presents for the Indians along the route. In May 1765 Croghan left Fort Pitt accompanied by a few soldiers and a number of friendly Shawnee and Delaware chiefs. Near the mouth of the Wabash a prowling band of Kickapoos attacked the party, killing several and making prisoners of the rest. Croghan and his fellow-prisoners were taken to the French traders at Vincennes, where they were liberated. They then went to Ouiatanon, where Croghan held a council, and induced many chiefs to swear fealty to the British. After leaving Ouiatanon, Croghan had proceeded westward but a little way when he was met by Pontiac with a number of chiefs and warriors. At last the arch-conspirator was ready to come to terms. The French on the Mississippi would give him no assistance. He realized now that his people were conquered, and before it was too late he must make peace with his conquerors. Croghan had no further reason to continue his journey; so, accompanied by Pontiac, he went to Detroit. Arriving there on August 17, he at once called a council of the tribes in the neighbourhood. At this council sat Pontiac, among chiefs whom he had led during the months of the siege of Detroit. But it was no longer the same Pontiac: his haughty, domineering spirit was broken; his hopes of an Indian empire were at an end. 'Father,' he said at this council, 'I declare to all nations that I had made my peace with you before I came here; and I now deliver my pipe to Sir William Johnson, that he may know that I have made peace, and taken the king of England to be my father in the presence of all the nations now assembled.' He further agreed to visit Oswego in the spring to conclude a treaty with Sir William Johnson himself. The path was now clear for the advance of the troops to Fort Chartres. As soon as news of Croghan's success reached Fort Pitt, Captain Thomas Sterling, with one hundred and twenty men of the Black Watch, set out in boats for the Mississippi, arriving on October 9 at Fort Chartres, the first British troops to set foot in that country. Next day Saint-Ange handed the keys of the fort to Sterling, and the Union

Jack was flung aloft. Thus, nearly three years after the signing of the Treaty of Paris, the fleurs-de-lis disappeared from the territory then known as Canada.

There is still to record the closing act in the public career of Pontiac. Sir William Johnson, fearing that the Ottawa chief might fail to keep his promise of visiting Oswego to ratify the treaty made with Croghan at Detroit, sent Hugh Crawford, in March 1766, with belts and messages to the chiefs of the Ottawa Confederacy. But Pontiac was already preparing for his journey eastward. Nothing in his life was more creditable than his bold determination to attend a council far from his hunting-ground, at which he would be surrounded by soldiers who had suffered treachery and cruelty at his hands—whose comrades he had tortured and murdered.

On July 23 there began at Oswego the grand council at which Sir William Johnson and Pontiac were the most conspicuous figures. For three days the ceremonies and speeches continued; and on the third day Pontiac rose in the assembly and made a promise that he was faithfully to keep: 'I take the Great Spirit to witness,' he said, 'that what I am going to say I am determined steadfastly to perform... While I had the French king by the hand, I kept a fast hold of it; and now having you, father, by the hand, I shall do the same in conjunction with all the western nations in my district.'

Before the council ended Johnson presented to each of the chiefs a silver medal engraved with the words: 'A pledge of peace and friendship with Great Britain, confirmed in 1766.' He also loaded Pontiac and his brother chiefs with presents; then, on the last day of July, the Indians scattered to their homes.

For three years Pontiac, like a restless spirit, moved from camp to camp and from hunting-ground to hunting-ground. There were outbreaks of hostilities in the Indian country, but in none of these did he take part. His name never appears in the records of those three years. His days of conspiracy were at an end. By many of the French and Indians he was distrusted as a pensioner of the British, and by the British traders and settlers he was hated for his past deeds. In 1769 he visited the Mississippi, and while at Cahokia he attended a drunken frolic held by some Indians. When he left the feast, stupid from the effects of rum, he was followed into the forest by a Kaskaskia Indian, probably bribed by a British trader. And as Pontiac lurched among the black shadows of the trees, his pursuer crept up behind him, and with a swift stroke of the tomahawk cleft his skull. Thus by a treacherous blow ended the career of a warrior whose chief weapon had been treachery.

For twelve years England, by means of military officers, ruled the great hinterland east of the Mississippi—a region vast and rich, which now teems with a population immensely greater than that of the whole broad Dominion of Canada—a region which is to-day dotted with such magnificent cities as Chicago, Detroit, and Indianapolis. Unhappily, England made no effort to colonize this wilderness empire. Indeed, as Edmund Burke has said, she made 'an attempt to keep as a lair of wild beasts that earth which God, by an express charter, had given to the children of men.' She forbade settlement in the hinterland. She did this ostensibly for the Indians, but in reality for the merchants in the mother country. In a report of the Lords Commissioners for Trade and Plantations in 1772 are words which show that it was the intention of the government to confine 'the western extent of settlements to such a distance from the seaboard as that those settlements should lie within easy reach of the trade and commerce of this kingdom,... and also of the exercise of that authority and jurisdiction... necessary for the preservation of the colonies in a due subordination to, and dependence upon, the mother country... It does appear to us that the extension of the fur trade depends entirely upon the Indians being undisturbed in the possession of their hunting-grounds... Let the savages enjoy their deserts in quiet.

89

Were they driven from their forests the peltry trade would decrease, and it is not impossible that worse savages would take refuge in them.'

Much has been written about the stamp tax and the tea tax as causes of the American revolution, but this determination to confine the colonies to the Atlantic seaboard 'rendered the revolution inevitable.'[2] In 1778, three years after the sword was drawn, when an American force under George Rogers Clark invaded the Indian country, England's weakly garrisoned posts, then by the Quebec Act under the government of Canada, were easily captured; and, when accounts came to be settled after the war, the entire hinterland south of the Great Lakes, from the Alleghanies to the Mississippi, passed to the United States.

---

2. Roosevelt's The Winning of the West, part 1, p. 57.

Bibliographical Note

The main source of information regarding the siege of Detroit is the 'Pontiac Manuscript.' This work has been translated several times, the best and most recent translation being that by R. Clyde Ford for the Journal of Pontiac's Conspiracy, 1763, edited by C. M. Burton. Unfortunately, the manuscript abruptly ends in the middle of the description of the fight at Bloody Run.

The following works will be found of great assistance to the student: Rogers's Journals; Cass's Discourse before the Michigan Historical Society; Henry's Travels and Adventures in Canada and the Indian Territories; Parkman's Conspiracy of Pontiac (the fullest and best treatment of the subject); Ellis's Life of Pontiac, the Conspirator (a digest of Parkman's work); Historical Account of the Expedition against the Ohio Indians, 1764 (authorship doubtful, but probably written by Dr William Smith of Philadelphia); Stone's The Life and Times of Sir William Johnson; Drake's Indians of North America; Handbook of American Indians North of Mexico and Handbook of Indians of Canada; Ogg's The Opening of the Mississippi; Roosevelt's The Winning of the West; Carter's The Illinois Country; Beer's British Colonial Policy, 1754-1765; Adair's The History of the American Indians; the Annual Register for the years 1763, 1764, and 1774; Harper's Encyclopedia of United States History; Pownall's The Administration of the Colonies; Bancroft's History of the United States; Kingsford's

History of Canada; Winsor's Narrative and Critical History of America and his Mississippi Basin; Gordon's History of Pennsylvania; Lucas's A History of Canada, 1763-1812; Gayarre's History of Louisiana; and McMaster's History of the People of the United States.

In 1766 there was published in London a somewhat remarkable drama entitled Ponteach: or the Savages of America. A part of this will be found in the appendices to Parkman's Conspiracy of Pontiac. Parkman suggests that Robert Rogers may have had a hand in the composition of this drama.

Pontiac

by Edson L. Whitney and
Frances M. Perry

Pontiac

The Meeting of Pontiac and the English

Though the French were still fighting stubbornly at sea, the French war was over in America. Canada had been surrendered to the British, and England's banners waved over Quebec. Yet the tidings of defeat had not reached the French garrisons on the Great Lakes.

In the fall of 1760 Major Robert Rogers, with two hundred British rangers, set out in fifteen whale boats, to carry to the interior the news of the surrender and to take possession of the French forts on the lakes.

This was a somewhat dangerous task. For, although no resistance was to be feared from the French, the savages who were in league with them could not be counted on to understand or believe the changed state of affairs. Indeed, it was doubtful if they would even allow the British a hearing before attacking them.

Rogers and his men, however, coasted along the shores of Lake Erie without adventure until early in November. Then the weather became so stormy and the lake so rough that the commander decided to go ashore and camp in the forest until the tempest had passed.

The rangers were glad to feel the solid earth under their feet and to find shelter from the driving wind and rain. Nevertheless, they soon realized that the forest was not without its dangers.

They had not been long ashore when a large band of Indians entered the camp. These Indians said that Pontiac, chief of the Ottawas, had sent them before him to demand of the Englishmen how they dared to come into his country without his permission.

Before nightfall the famous warrior himself stood in the presence of the English commander and his officers and spoke in this fashion: "Englishmen, I am Pontiac, greatest councillor and warrior of the Ottawas. This land belongs to my people. You are the enemies of my people. You are the enemies of our brothers, the French. Why do you bring armed warriors into my country without asking my consent? You can not go farther until Pontiac leaves your path."

To this haughty speech Rogers answered: "Brother, we come to tell you that the war is over. Our mighty English warriors have made your French brothers shake with fear. We have slain their war chiefs; we have taken their strong villages. They have begged us for mercy. They have promised to be the dutiful and obedient children of the English king if we will lay down the hatchet and fight against them no more. They have given us their guns, their forts, and all the land of Canada. I have come into your country to take Detroit. I shall not fight with your brothers, the French; I shall not shoot them. I shall show their commander a paper and he will pull down his flag and he and his men will come out of the fort and give me their guns. Then I shall go in with my men and put up my flag.

"The English king is terrible in war. He could punish the Indians and make them cry for mercy, as he has the French. But he is kind and offers to his red children the chain of friendship. If you accept it he is ready to shut his eyes to the mischief the French have put you up to in the past, and to protect you with his strong arm."

PONTIAC AND ROGERS

Pontiac listened gravely to every word the white man spoke. But his dark face gave no token of what was passing in his mind. Now, Indians despise rashness, and it is their custom to deliberate over night before answering any important question. So, with the dignity of one who knows no fear and craves no favour, the greatest councillor of the Ottawas replied simply: "Englishmen, I shall stand in your path till morning. In the meantime if your warriors are cold or hungry the hands of my people are open to you." Then he and his chiefs withdrew, and slipped silently back through the dripping forest to their camp.

The English rangers slept with their guns at hand that night. They knew the pride and might and treachery of Pontiac, and they feared him. They felt as if they were in a trap, with the raging sea before them and the forest alive with pitiless savages behind.

But they need have had no fear, for the great chief thought not of massacre that night. He thought of the English who stood ready to avenge any harm done to their brothers; of his own race dependent on the white men for rum, for *wampum*, for guns and powder and bullets. Clearly the Indians must have friends among the palefaces. The French were their "brothers." They had given them presents, had married their maidens, had traded, hunted, and gone to battle with them. The English were their foes. But they were many and strong. They had beaten the French and taken their guns. The red men must let their hatred sleep for awhile. They would smoke the pipe of peace with the English, and the English would give them presents: tobacco and rum, guns and powder.

Having reached this conclusion, Pontiac and his chiefs returned to Rogers's camp on the following morning. There they smoked the calumet with the English and exchanged presents and promises of kindness and friendship. The men who had met as enemies parted as friends.

Years later, when British armies were marching against Indians whose tomahawks were red with English blood, Pontiac's faith in the friendship of Rogers remained unshaken. The latter sent to the chief a bottle of rum. When advised not to drink it lest it should contain poison, Pontiac replied: "I did not save from death on the shores of Lake

Wampum

98

Erie a man who would to-day poison me," and he drained the bottle without hesitation.

Though a single Indian and a single English-man could thus overcome their distrust for each other, the feelings of the two races could not be so easily altered. The Indians looked upon the English as cruel robbers, whose ob-ject was to drive them from their homes and possess their lands. They thought of them as enemies too powerful to be withstood by open force and therefore to be met only with cunning and deception. Many of the English looked upon the savages as ignorant, filthy, and treacherous beings, lit-tle better than wild beasts, and thought that the world would be better off without them. Yet for the present both were glad to be at peace.

CALUMET

The Indians found that Major Rog-ers had spoken truly about Detroit. When they saw the large French garrison yield without resistance they were filled with wonder, and said to one another: "These English are a terrible people. It is well we have made friends with them."

By "making friends" with the English, the Indians had no notion of accepting them as masters. The French had seemed pleasant neighbours and valuable friends. When they occu-pied the fort the Indians had always found a warm welcome there. Their chiefs had been treated with great pomp and cer-emony. They had received rich presents and great promises. They expected the English to show them the same considera-tion. But they were disappointed. The new masters of the fort had little patience with the Indian idlers, who loafed about at the most inconvenient times in the most inconvenient places, always begging, and often sullen and insolent. They frequently ordered them in no mild terms to be off. The chiefs received cold looks and short answers where they had looked for flattery and presents.

The Indians resented the conduct of the English bitterly, and when Pontiac learned that they claimed the lands of his tribe, he said within himself: "The hatred of the Ottawas has slept long enough. It is time for it to wake and destroy these British who treat the red man as if he had no right to the land where he was born."

PONTIAC'S CHILDHOOD

We love our country principally because of the political freedom its government allows us. As we study its history, the lives of its heroes, and the struggles they have made for the liberties we enjoy, our patriotism grows stronger.

Pontiac loved his country, too, but in a much simpler and more personal way, as you will understand when you have learned about the proud chieftain's boyhood and youth.

The birds scarcely know the forest so well as he did. When he was a tiny baby,—a fat, brown, little *papoose*,—his mother used to bundle him up in skins, strap him to a board, and carry him on her back when she went to gather the bark of the young basswood tree for twine. As the strong young *squaw* sped along the narrow path, soft and springing to her moccasined feet with its depth of dried pine needles, the baby on her back was well content. Even if he felt cross and fretful the regular motion pleased him; the cool dim green of the forest rested him; the sweet smell of the pines soothed him; and the gentle murmur of the wind in the tree tops soon lulled him to sleep.

When the mother clambered over a large tree trunk that

had fallen across the path and the little *papoose* was jolted wide awake, he did not cry. His beady black eyes fol- lowed every stray sunbeam and every bounding rabbit, or chance bird with wonder and de- light. When his moth- er went to work she placed his rude cradle beside a tree where he could look on, out of harm's way. He was very little trouble, and she always took him with her when she went to get cedar bark, to gather rushes for mats and herbs for dyes, to pick up fagots for the fire, or to get sap from the sugar tree. So it hap- pened that when he grew up

SQUAW WITH PAPOOSE

Pontiac could not remember a time when the dark forest did not seem like home to him.

As soon as he was old enough to understand words, he heard his mother laughing with her neighbours about the men in the village who stayed about their wigwams like women. Now, he thought that a wigwam or bark lodge was a very pleasant place. The small, dark, oven-shaped room, smoky and foul with the smell of fish and dirt, was home to him—the mud floor, worn smooth and hard with use, was strewn with mats and skins which served for chairs and beds. There was a fireplace in the centre, and over it a rack on which smoked

Indian squaw at work

fish hung, well out of the reach of the wolf-like dogs that lay about gnawing at old bones. It was usually dry in wet weather, warm in cold weather, and cool when the sun was hot. It was where he went for food when he was hungry; it was where he slept on soft buffalo robes and bear skins when he was tired; it was where he heard good stories, and, best of all, it was where his mother spent most of her time.

But before Pontiac was many years old he knew that the wigwam was the place for women and children, and that it was a shame for a man not to follow the deer through the forest, and go upon the warpath. He saw that if a man stayed at home and loved ease and comfort his *squaw* would scold him with a shrill tongue. But if he went off to hunt, it was different. Then, when he came home for a short time, he might lounge on a bear skin while his *squaw* worked hard to make him happy, cooking his meals, fetching clear water from the spring, and dressing the skins he had brought from the hunt.

Pontiac liked to watch his mother while she stood weaving the wet rushes into mats to cover the lodge in summer, or while she sat on the floor with her feet crossed under her, making baskets out of sweet grass or embroidering with brightly dyed porcupine quills. But if he showed his pleasure or offered to help her, she looked stern and shook her head, saying, "Go out into the field and run; then you will be swift when you are a man;" or "go into the forest and shoot rabbits with your little bow and arrow, so that you may one day be a great hunter like your father."

All this made little Pontiac feel that the great fields and forests were his—his to find his pleasure in while he was a boy; his to find his work in when he should become a man.

He learned, too, that his very life depended on the forests he loved. He could never forget the cruel winter days when he had asked his mother again and again for fish and meat, and she had told him to be still and wait till his father brought meat from the forest. And he had waited there long with his hollow-eyed mother, crouching before the feeble fire, starving with hunger. He had strained his ears toward the great white forest only to hear the wail of the winds and the howl of the wolves. But at last the yelp of the dogs was sure to be heard, and then the half-frozen hunters would appear, dragging the deer over the crusted snow.

PONTIAC'S EDUCATION

Pontiac's father was a war chief. But it did not follow that therefore Pontiac would be a war chief. He would have to prove himself strong and brave, a good hunter and a good warrior, or his tribe would choose some more able leader.

Pontiac, like most small boys, took his father for his pattern. His ambition was to be like him. But he was told early, "Be a good Indian. Be a good Ottawan. Be true to your tribe. Be a strong man and help your people. But don't think about being chief. The greatest brave must be chief of the Ottawas."

Yet, Indians love glory and perhaps in the bottom of their hearts Pontiac's father and mother hoped that he would one day be a chieftain. At any rate they did all they could to train him to be a worthy Indian. They were sometimes very severe with him. If he was rude to strangers or to old people; if he lost his temper and threw ashes at his comrades; if he told a falsehood, he was beaten. He had broken the laws of the Great Spirit, and the Great Spirit had commanded that parents should beat their children with rods when they did wrong. The boy understood this and he tried to take his punishment bravely that he might regain the good will of the Great Spirit. He stood quite still and endured heavy blows without whimpering or flinching. He learned, too, to endure hunger and great fatigue without complaint. He raced, and swam, and played ball, and wrestled with other boys till his body was strong and straight and supple. He played at hunting and war in the forest, until his eyes became so sharp that no sign of man or beast escaped them.

INDIAN WARRIOR

But he did not depend altogether on his eyes for information. He could find his way through a forest in the dark, where the dense foliage hid the stars. Perhaps the wind told him the direction by the odours it brought. He could tell what kind of trees grew about him by the feel of their bark, by their odour, by the sound of the wind in the branches. He did not have to think much about his course when on a journey. His feet seemed to know the way home, or to the spring, or to the enemy's camp. And if he had travelled through a wilderness once he knew the way the next time as well as any boy knows his way to school.

While Pontiac was training his body, his parents took care that he should not grow up in ignorance of the religion and the history of his people. He heard much about the Great Spirit who could see all he did and was angry when he said or did anything dishonest or cowardly.

The laws of the Great Spirit were fixed in the boy's mind, for his mother was always repeating them to him. She would say as he left the wigwam:"Honour the grey-headed person," or "Thou shalt not mimic the thunder;" "Thou shalt always feed the hungry and the stranger," or "Thou shalt immerse thyself in the river at least ten times in succession in the early part of the spring, so that thy body may be strong and thy feet swift to chase the game and to follow the warpath."

In the evenings the older members of the family and some visiting Indians sat around the fire and told stones about the Great Spirit and many other strange beings, some good and some evil. They told, too, wonderful tales about omens and charms. The same story was told over and over again, so that in time little Pontiac knew by heart the legends of the Ottawas. He remembered and firmly believed all his life stories that as a child he listened to with awe, in his father's wigwam.

In the same way he heard about the great deeds of the warriors of his tribe; and he came to think there were no people in the world quite equal to the Ottawas. He heard of other tribes that were their foes and he was eager to go to war against them.

As he grew older he heard a good deal about men, not only of another tribe but of another race, the palefaces, who were trying to get the lands of the Indians. Then he thought less about being an Ottawa and conquering other Indians; while every day he felt more and more that he was an Indian and must conquer the white man. He wished he could unite the tribes in friendship and lead them against these strangers who were so many and so strong, and who had come to drive the Indians from their homes and hunting grounds.

Such thoughts made Pontiac very serious. Obeying the commands of the Great Spirit, the young Indian often blackened his face with a mixture of charcoal and fish-oil, and went into the depths of the forest, where he remained for days without food, praying and thinking earnestly about the future.

He formed his own plans, but he hid them in his heart. He practised keeping his feelings and thoughts to himself, and spoke only when he was very sure he was right. This habit soon gained him a reputation for gravity and wisdom.

THE CHIEF

When he was old enough to go to battle with the tried warriors, Pontiac took many scalps and distinguished himself for courage. He was, therefore, amid great feasting and rejoicing, made a war chief of the Ottawas.

His influence increased rapidly. The young men of his tribe felt sure of success when they followed Pontiac to battle. His very name made his foes tremble.

In the council, too, his power grew. His words seemed wise to the grey heads, and the young warriors were ready to take up the hatchet or lay it down at his bidding. Because of his eloquence and wisdom, Pontiac was made sachem, so that he not only led his people to battle, but also ruled them in time of peace. He was called the greatest councillor and warrior of the Ottawas; yet he was not content.

In Michigan, where the Ottawa Indians lived, there were other tribes of the Algonquin Indians. Chief among these were the Ojibwas and the Pottawottomies. These tribes, though related by marriage and on friendly terms, had separate chiefs. But gradually they came to recognize the great Pontiac as their principal ruler.

Among the Indians of his own tribe Pontiac's word was law. Among kindred tribes his friendship was sought and his displeasure feared. Through all the Algonquin territory, from the Lakes to the Gulf, from the mountains to the river, the great chief's name was known and respected.

Pontiac was no doubt proud and ambitious. But if he was glad to gain glory for himself he considered the good of his people also. To unite them and overpower the palefaces was the end toward which he planned.

By this time he had learned that all palefaces were not alike. There were two great nations of them, the French and the English, and the Indians had found a great difference between them. The English had treated them with contempt and helped themselves to their lands. The French had come among them as missionaries and traders, with kind words and gifts. To be sure, they had built forts in the land, but they told the Indians they did this for their sake that they might protect them from the English, who wished to take their lands. The French seemed to hate the English no less than the Indians did.

It is said that Pontiac planned to use the French to help him conquer the English, and then intended to turn upon them and drive them away. No doubt if the French had openly claimed the territory of the Indians, or in any way had shown that their professions of friendship were false, Pontiac would have been their enemy. But he evidently took them at their word and looked upon them as friends who wished to help his people.

In all his dealings with the French, Pontiac was true and honourable. He joined them in their wars against the English. He and his Ottawas helped to defeat the British regulars under General Braddock at Fort Duquesne. He saved the French garrison at Detroit from an attack by hostile Indians. He trusted them when all appearances were against them. His acceptance of the peace offered by Major Rogers on the shore of Lake Erie was not a betrayal of the French. Pontiac did not forsake their cause until they had given it up themselves. He took a step which seemed for the best interests of his own people, and, at the same time, not hurtful to the French. We have seen that he was disappointed in the reward he expected.

The English, having subdued the French, felt able to manage the Indians without difficulty. They were, therefore, more careless than ever about pleasing them. They refused to give the supplies which the French had been accustomed to distribute among the Indians. The Indians were obliged to provide for themselves, as in the days of Pontiac's childhood.

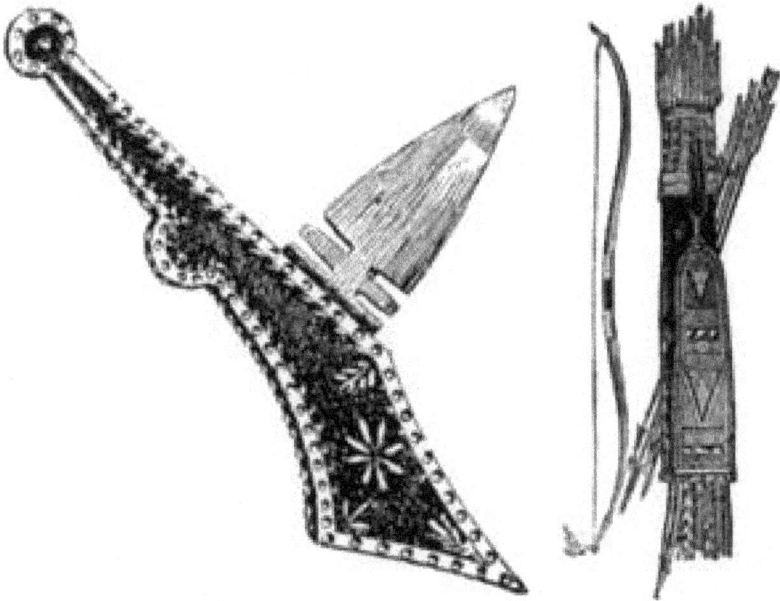

INDIAN WEAPONS

They had no powder or bullets and the young men had lost their skill with the bow. There was suffering and death for want of food.

Even Pontiac had been willing to profit by the generosity of the French. He had not only cheered himself with their firewater, but, like other Indians, he had been glad to give up his bow and arrow for a gun; he had been ready to accept corn and smoked meats in winter when game was scarce, and to protect himself from the cold with the Frenchmen's blankets.

He realized now that in adopting the white men's customs, in using their food and blankets and arms, his people had become dependent upon them. He remembered the stories he had heard in his childhood about the might of the Ottawas in the days when they depended on the chase for their food, and fought their battles with bows and arrows and stone hatchets. He wished his people would return to the old customs. In that way only could they regain their native hardihood and independence.

While Pontiac's hatred of the English grew more bitter daily, other Indians were not indifferent. Through all the Algonquin tribes spread this hatred for the English. The insolence of the garrisons at the forts provoked it; the cheating, the bad faith, and the brutality of the English trappers and traders increased it; the refusal of supplies, the secret influence of the French, the encroachments of English settlers, fanned it into fury. And when at last, in 1762, word came that the English claimed the land of the Algonquins their rage could no longer be restrained.

THE PLOT

The time was ripe for rebellion and Pontiac was ready. All over the land should council fires be lighted. All over the land should the hatchet be raised. By wile and treachery the forts should fall. By fire and bloodshed the settlements should be laid waste and the Englishmen driven into the sea. Thus spoke Pontiac, and thus spoke his messengers, who with war belts of black and red *wampum* and hatchets smeared with blood sought out the villages of the Algonquins. Far and wide this dark company went its way through forests, across prairies, in spite of storm or flooded stream, or mountain barrier. No camp was so secret, no village so remote, that the messengers of war did not find it out. Wherever they went the bloody plan found favour; the tokens of war were accepted and pledges of warlike purpose sent to Pontiac.

Not far from the summering place where clustered the lodges of Pontiac and his kinsmen rose the walls of Fort Detroit. There Pontiac had suffered humiliation at the hands of the English, and upon it he planned to visit his vengeance.

The little French military station planted on the west bank of the Detroit River had reached half a century's growth. It had become a place of some importance. Both banks of the river were studded with farmhouses for miles above and below the "fort," as the walled village where the soldiers lived was called.

The fort consisted of about one hundred small houses surrounded by a palisade, or wall of heavy stakes, twenty-five feet high. Since gates are easily broken down, over every gate a block house had been built, from which soldiers could fire upon the approaching enemy. At the four corners of the palisade were bastions, or fortified projections, from which the inmates could see the whole length of the wall and shoot any one attempting to climb it, set fire to it, or do it any harm.

The small log houses within were crowded together with only narrow passage-ways between. They were roofed with bark or thatched with straw. To lessen the danger of fire a wide road was left between the wall and the houses. Besides dwelling houses, there were in the fort the barracks where the soldiers stayed, the church, shops, and the council house, where meetings with the Indians were held.

At this time the garrison consisted of about one hundred and twenty men. But counting the other inmates of the fort and the Canadians who lived along the river, there were about two thousand five hundred white people in the Detroit settlement. On the outskirts of the settlement hung the Indian villages, much as the Indian villages crowd around the white settlements of Alaska to-day.

In the midst of the wilderness this little band of English lived protected by their log walls. No friends were near. Their nearest neighbours were the conquered French, who regarded them with jealousy and dislike. Not far away were their Indian enemies. Yet they thought little of danger.

Occasionally some story of Indian treachery, some rumour of Indian hostility, or some omen of evil filled the garrison with vague alarm. In October, 1762, dense clouds gathered over the fort, and soon rain black as ink fell from them. This strange occurrence stirred up the fears of the settlers. Some said that it was a sign that the end of the world was at hand; others, that it was a sign of war. But by the spring of the next year the settlers of Detroit had ceased to think of the black rain and war.

If a few had suffered unrest because of the Indians, their fears were put to flight by a visit which Pontiac made to Detroit late in April. With forty of his chiefs he came to the fort asking to be allowed to perform the peace dance before the commander. The request was granted, and a good-natured crowd gathered near Major Gladwin's house to see the Indian dance.

No one thought anything of the fact that ten of the party took no part in the dance, but strolled around the fort prying into everything. Those who noticed them at all, thought their conduct showed nothing more than childish curiosity.

No one dreamed that these men were spies, and that the sole purpose of the visit was to discover the strength of the garrison. The Indians left with promises to come again to smoke the calumet with the English when all their chiefs should assemble after the winter's hunt.

After visiting Detroit, Pontiac sent swift-footed runners to all the tribes in the neighbouring country, calling the chiefs to a council to be held in the village of the Pottawottomies.

When the day for the great council arrived, all the women were sent away from the village so that they could not overhear the plans of the chiefs. At the door of the great bark lodge where the chiefs met, sentinels were posted to prevent interruption.

When all had taken their places in the council room Pontiac rose and laid before his trusted chiefs his crafty plans. On the seventh of May the young warriors should gather on the green near Detroit to play ball, while the older men lay on the ground looking on, or loitered in and about the fort. The squaws should go about the streets with guns and tomahawks hidden under their blankets, offering mats and baskets for sale, or begging. Later Pontiac, with the principal chiefs would arrive, and ask to hold a council with the commander and his officers. While speaking in the council he would suddenly turn the *wampum* belt that he held in his hand. At that signal the chiefs should throw off the blankets that hid their weapons and war paint, and butcher the English before they could offer resistance. When the Indians outside heard the clamour within the council house they should snatch the guns and knives that the squaws carried, fall upon the surprised and half-armed soldiers, kill them and plunder and burn the fort, sparing only the French. From the Indians' point of view this seemed a brave plot. No one objected to the treachery. All the guttural sounds that broke from the throng of listeners were made for approval and applause.

THE SEVENTH OF MAY

The Indians kept their secret well. A Canadian saw some Indians filing off their guns to make them short enough to hide under their blankets. But if his suspicions were aroused he held his peace and said no word of warning to the English. The appointed seventh of May was at hand and no alarm had been taken at the garrison.

But on the evening of the sixth, Major Gladwin talked long in secret with his officers, then ordered half the garrison under arms. He doubled the guard and himself went from place to place to see that every man was at his post. The soldiers did not know the reason for this unusual watchfulness, but they understood that it meant danger.

It is said that in the afternoon an Indian girl who was deeply attached to the English Major had brought him a pair of moccasins she had been embroidering for him. She lingered at the fort and seemed unwilling to leave. At last she begged Gladwin to go away from the fort for a day or two. Her conduct and request excited suspicion. The Major questioned her closely and discovered Pontiac's plot.

Be that as it may, on the night of the sixth Major Gladwin was on the alert.

Nothing disturbed the peace of the mild May night. In the morning one watchman on the walls said to another, "See, yonder they come."

The man addressed looked up the stream and saw many birch canoes rapidly approaching the fort. "A perfect fleet!" he exclaimed.

"Yes; plenty of boats, but not many Indians; only two or three in each canoe," replied the first.

"That's true. But see how deep the canoes are in the water, and what heavy paddling those fellows are doing! A dozen beaver skins to one, every canoe's got a load of those red rascals stretched on their backs well out of sight."

"You may be right," said the other, shaking his head. "It looks as if there might be some ugly work before us. They say the Major has ordered the whole garrison under arms. Even the shops are closed and the traders armed to the teeth."

Most of the Indians who came in the boats went to a

BETRAYAL OF PONTIAC'S PLOT

green near the fort and began a game of ball. Soon Pontiac himself was seen approaching along the river road at the head of sixty of his chiefs. They wore blankets and marched in single file without a word. When they reached the gate Pontiac, with his accustomed dignity, asked that he and his chiefs might meet their English brothers in council to discuss important questions.

In answer to his request the gates swung open. Lines of armed soldiers appeared on either side. The Indians, trained to read signs, knew at once that their plot was discovered. Perhaps they felt that the treachery they had planned would be visited on their own heads. But if they feared, they gave no token; they said no word. They walked undaunted through the narrow streets, meeting armed soldiers at every turn.

At the council house they found Major Gladwin, his assistant, Captain Campbell, and other officers already assembled and waiting for them. If any Indian had doubted the discovery of their plot, he was certain of it when he saw that the officers wore swords at their sides and pistols in their belts. It was with some reluctance that they seated themselves on the mats arranged for them. This was a trying moment for Pontiac. He stood there discovered, defeated. But he did not quail before the steady gaze of the English. His brow was only more haughty, his face more stern.

"And why," he asked, in a severe, harsh voice, "do our brothers meet us to-day with guns in their hands?"

"You come among us when we are taking our regular military exercise," answered the commander calmly.

With fears somewhat soothed, Pontiac began to speak: "For many moons the love of our brothers, the English, has seemed to sleep. It is now spring; the sun shines bright and hot; the bears, the oaks, the rivers awake from their sleep. Brothers, it is time for the friendship between us to awake. Our chiefs have come to do their part, to renew their pledges of peace and friendship."

PONTIAC'S SPEECH

Here he made a movement with the belt he held in his hand, as if about to turn it over. Every Indian was ready to spring. Gladwin gave a signal. A clash of arms sounded through the open door. A drum began beating a charge. Within the council room there was a startled, breathless silence. Pontiac's hand was stayed. The belt fell back to its first position. The din of arms ceased. Pontiac repeated his promises of friendship and loyalty, and then sat down.

Major Gladwin answered briefly: "Brothers, the English are not fickle. They do not withdraw their friendship without cause. As long as the red men are faithful to their promises they will find the English their steadfast friends. But if the Indians are false or do any injury to the English, the English will punish them without mercy."

The one object of the Indians was now to turn aside the suspicion of the English. After Gladwin's speech presents were exchanged, and the meeting broke up with a general hand-shaking. Before leaving, Pontiac promised that he would return in a few days with his squaws and children that they might shake hands with their English brothers.

"Scoundrels!" laughed one officer, when the last Indian had left. "They were afraid to sit down. They thought they had been caught in their own trap. It's a pity to let them off so easily."

"No," replied another, more seriously. "The Major is right. If there is an outbreak, the Indians must take the first step. They depend more on treachery than force for success; now that their plan is foiled, the whole trouble will probably blow over."

The next day this opinion seemed verified by the appearance, of Pontiac with three of his chiefs. He brought a peace-pipe and approached the commander with smooth speeches: "Evil birds have whistled in your ears, but do not listen to them. We are your friends. We have come to prove it. We will smoke the calumet with you."

INDIANS PLAYING BALL

Pontiac then offered his great peace-pipe. After it had been smoked in all solemnity, he presented it to Captain Campbell as a high mark of friendship.

Hostilities Begun

Bright and early the next morning hordes of naked savages gathered on the pasture land near the fort. A long quadrangle was marked out on the grass with lines across it. At each end of this "gridiron" two tall posts were erected five or six feet apart. This, as you may have guessed, was to prepare for an Indian game of ball.

When all was ready the young men of the Ottawa tribes took their places on one side of the field. Opposite to them were the Pottawottomies. Each Indian had a long racket or bat with which he tried to drive the ball to the goal against the opposition of the players of the other nation. Such a yelling as they kept up, running and pushing and plunging and prancing the while! Small wonder that squaws, warriors, and chiefs should have come to watch so exciting a game!

Still the men in the fort kept the gates closed and stayed behind their walls, as if they took no interest in the game. They were really watching with some uneasiness the vast crowd of Indians so close at hand.

When the game was finished Pontiac went to the gate of the fort. His chiefs attended him and a motley crowd of warriors, squaws, and children came trooping after. The great chief shouted in a loud voice, demanding admission. He received answer that he might come in if he wished, but the rest would have to keep out. With injured dignity he asked if his followers were not to be allowed to enjoy the smoke of the calumet.

The English commander, tired of false speech, gave a short answer, refusing flatly to let the Indians in. Thereupon Pontiac's brow darkened and he strode off to the river in high dudgeon.

The others withdrew a little and stood in groups, muttering and gesticulating. Then with wild whoops they bounded off to join their comrades who lay stretched on the earth around the ball grounds. After a brief parley, some started with blood-curdling yells toward a house across the fields where an English woman lived with her children; others leaped into their canoes and paddled off to an island where an English farmer lived alone.

Before sunset the men at the fort heard the exultant scalp yell of the Indians, and knew that the first blood of the war had been shed.

In the meantime Pontiac hastened with gloomy rage to his own village across the river. It was deserted by all but a few squaws and old men. These Pontiac ordered to pack the camp luggage and make all ready for removal, as soon as the men came with their canoes to carry the camp equipment to the Detroit side of the river.

All laboured to do their chief's will, while he went apart and blackened his face.

At nightfall the braves came in with the scalps they had taken. A pole was driven into the ground in the open space where the tents had been. The warriors gathered about it, their bodies decked with paint and eagle feathers.

Pontiac sprang into their midst, brandishing his hatchet and striking violently at the pole. As he danced about, he recited the great deeds he and his fathers had done in war. His appalling cries, his terrible words, stirred the hearts of his Indians and fired their blood. All were in a frenzy of excitement. With wild cries they joined their chief in his war dance.

Even the faint echo of the din these blood-thirsty demons made struck terror into the hearts of the watchers in Detroit. The soldiers kept close guard all night, expecting an attack at any moment.

But not till early dawn did the war cry sound. Shrill and near it rose from hundreds of throats. Strong men turned pale at the clamour of yells and cracking rifles. It seemed that the Indians must be at the very walls of the fort.

The guards on the ramparts, however, could see no enemy in the faint grey light. From behind every tree, every stone, every rise of ground, came the incessant flash of muskets. Bullets and blazing arrows rattled against the palisades. The Indians aimed at the loopholes and succeeded in wounding five of the English. The soldiers returned a cautious fire, unwilling to waste powder on an invisible foe.

After an attack of six hours' duration the Indians, weary with their night's activity, gradually withdrew to their camps, having suffered no loss, but at the same time having inflicted little.

Gladwin, whose spirit was manly and humane, wished if possible to avoid further bloodshed. The Canadians took no part in the war, and could, therefore, be safely used as messengers. As soon as the battle had subsided Major Gladwin sent a deputation of them to tell Pontiac that he was willing to listen to any real grievance of the Indians, and do his best to redress whatever wrongs they had suffered.

Pontiac knew that his chief charge of injustice against the English, their presence in and claim to his lands, would not be considered by the English a real grievance. He thought the hour for talking had passed; the time for action had come. Treachery was his readiest weapon and he used it. He replied that he could consent to no terms unless they were made with the English in person, and asked that Captain Campbell, second in command at the fort, come to a council in his camp.

Captain Campbell had no fear, and urged Major Gladwin to permit him to go. He and another Englishman, accordingly, hastened to the Indian village. The women and the warriors were so enraged at the sight of their red coats, that they would have stoned them had not Pontiac interfered and led them to his lodge.

After a long but fruitless talk around the council fire, the English rose to go. But Pontiac said: "Brothers, you will sleep to-night on the couches the red men have spread for you." He then gave orders that his prisoners should be taken to the house of a Canadian, where they should be treated with respect, but closely guarded.

THE TWO LEADERS

When the officers at Detroit learned that their deputies were detained by the Indians, they realized that there was no hope of peace. Before the fort two armed schooners rode at anchor. Most of the officers wished to abandon the fort and seek safety by sailing away on these boats.

"There is no use trying to hold the old fort against eight times our number," they said impatiently.

But Major Gladwin had no thought of surrender. "We could not," he answered, "if the Indians should attempt to force the walls. But there is no danger of their venturing within gunshot in any numbers. They won't risk their red skins that way. They'll simply waste their powder and lead in such firing as they did this morning, and pretty soon they'll lose heart and drop off, leaving Pontiac to beg for peace."

"I don't suppose they will unite in a charge," assented one of the officers. "But they will keep a sharp lookout day and night to do us injury. We have four walls to guard and only one hundred and twenty men to do it. The garrison will be exhausted in no time."

"Yes, we have hard work before us," agreed the commander, "but we can do it. Our case is not so bad as you represent. The ship's guns protect two walls, so that virtually only two sides of the fort are exposed to the enemy. To me the most alarming feature of the siege is short rations."

"The supplies are low and we cannot hope for more within three weeks. We'll starve to death, penned up here with no hunting and no provisions from the Canadian farmers," complained some, ready in their alarm to magnify every danger.

"By taking care to prevent waste we can make the supplies last," the commander interrupted. "I shall buy up at once everything in the fort that can serve as food, put it into a common storehouse, and give to each person a daily allowance. If even with this care the food runs short, Canadians may be found who love gold better than Indians." In this way the courageous leader argued, until, at last, he overcame the fears of his aids and roused in them a spirit of resistance.

Pontiac had no lack of warriors, nevertheless he, as well as the British leader, had his fears and difficulties.

His own followers were not easily managed. He had brought them together from near and far with promise of easy victory over the English. After a short struggle many of the tribes lost heart and were ready to go back to their villages.

The Canadians were neutral and were supposed to sympathize with the Indians; but Pontiac knew that many of them favoured the English, and were ready at the slightest offense to take the side of his enemies.

His campaign against the English had begun with failure. Treachery had failed. He had put the English on their guard and must now use open force.

To hold a horde of savages together, to keep the fickle Canadians friendly, to take without cannon all the fortifications on the frontier, were the tasks the Indian general had set himself.

Pontiac's personal influence over the Indians was unparalleled. He had lost none of his power over them by the defeat of his plan to take Detroit. No Indian dared reproach him with failure. All quailed before his terrible rage and disappointment. They brought him the scalps of the English they had slain. They sought to please him with loud outcries against the English, and promises of the bloody work they would do. He held all in awe of him. He commanded as if

PONTIAC'S ELOQUENCE

sure of being obeyed, and punished the slightest disobedience with extreme severity.

But he did not govern by fear alone. He took care that his warriors should not want for food; he took care to give them grounds for hope and to keep them busy.

No preparations had been made for a long siege. When provisions failed and the tribes were on the point of leaving, Pontiac had a conference with some Canadians and arranged that they should furnish his people with corn and meat. He had no money to pay for provisions, but he made out notes promising to pay for them at some future time. These notes were written on birch bark, and signed with the figure of an otter, the totem of the great chief. Many of the farmers feared they would never see the money promised them in these notes, but Pontiac paid them all faithfully.

Pontiac knew how wasteful his people were, feasting in the day of plenty without thought of the morrow. He therefore employed a Canadian as his provision officer. This man had charge of the storehouse, and doled out each morning the provisions for the day.

This novel arrangement increased the Indians' confidence in their leader. Yet some grew restless and were on the point of giving up the struggle as a failure.

On learning this, Pontiac sent out messengers to the Wyandot Indians, ordering them to join him in his war against the British or prepare to be wiped off the face of the earth. By this stroke Pontiac turned threatened loss into gain. The support of the warlike Wyandots renewed the courage of the faint-hearted, and for a time all thought of failure ceased.

The chiefs conduct toward the Canadians was highly praiseworthy. They had encouraged him to make war against the British by promising that the French king would send him help. Week after week passed and no help came. Pontiac's expectation of the arrival of a French army grew fainter and fainter. Still he did not lose faith in the truth of the Canadians.

He protected them and their property from injury and theft; for there were many lawless young warriors who were ready to do violence to the French as well as to the English.

While pretending to sympathize with the Indians, many of the French farmers were secretly helping the English by selling them food and reporting the movements of the Indians. Pontiac heard many reports of their faithlessness.

One stormy evening the chief entered the cabin of a Frenchman whom he had known for many years. With only a nod for his host he sat down before the dying fire. He sat there wrapt in his blanket for a long time without a word. At last he faced the Frenchman and said: "Old friend, I hear that the English have offered to give you a bushel of silver if you will take them my scalp."

"It is false," cried the Frenchman in alarm. "I would not injure my friend for many bushels of silver."

"Pontiac has no fear. Pontiac trusts his brother," the Indian replied, and stretching himself upon a bench he was soon sound asleep. The Frenchman could not be false to such faith and the chief slept unharmed.

While successfully keeping together his warriors and strengthening the bond of friendship between the French and the Indians, Pontiac was carrying on the war against the English with vigour. His camp near Detroit was the centre of action. From it Pontiac directed the war and kept constant watch over the garrison. He prevented the besieged from leaving their walls; he sent out parties to waylay the supplies the British were expecting from the East; he planned and managed expeditions against other forts held by the British.

THE SIEGE OF DETROIT

The English at Detroit soon became accustomed to the discomforts and alarms of the siege. The women no longer trembled when the Indian war whoop sounded. The men no longer ran to the walls at the popping of muskets. The smell of gunpowder, the whiz of bullets, had lost their power to quicken the pulse.

The days dragged slowly on. A few wan-faced men worked, many lounged in the narrow streets, playing games of chance, betting on the outcome of the war, quarrelling, complaining, boasting. Now they talked vauntingly, telling tales of the Englishman's prowess and the Indian's cowardice. Again, they told dismal stories of Indian cruelty and massacre, and shook their heads over their own prospects.

But every idler had his firelock close at hand, and all the time the sentinels on the bastions kept a sharp lookout. Every little while rapid firing broke the monotony of the long watch; the rolling drum called the garrison to the ramparts; wounded men groaned under the rough kindness of the fort surgeon; the dead received the soldiers' burial. But over all the old flag with its red cross, stained with rain and smoke, flapped defiantly.

Major Gladwin went about with a cheerful face, but a heavy heart. Provisions were fast melting away. It seemed scarcely possible that the garrison would be able to hold out till the expected supplies arrived. He decided to send one of the schooners to meet the provision boats, to warn them of the hostility of the Indians and urge them to all speed.

They could ill spare any of the garrison, but food must be had. So, on a bright spring morning one of the vessels weighed anchor and started for the East. Before she left the Detroit River the wind died and her sails hung limp.

As the boat lay helplessly drifting with the current a hundred canoes darted out from the shore. In the foremost one the Indians had bound their prisoner, Captain Campbell. The British saw, and were afraid to fire lest they should shoot their countryman. Noticing their hesitation, the brave old man called out: "Don't think of me. Do your duty and fire." The man at the cannon still paused. A breeze stirred, swelled the canvas, and the schooner flew like a great gull over the blue waters far out of reach of the canoes.

After the boat left, a gloom settled upon the little garrison at Detroit. With two boats in the harbour flight had seemed possible. Now that one of them had gone, all felt that the siege meant victory or death. The daily allowance of food grew smaller. The men became exhausted with ceaseless watching. All hope was fixed on the expected reinforcements.

On the thirteenth of May the sentinel announced that the long looked for convoy was in sight. The good news spread rapidly. Soon the entire population of the village was hurrying to the gate that led to the river.

The hungry, haggard-looking men that crowded the wharf sent up cheer after cheer as the boats approached with flags flying. Days of rest and plenty seemed theirs again. Here were comrades to share their vigils. Here was food to satisfy their hunger.

As the boats drew nearer, the cheers died in throats hoarse with horror. No answering shout came from the boats. The English at the oars were not their own masters. The long expected supplies had fallen into the hands of the Indians. The men to whom the garrison had looked for help were the prisoners of the enemy.

Two Englishmen escaped from their guards and succeeded in reaching the fort where they told their story: Ninety men had started with large stores of food and ammunition, early in the spring to reinforce Detroit. Meeting the schooner from the fort and learning the danger and need of the garrison, they had pushed on with all possible speed until they reached the mouth of the Detroit River. That night, as the boats were drawn up on the shore and the men were getting supper, their camp was suddenly surprised by a horde of Wyandot Indians. The British made an attempt to defend themselves. But the Indians were upon them brandishing their tomahawks and yelling like demons. Panic fear seized the white men. They dropped their guns, fled to the boats, jumped in and pushed off. The exultant Indians pressed after them and succeeded in retaking all but two of their over-loaded boats. The savages were now taking their prisoners, about sixty in number, to the camp of Pontiac, where they would be tortured and put to death.

The success of this bold venture probably would have ended the siege of Detroit with victory for Pontiac, had the Canadians been as loyal to the Indians as they pretended. But while they were giving the chief assurances of good will and future help, some of them were secretly succouring the English. Under the cover of night they smuggled cattle and sheep and hogs to the famishing garrison.

Even with this aid the prospects of the little garrison were dark enough. Every wind seemed to blow them ill news.

One afternoon the guard at the fort heard a weird chant and saw issuing from the distant forest a file of warriors whose naked bodies were smeared with black paint. Every one of them carried a pole over his shoulder, and the horrified watchers knew well enough that from the end of each pole fluttered the scalp of some Englishman. They learned from the Canadians that night that Fort Sandusky had been burned and its garrison murdered.

A little later the Indians offered to exchange some prisoners with the English. The victims thus released by the Indians proved to be from Fort St. Joseph. They told how that fort had been treacherously taken and burned, and all the inmates but themselves slain.

A travelling priest brought word that the plot which had failed at Detroit had succeeded only too well at Michillimack-inac. Next came tidings of the massacres at Fort Ouatanon on the Wabash River and at Fort Miamis, on the Maumee.

Nor was the tale of fire and blood yet ended. A fugitive from the camp of Pontiac reached Detroit one afternoon. It proved to be Ensign Christie, the commanding officer at

Presqu' Isle, near the eastern end of Lake Erie. His story was a thrilling one. He told how his little garrison of twenty-seven men had fortified themselves in their block house and made a fierce struggle to keep back the Indians and save their stronghold from the flames; how at last the Indians had undermined their fort and threatened to apply the torch above and below at once. Then to escape death by fire the little band had listened to the promises of the Indians and yielded themselves prisoners.

If these reports terrified the English at Detroit, they also strengthened their determination not to surrender. In spite of fatigue, hunger, and discouragement they fought stoutly on, until, at length, there came a turn in the tide of ill fortune that had surged against them.

On the nineteenth of June news reached them that the schooner which had been sent to meet the provisions had returned and was entering the Detroit River. This cheered all, for they knew that the boat had been to Niagara for more supplies and more men. Still, they remembered the fate of the provision boats, and were worried lest mischance should befall the schooner.

Their anxiety increased when they saw the Indians going in large companies down the river and heard from the Canadians that they were planning to attack the schooner. The British at the fort fired two cannon shots to let their countrymen know that they still held Detroit. But several days passed before they heard anything of the boat. At last they saw her sailing safely toward them.

There were waving caps, shouts of joy, and prayers of thanksgiving among the little company of half-starved men who thronged at the gate to welcome the newcomers.

They had heard that eight hundred more Ojibwa Indians were on their way to increase the forces of Pontiac. But what were eight hundred Ojibwas to sixty hardy sons of England and a schooner loaded with supplies and cannon!

Hope grew strong in Pontiac's heart as week after week his tribes and allies brought to his camp trophies of victory—guns, prisoners, scalps. But Detroit troubled him. The most violent attacks produced no effect. To starve the garrison seemed the only way to conquer it.

When, therefore, Pontiac's messengers had brought word that the schooner was approaching he bent his whole energy to prevent her reaching Detroit. Along the river where dense underwoods grew, hundreds of Indians lay concealed with their canoes, waiting for the schooner.

When, in the darkness of a moonless night, they saw the great boat sailing steadily up the narrow channel they paddled silently toward her, dark specks on the breast of the dark, shining river.

Nearer and nearer they pressed. All was silent on the vessel. Surely no one had taken alarm. Not a shot and they had reached the boat; they were clambering like rats up its bulky sides—when lo! a sharp hammering on the mast head, a flash of muskets in the dark, a cry of defeat and rage above the din of battle! Cannon boomed; canoes flew high into the air; bullets did their work.

For fourteen Indians the long struggle against the palefaces was over. The rest scurried to the shore as best they could, some paddling, some swimming. Once there, they took shelter behind some temporary earthworks, and opened such a fierce fire on the schooner that it was forced to drop down stream to a broader part of the river. For several days they delayed the ship, but at length she sailed boldly past, and was but little injured by the fire.

Pontiac was sorely vexed that the ship had succeeded in reaching the garrison. He and his people looked upon the boats with almost superstitious horror. Their dislike was not lessened when one day the smaller schooner made her way against wind and current up to Pontiac's village, and there sent shot and shell roaring through the frail dwellings.

Though no loss of life resulted, the Indians were greatly alarmed. Pontiac moved his camp to a safer place and then turned his attention to destroying the ships. Early in July he made his first attempt.

Two large boats filled with birch bark and pitch pine were tied together and set on fire. They were then cut loose and left to float down stream. Keenly the Indians watched; keenly, the English. Would the fireboats go close enough? the first wondered with bated breath. Would they come too close? questioned the British. Woe on the one hand, joy on the other! the space between the ships and the flaming craft widens— the fireboats float harmlessly down the river. A second and a third attempt to burn the boats failed. Fortune seemed to favour the English.

Pontiac began to despair of taking Detroit unaided. He called a council of the French. He reminded them that the English were their enemies as well as his. He charged them with helping the English and told them that the time had come for them to choose sides and fight with him or against him. He then offered them the war belt. His hope was that they would take it up and join him against the English.

Now, the Canadians had become by the terms of the treaty that closed the French war, British subjects, but they were ashamed or afraid to admit it, and still deceived the Indians. They told Pontiac that much as it would please them to fight with him against the English, they must obey the commands of their father, the King of France, who had bidden them to remain at peace until his coming. They added that he, with a great army, was already on the St. Lawrence and would soon arrive to punish the enemies of his children and reward their friends. They advised the chieftain not to make an enemy of his mighty friend.

When the French speaker had finished, there was a short

silence. Then an old trapper came forward, and, picking up the war belt, declared that he was ready to take sides with the Indians against the English. Several of his rough comrades followed his example.

Pontiac's hope of gaining aid from the French was thus not utterly defeated. Besides, he still believed their talk about the coming of the French king. So the French and Indians continued friends.

Some of the tribes growing restless, now made peace with the English and deserted Pontiac. But a greater blow than the desertion of a few tribes was in store for the chief.

Late in July he learned that twenty-two barges bearing large supplies of food and ammunition and almost three hundred men had made their way up the Detroit River in safety, protected by a dense fog. The news came so late that it was impossible for the Indians to oppose the progress of the boats, and they reached the fort with little resistance.

At about two o'clock in the morning of the second day after the arrival of this convoy, Pontiac's spies brought him word that the English were coming against his camp with a great force. Swiftly and silently the Ottawas broke their camp, and with some Ojibwas started to meet the British. On reaching the site of their former camp, about a mile and a half above the fort, near the bridge that crossed a little stream, called from that night Bloody Run, they formed an ambush and waited for the British.

They had barely time to hide behind their old earthworks, natural ridges and piles of brush. Already they heard the barking of watchdogs at the farmhouses along the river road, and the tramp of many feet. They listened and discovered that the enemy outnumbered them. What of that! The night was dark. They knew their ground. Their scouts would soon bring other tribes to help them.

Every Indian was out of sight; every gun was loaded. The tramp of feet drew nearer. A dark mass of marching men came in sight. The quick steps of the advanced guard rang on the wooden bridge. All else was still. The vanguard had crossed the bridge and the main body of the English had started over, when, in front, to right, to left, burst blood curdling yells, blazed a fatal volley of muskets.

Back only, lay safety. Those who had not fallen in the first charge turned and fled, followed by a rain of bullets. Panic spread along the line. But the brave leader of the English, Captain Dalzel, sprang to the front and rallied his men. They made a bold charge, as they thought, into the midst of the enemy; but they found none to resist them. Every Indian had vanished. They pressed bravely on in search of their assailants; but the night was black and the way was rough and unfamiliar. Whenever they reached a place of difficulty the Indians unexpectedly renewed their attack.

The savages, whose eyes were accustomed to the darkness, saw the enemy after a parley return to the bridge. There, half of the men mounted guard while the others took up the dead and wounded and carried them to two armed boats that had accompanied them down the river.

Seeing that a return to the fort was intended, the Indians turned back in large numbers to form another ambuscade at a point where several houses and barns stood near the road and cut the English off from the fort.

They again allowed the vanguard to pass unmolested and surprised the centre with a galling fire. The soldiers, confused by the weird and terrible cries of the savages and the blaze of musketry, blinded by smoke and flash, and stung by pelting bullets, huddled together like sheep.

Captain Dalzel, though severely wounded, by commanding, imploring, fairly driving his men with his sword, at last succeeded in regaining order. He made a charge and as usual the Indians fled before the attack. As soon as the English attempted to continue their retreat the Indians were upon them again, firing from every fence and thicket.

The gallant Dalzel was among those shot down by this fire. He died trying to save a wounded soldier from the scalping knife of the Indians. In the confusion he was scarcely missed. The officers next in command took charge of the retreat. In the grey dawn the remnant of Dalzel's army reached the fort. The Indians went off, well satisfied with their night's work, to count their scalps and celebrate.

While the English lost about sixty men in this engagement, called the battle of Bloody Ridge, the number of Indians killed and wounded was not greater than fifteen or twenty. The Indians considered it a great victory and fresh warriors flocked to the camp of the Indian commander who seemed to be a match for the English.

THE END OF THE SIEGE

We have seen that after the battle of Bloody Ridge many tribes that had before been afraid to take up the hatchet against the English, presented themselves at the camp of Pontiac, eager for a share in the victory at Detroit, which they thought would follow.

Yet that English stronghold, that log palisade, was a prize out of reach of the chief and his warriors. The Indians kept close watch. If a head appeared at a loophole, bang went an Indian's gun. If a point was left unguarded, there was the torch applied. Fire arrows whizzed over the rampart in the darkness, only to burn themselves out in the broad roadway between the wall and the buildings. Again and again hundreds of painted warriors danced about the fort yelling as if Detroit, like Jericho, might be taken with shouting. Their spent bullets pelted the old fort like harmless hail. They tried to rush upon the gate, but the fusillade from the block house and the fire-belching cannon of the British drove them back helter-skelter.

Late in September an incident occurred which increased

the Indians' awe of the British. A scout brought word to Pontiac that a dispatch boat with a large store of provisions was on her way to the fort. As there were only twelve men aboard, her capture seemed an easy matter.

The Indians planned a midnight attack. Three hundred of them drifted down the river in their light birch canoes. The night was so dark and they came so noiselessly that the watching English did not know of their approach until they were within gunshot of the boat.

A cannon was fired, but its shot and shell went over the heads of the Indians and ploughed up the black water beyond. The canoes were all about the ship and the savages, with knives in their teeth, were climbing up its sides. The crew fired once. One or two Indians fell back into the water; the rest came on. As they climbed nearer, the British charged them with bayonets, and hacked them with hatchets and knives. But where one man was driven back a dozen gained the deck.

The little crew defended themselves desperately; they were surrounded by brandished tomahawks; their captain had fallen; more than half their number were cut down. The Indians were raising their shout of triumph. Then the order of Jacobs, the mate, rang out: "Blow up the ship!" he said. One Indian understood and gave the alarm to his fellows. With one accord they threw down hatchets and knives and leaped into the river. They made haste to reach the shore and left six bloodstained British sailors to take their boat in triumph to Detroit.

As autumn advanced the Indians grew weary of the long siege. The prospect of winter with no food, the continued resistance of the British, and the report that a large force of armed men was coming to relieve Detroit, discouraged them.

One tribe after another sent delegations to Major Gladwin to sue for peace. They told smooth stories. They had always loved the English, but Pontiac had compelled them to go to war. Now they were sorry they had obeyed him and longed to be at peace with their English brothers.

Gladwin understood their deceit, but as he was in need of winter supplies, readily granted them a truce. The various tribes broke up their camps and separated for the long winter hunt.

Pontiac and his Ottawas still held their ground without flinching. "Surely," thought the proud-hearted chief, "our French father will send us help before long."

One day, near the close of October, a messenger did come from the French. The letter he brought was from M. Neyon, the commandant of Fort Chartres, in the Illinois country. Pontiac had written to him asking for aid. What had he answered? He had told the truth. He had told Pontiac that the French in America were now the subjects of the English king, and so could not fight against his people.

When the great chief heard this he did not put on his war paint and lead his warriors against the defenceless French who had so long dealt falsely with him. He sat alone for a long time, thinking. The next day he sent a letter to Major Gladwin saying that he was now ready to bury the hatchet, and begging the English to forget the past.

Major Gladwin thought that the French were more to blame than the Indians in the war, and was willing to be at peace with his red neighbours. So he sent Pontiac a favourable reply. A few days later the stern-faced chief turned his back on Detroit, and began his march to the Maumee River, followed by his faithful braves.

ALL ALONG THE FRONTIER

The plan of Pontiac had been to take the forts all along the frontier by strategy and then destroy the defenceless English settlements.

We have seen that while there were many French farmers living outside of the walls of Detroit there were very few English. And, in truth, in 1763, there were not many English settlers east of the Alleghany Mountains. Most of the forts that had been taken from the French, except those on the Mississippi River, were garrisoned with English. Within reach of the protection of these forts, lived some British traders and trappers, and a few venturesome settlers. But the Mohawk Valley in New York, and the Susquehanna, in Pennsylvania, really formed the western limit of extensive English settlement.

Pontiac's war belts had stirred up the Indians all along the border. In the summer of 1763, while he and the Ottawas and Ojibwas were besieging Detroit, the Delawares and Shawnees were laying waste the Pennsylvania frontier.

Backwoodsmen, trappers or travellers, venturing into the wilderness were shot down without warning. Men, women, and children were miserably slain. Isolated farmhouses were attacked, their inmates scalped, the cabins burned. Churches and schools added to the blaze that swept the wilderness from the Great Lakes to the Ohio. One after another the smaller forts were taken by the Indians.

Panic seized the settlers. Women left the kettle on the hearth, men the plough in the furrow, and fled. Some crowded for refuge into the nearest fort. Others feared to stop until they had reached Lancaster or even Philadelphia.

The terrible butcheries committed by the Indians so maddened the frontiersmen that they forgot their civilization and resorted to methods as inhuman as did the Indians. Peaceable, friendly Indians were massacred by bands of ruffian borderers, organized for vengeance as well as protection. Even men in high places forgot their usual humanity. The commander-in-chief of the army, Sir Jeffrey Amherst, and Colonel Henry Bouquet planned to send smallpox among the Indians by giving them infected blankets. They even talked of fighting them with bloodhounds instead of soldiers. The Governor of Pennsylvania issued a proclamation offering a reward for Indian prisoners and Indian scalps.

Fort Pitt, one of the most important posts on the frontier,

held out against the attacks of the Delawares and the Shawnees. When the commander-in-chief of the army learned of the distress of the fort he sent a strong force under Colonel Bouquet to relieve it.

In August, when crossing the Alleghany Mountains, Bouquet's army was assailed by a horde of Indians that had been lying in wait for them at Bushy Run. The battle which followed was hot. The British were courageous, but they fell in large numbers under the fire of the Indians, who fled before every charge, only to return like infuriated wasps at the moment the English fancied they had repulsed them. Night brought relief from the galling fire. But the battle was not over.

The English were held penned up on the road without water till dawn, when the charge was renewed with such zest that for a time it looked as if there were no escape for the forces of Bouquet. The unusual boldness of the Indians suggested to him a stratagem.

REDOUBT AT FORT PITT

He feigned a retreat. Thus encouraged the Indians rushed upon the British with war whoop and scalp cry. The forces of Bouquet divided; the Indians filled the breach. Then at the word of command the troops closed on them, charging with bayonets. Many of the Indians entrapped in this way fell; the rest fled.

After that the English made their way to Fort Pitt without serious interruption. In the battle of Bushy Run the loss on both sides was heavy for an Indian battle. The English lost eight officers and over one hundred soldiers; the Indians, several chiefs and about sixty warriors. Though the English loss was greater than that of the Indians, it could be more easily made up. For that reason, and because the English had succeeded in reaching Fort Pitt, the expedition was regarded as a splendid victory for the palefaces.

As winter advanced the Indians were obliged to desist from war and go into the forest in small companies to hunt. During the winter that followed the rebellion, the Indians had no help from the white people, and the bitter hardships they suffered did much to put them into a pacific frame of mind.

Sir William Johnson, the king's sole agent and superintendent of Indian affairs, understood the red men better than most of his countrymen did. He lived among them on a great estate in the Mohawk Valley. He spoke their language and often dressed in Indian suit of slashed deerskin.

In his opinion it was wasteful and unwise to fight with the Indians. He said the English were largely to blame for the Indian war because of their injustice and their want of policy in dealing with the savages. He advocated following the example of the French, and winning the good will of the Indians by flattery and presents. He believed that under that policy the Indians would become so dependent on the white man that they could be easily subdued.

Early in the spring of 1764 he sent messages to the various tribes, warning them that two great armies of English soldiers

were ready to start into the western forest to punish the enemies of the English, and inviting all who wished to make
peace to meet him at Niagara.

Accordingly, early in the spring, the fields around the fort
at Niagara were dotted with Indian encampments. Among
the savages were friendly Indians who had come to claim
their reward; enemies who, through want or fear, were ready
to make a temporary peace, and spies, who wanted to see
what was going on.

For many a long day Sir William Johnson sat in the council
room at the fort making treaties with various tribes. All day the
fumes of the peace-pipe filled the hall, and threats and promises were made, and sealed with long strings of *wampum*.

It would have taken much less time to make one treaty
with all the Indians, but Sir William Johnson sought to dis-
courage the idea of a common cause, which Pontiac had done
so much to arouse among the Indians. He treated each tribe as
if its case were quite different from that of every other tribe.

Some Indians were so bold that they would not even pre-
tend to be friendly. The Delawares and the Shawnees replied
to the Indian agent's message summoning them to Niagara,
that they were not afraid of the English, but looked upon
them as old women.

The armies to which Sir William Johnson had referred
were under the command of Colonel Bouquet and Colonel
Bradstreet. The latter went by way of the Lakes to relieve Detroit, offer peace to the northern Indians, and subdue those
who refused to submit. Bouquet, with a thousand men, penetrated the forests further south to compel the fierce Delawares
and Shawnees to submission. Both succeeded.

Bradstreet found the northern Indians ready to come to
terms. He has been criticised for requiring the Indians to sign
papers they did not understand and make promises that they
did not fulfil. He did not see Pontiac, but sent a deputation to
find him and confer with him.

COUNCIL WITH COLONEL BOUQUET

Colonel Bouquet, on the other hand, was stern and terrible. In council he addressed the Indians as chiefs and warriors, instead of "brothers." He refused to smooth over their wrong doing or listen to the excuses they offered for going to war. He charged them openly with the wrongs they had done, and required them to surrender all their white prisoners and give him hostages from their own race.

Many of the captives had lived among the Indians so long that they had forgotten their white relatives and friends. They left the Indian life and Indian friends with tears, and would have remained in captivity gladly. But Colonel Bouquet would make no exceptions.

His stern measures subdued the warlike tribes completely. In the fall of 1764 Bouquet returned to the East to receive honours and rewards for his services.

The Last of Pontiac

While other Indians were promising to bury the hatchet, Pontiac, the soul of the conspiracy, made no promises and smoked no peace-pipe. Surrounded by hundreds of warriors the chief camped on the Maumee River. His messengers brought him news of what was going on, and until the white men had taken their soldiers from the land he was content to wait and plan.

Captain Morris, who had been sent to Pontiac's camp by Colonel Bradstreet, was coldly received by the great chief. Pontiac, indeed, granted him a hearing, but he bent upon his guest dark looks and refused to shake his hand. He made no flowery speeches, but declared that all the British were liars, and asked what new lies he had come to tell. After some talk Pontiac showed the captain a letter which he supposed to have been written by the King of France. It told the old story of the French army on its way to destroy the English. Captain Morris did his best to persuade him that the report was false. He was much impressed with the influence, knowledge, and sense of Pontiac—an Indian who commanded eighteen nations and was acquainted with the laws that regulated the conduct of civilized states.

Pontiac would make no official promises of peace, but he was so much discouraged by the communications Captain Morris brought, that he said to one of the followers of the latter: "I shall never more lead the nations to war. As for them, let them be at peace with the English if they will; for me, I shall be at war with them forever. I shall be a wanderer in the woods, and if they come to seek me I will fight them single-handed." With much bitterness of soul did Pontiac learn that the forts he had taken with so much effort and loss of Indian blood, had been retaken by the enemy; that the war spirit he had with so much labour aroused had been put to sleep.

But his hopes were not easily dashed. There were the letters from the French. The English said they were false, but the English were his enemies. The French were his friends. Enemies might deceive each other, but friends must trust each other.

His confidence in the French was encouraged by the fact that several of the forts in the Illinois country were still occupied by French garrisons.

Pontiac resolved to make another effort to rouse his people. He set his squaws to work on a *wampum* war belt, broad and long, containing symbols of the forty-seven tribes which belonged to his confederacy. When the belt was done he sent a delegation of chiefs to the south with it. These messengers were instructed to show the war belt and offer the hatchet to all the tribes along the Mississippi River as far south as New Orleans. They were then to visit the French Governor at New Orleans and invite him to assist them in war against their common enemy.

Pontiac, in the meantime, went about among his old French friends asking for their help, and among the Illinois Indians urging them with threats and promises to join him in making war against the English. He met with some success, but his dreams were rudely broken by the return of his chiefs with the news that the Governor of New Orleans had indeed yielded to the British, and by the arrival of a company of British from Fort Pitt, offering terms of peace to the Illinois Indians. Daily Pontiac's allies deserted him, and accepted the terms of the English.

Again the day had come when it seemed to Pontiac wise to let his hatred of the English sleep. He sent his great peace-pipe to Sir William Johnson and promised to go to Oswego in the spring to conclude a treaty with him.

True to his promise, in the spring of 1766, Pontiac, greatest war chief and sachem of the Ottawas, presented himself in the council chamber of Sir William Johnson. There was nothing fawning in his attitude; he conducted himself with the dignity of a fallen monarch. "When you speak to me," he said, "it is as if you addressed all the nations of the west." In making peace he submitted not to the will of the British but to that of the Great Spirit, whose will it was that there should be peace. He made it clear that in allowing the English to take the forts of the French the Indians granted them no right to their lands. When he promised friendship for the future, he called his hearers to witness how true a friend he had been to the French, who had deceived him and given him reason to transfer his friendship.

It would be hard to say how sincere Pontiac was, or how readily he would have let go the chain of friendship he had been forced to take up, had opportunity offered. He went back to his camp on the Maumee River, and there among his own people tried to live the life of his fathers. Little was heard of him for a year or two, but whenever an outbreak occurred among the Indians there were those who said Pontiac was at the bottom of it.

In the spring of 1769, anxious to see his French friends once more, he made a visit to St. Louis. He was cordially received and spent several days with his old acquaintances. Then he crossed the river with a few chiefs to visit an assembly of traders and Illinois Indians.

After feasting and drinking with some of the Illinois, Pontiac sought the quiet of the forest. He wandered through its dim aisles, living over again the hopes and ambitions of the past, which his visit with the French and the Illinois had vividly recalled. He had forgotten the present and was again the mighty warrior who had made the hearts of the palefaces quake with fear. Little he dreamed that behind him stood an assassin with up-raised tomahawk.

The murderer of the great chief was an Illinois Indian who had been bribed to do the deed by an English trader.

During his life Pontiac had tried to overcome the tribal feeling of the Indians, and to unite them as one people. Over his grave the old tribal instinct awoke. The Illinois rallied about their kinsman to protect him; the Ottawas flew to arms to avenge their chief—such a sachem, such a chief, could not be forgotten. Wrong to him could not be forgiven. The fury of the Ottawas was not slaked until they had avenged the death of their chief, through the destruction of the powerful tribes of the Illinois.

Ponteach—
or The Savages of America

A Tragedy

by Robert Rogers

with an introduction and notes by
Allan Nevins

Introduction

The importance of Rogers *Ponteach* does not lie in any purely artistic qualities. It is only the historian, whether of events or letters, in whom it can nowadays inspire more than a .transiently curious interest; for while it is the product of a fresh acquaintance with savage character and the various causal trains which exploded the spectacular rebellion of the Indian ruler while it has, too, a factitious importance as almost the first of American dramatic compositions, and even yet remains one of our few specimens of poetic tragedy, it must seem to any reader who picks up the play for its own sake almost pitifully devoid of intrinsic merits. The web and woof of its style never rise from the commonplace to the even faintly poetical, and all too frequently sink to doggerel and empty declamation; the larger outlines of the plot reveal manifold absurdities. Even over one or two passages of comparative force and eloquence, such as those in Acts II and III in which *Ponteach* throws fuel upon his anger and reveals the main outlines of his great plan to his sons and warriors, few readers would linger long. As we wonder at the temerity with which Rogers, author a month before of the shrinkingly modest preface to the *Concise Account*, left his production to the caustic mercy of the great reviews, we can only reflect that it was completed in haste, at the moment he was called back to take command at Mackinac, and that to an untutored and ambitious man it might have seemed that its faults could hide behind its novelty, and that, helping *"to give a just idea of the genius and ideas of the Indians,"* it would interest many by the picturesqueness of its scenes and the fame of its central character.

And in a measure Rogers was right; for the tragedy is one that can scarcely be forgotten; and waiving its merely curious attraction as the strange product of an American backwoodsman suddenly transported to the centre of Anglo-Saxon civilization and fashion, its chief claim to a reprieve from oblivion lies in those historical elements upon which Rogers mistakenly hoped to base a temporary appeal. Parkman and other writers upon the period have attested its value by a liberal use of it as a source. In his military service at Albany and the forts immediately north, in his rangings over upper New York and lower Canada, and in his survey of the lake posts at the close of the Seven Years War, Rogers had by 1762 familiarizes himself with the conditions of Indian life and the strange facts evoked by the attempted adjustment to it of English authority, commerce, and agriculture; he had, indeed, engaged in the trade himself, and so had felt both a soldier s and a merchant's concern in inter-racial relations. Participation in the suppression of Pontiac's rebellion in 1763 finally equipped him with the adequate knowledge of the chief and his conspiracy which the tragedy manifests. Indeed, Rogers informing historical accuracy is beyond the many definite parallels between the language of the play and that of the *Concise Account* one of the surest establishments of the authorship which he never formally claimed. No other hand in London could have written with such directness and truth to fact the two first and expository acts of the drama.

The specification of the grievances of the Indians is accomplished with a detail which is kept fresh and interesting by a grimly effective sense of humour. The traders Murphy and McDole, with their use of rum *"more powerful made by certain strengthening drugs,"* and scales *"so well conceived that one small slip will turn three pounds to one,"* so that they secure ninety pounds of beaver skin for six quarts of a vile alcoholic decoction; the hunters Osborne and Honeyman, who shoot two braves for their loads of fur; Colonel Cockum and Captain Frisk, of the English fort, who requite the chiefs pleas for justice with unsoldierly insults; Governors Sharp, Gripe, and Catchum, who, quoting scripture to their own wretched purposes, steal all but a beggarly remnant of the £1000 worth of goods given them for presents to the Indians; all are drawn by a satirical pen that makes of the scenes in which they appear rather more than a mere explanation of the central action. With the transition to a direct study of the Indian point of view, the play assumes a greater elevation of tone; and the pride of Pontiac, his haughty sense of humiliation, his brooding jealousy of his kingly prerogatives, are expressed in what, despite Rogers deficiencies of expression, approaches the force ascribed to his oratory, and the stateliness to his person and character. The development of his plot, moreover, from his sudden determination:

> *The broken accents murmured from his tongue,*
> *As rumbling thunder from a distant cloud,*
> *Distinct I heard, 'T is fixed, I'll be revenged.*

and the moment when, in his poor cabin, he gathers his sons and chiefs to denounce the *"false, deceitful, knavish, insolent band. . . . Who think us conquered and our country theirs,"* to that in which he secures the adhesion of the western tribes to his design, is traced with considerable spirit. With the entrance, however, of the romantic element, which after Act II almost dominates the play, its historical interest reappears only in flashes, for the value even of the impression Rogers gives of Indian character is greatly diminished. The part played in the story by Pontiac s negotiations for Mohawk aid has no basis in fact, for this easternmost tribe of the Iroquois Confederacy was a fast-rooted ally of the English, and would have offered a field of discouragingly scant promise to his emissaries. We know nothing of Pontiac s sons or Hendrick's daughter; Hendrick himself was eight years dead at the time of the revolt; and private calamities had nothing to do with Pontiac s retirement to the Illinois. But, altogether, Rogers picture of the vices and abuses of the soldiers and traders, lying at the source of the rebellion, of the galled resentment of the Indians, and, in fact, of the whole fundamental characteristics of much of border life, is proved by con temporary documents to be faithful and authoritative. In particular, the portrait of Pontiac, partially idealized as it is, must always be matter for the study of those who are interested in the character of the greatest of North American Indians.

From the point of view of American literary history the influence of Rogers production upon the development of the stage was nil; for at the time, and until long after, there was no native American stage. One may perceive by a moment s reflection the paucity of the author s opportunities to familiarize himself with the theatre. The first American playhouse was opened at Williamsburg, Virginia, in the second decade of the eighteenth century; the second at New York, in 1732; the third at Charleston, in 1736. Throughout virtually all New England the theatre lay under a ban, and players were subject to arrest, during the whole colonial period; in Massachusetts until 1792. Even elsewhere, performances were so infrequent that Rogers may very probably never have watched one until he reached London, and saw the spacious stage of Betterton and Garrick. As for playwriting, if we waive consideration of a few wretchedly obscure manuscripts of interest only to the antiquarian, *Ponteach* is the second drama penned by an American, and narrowly escaped being the first in print; for Rogers published his play in January, 1766, and it was antedated in book form by Thomas Godfrey's *The Prince of Parthia* by only a few months. It must needs be added that Godfrey, a Philadelphian, the son of a member of Franklin s Junto, was already dead, and that his tragedy had been written about 1760; that, beaten out in smooth blank verse, and with considerable merit of construction, it was much superior both poetically and dramatically to Rogers work; and that it enjoyed later (April 24, 1767) a single representation, a distinction which its successor never achieved. But Rogers remained for a full generation the only son of New England to permit his dramatic ambitions to struggle up from under the *incubus* of prejudice and neglect which Puritanism had thrown upon all activities connected with the stage.

DRAMATIS PERSONÆ.

PONTEACH,   Indian *Emperor on the great Lakes.*

PHILIP *an.' * CHE-
KITAN,   }   *Sons of* Ponteach.

TENESCO,   *His chief Counsellor and Generalissimo.*

ASTINACO, -
The BEAR,   -   }   Indian *Kings who join with Ponteach.*
The WOLF,   -

TORAX *and* MO-
NELIA   -   }   *Son and Daughter to* Hendrick,
                 Emperor of the Mohawks.

Indian   -   -   -   *Conjurer.*

French   -   -   -   *Priest.*

SHARP,   -   -
GRIPE,   -   -   }   *Three* English *Governors.*
CATCHUM,   -

Colonel COCKUM   }   *Commanders at a Garrison in* Pon-
Captain FRISK   }   teach's *Country.*

M'DOLE *and*   }
MURPHEY   }   *Two* Indian *Traders.*

HONNYMAN *and*   }
ORSBOURN   }   *Two* English *Hunters.*

MRS. HONNYMAN   *Wife to* Honnyman *the Hunter.*

Warriors, Messengers, &c.

PONTEACH:

OR THE SAVAGES OF AMERICA.

ACT I.

SCENE I.— *An* Indian *Trading House.*

Enter M'Dole *and* Murphey, *Two* Indian *Traders,* *and their Servants.*

M'Dole.

So, *Murphey*, you are come to try your Fortune
Among the Savages in this wild Desart?
  Murphey. Ay, any Thing to get an honest Living,
Which 'faith I find it hard enough to do;
Times are so dull, and Traders are so plenty,[1]
That Gains are small, and Profits come but slow.
  M'Dole. Are you experienc'd in this kind of Trade?
Know you the Principles by which it prospers,
And how to make it lucrative and safe?
If not, you're like a Ship without a Rudder,
That drives at random, and must surely sink.
  Murphey. I'm unacquainted with your *Indian* Commerce.
And gladly would I learn the Arts from you
Who're old, and practis'd in them many Years.
  M'Dole. That is the curst Misfortune of our Traders,
A thousand Fools attempt to live this Way,
Who might as well turn Ministers of State.
But, as you are a Friend, I will inform you
Of all the secret Arts by which we thrive,
Which if all practis'd, we might all grow rich,
Nor circumvent each other in our Gains.
What have you got to part with to the *Indians?*

[1] Cf. *Johnson Mss.*, 24, 6. Abercrombie condemns the vast extent of the illicit fur-trade in Pennsylvania.

159

Murphey. I've Rum and Blankets, Wampum, Powder, Bells,
And such-like Trifles as they're wont to prize.

M'Dole. 'Tis very well: your Articles are good:
But now the Thing's to make a Profit from them,
Worth all your Toil and Pains of coming hither.
Our fundamental Maxim then is this,
That it's no Crime to cheat and gull an *Indian.*[2]

Murphey. How! Not a Sin to cheat an *Indian*, say you?
Are they not Men? hav'nt they a right to Justice
As well as we, though savage in their Manners?

M'Dole. Ah! If you boggle here, I say no more;
This is the very Quintessence of Trade,
And ev'ry Hope of Gain depends upon it;
None who neglect it ever did grow rich,
Or ever will, or can by *Indian* Commerce.
By this old *Ogden* built his stately House,
Purchas'd Estates, and grew a little King.
He, like an honest Man, bought all by Weight,
And made the ign'rant Savages believe
That his Right Foot exactly weigh'd a Pound:[3]
By this for many Years he bought their Furs,
And died in Quiet like an honest Dealer.

Murphey. Well, I'll not stick at what is necessary;
But his Device is now grown old and stale,
Nor could I manage such a barefac'd Fraud.

M'Dole. A thousand Opportunities present
To take Advantage of their Ignorance;

---

[1] Cf. *Johnson Mss.*, 5, 153. Egremont to Amherst; pointing to the necessity of correcting the trickery of Indian traders in their dealings with the Indians and compelling imitation of the more honorable French practice. Also *Idem*, 5, 108.

[2] "The English fur-trade had never been well regulated, and it was now in a worse condition than ever. Many of the traders, and those in their employ, were ruffians of the coarsest stamp, who vied with each other in the worst rapacity, violence, and profligacy. They cheated, cursed, and plundered the Indians, and outraged their families; offering, when compared with the French traders, who were under better regulation, a most unfavorable example of the character of their nation." Parkman, *The Conspiracy of Pontiac*, Chapter VII. See *Colonial History of New York*, VII, 995.

[3] This classic method of cheating the Indians is probably best known through Washington Irving's ludicrous description of its practice by the Dutch in his *Knickerbocker History of New York*.

But the great Engine I employ is Rum,[1]
More pow'rful made by certain strength'ning Drugs,
This I distribute with a lib'ral Hand,
Urge them to drink till they grow mad and valiant;
Which makes them think me generous and just,
And gives full Scope to practise all my Art.
I then begin my Trade with water'd Rum,
The cooling Draught well suits their scorching Throats.
Their Fur and Peltry come in quick Return:
My Scales are honest, but so well contriv'd,
That one small Slip will turn Three Pounds to One;
Which they, poor silly Souls! ignorant of Weights
And Rules of Balancing, do not perceive.
But here they come; you'll see how I proceed.
Jack, is the Rum prepar'd as I commanded?

   Jack. Yes, Sir, all's ready when you please to call.

   M'Dole. Bring here the Scales and Weights immediately.
You see the Trick is easy and conceal'd.

                       (Shewing how to slip the Scales.

   Murphey. By *Jupiter*, it's artfully contriv'd;
And was I King, I swear I'd knight th' Inventor.
—*Tom*, mind the Part that you will have to act.

   Tom. Ah, never fear, I'll do as well as *Jack*.
But then, you know, an honest Servant's Pains
Deserves Reward.

   Murphey. O! I'll take care of that.

Enter a Number of Indians with Packs of Fur.

   1st Indian. So, what you trade with *Indians* here to-day?

   M'Dole. Yes, if my Goods will suit, and we agree.

   2nd Indian. 'Tis Rum we want, we're tired, hot, and thirsty.

   3rd Indian. You, Mr. *Englishman*, have you got Rum?

---

   [1] "The Indians dwindle away . . . chiefly because when settled among the English they have better opportunity of procuring spirituous liquors, of which they are inordinately fond; and very little care has ever been taken to prevent those who are incl'ned to take advantage of them in trade from debauching them; by which means, where there were considerable settlements of them a few years since, their name is now almost totally extinct." Rogers, *A Concise Account of North America*, p. 152. See also *Johnson Mss.*, 24: 11, 12; Johnson, engaged (July, 1758,) in bringing an Indian party up to Fort Edward, disgustedly charges his delay to an illicit rum-trade, and asks power to quash it.

M'Dole. *Jack*, bring a Bottle, pour them each a Gill.
You know which Cask contains the Rum. The Rum?

1st Indian. It's good strong Rum, I feel it very soon.

M'Dole. Give me a Glass. Here's Honesty in Trade;
We *English* always drink before we deal.

2nd Indian. Good Way enough; it makes one sharp and
cunning.

M'Dole. Hand round another Gill. You're very welcome.

3rd Indian. Some say you *Englishmen* are sometimes Rogues;
You make poor *Indians* drunk, and then you cheat.

1st Indian. No, *English* good. The *Frenchmen* give no Rum.

2nd Indian. I think it's best to trade with *Englishmen.*

M'Dole. What is your Price for Beaver Skins *per* Pound?[1]

2nd Indian. How much you ask *per* Quart for this strong
Rum?

M'Dole. Five Pounds of Beaver for One Quart of Rum.

1st Indian. Five Pounds? Too much. Which is't you call
Five Pound?

M'Dole. This little Weight. I cannot give you more.

1st Indian. Well, take 'em; weigh 'em. Don't you cheat us now.

M'Dole. No: He that cheats an Indian should be hang'd.

(Weighing the Packs.

There's Thirty Pounds precisely of the Whole;
Five times six is Thirty. Six Quarts of Rum.
Jack, measure it to them; you know the Cask.
This Rum is sold. You draw it off the best.

(Exeunt Indians *to receive their Rum.*

Murphey. By *Jove*, you've gain'd more in a single Hour
Than ever I have done in Half a Year;
Curse on my Honesty! I might have been
A *little King*, and liv'd without Concern,
Had I but known the proper Arts to thrive.

M'Dole. Ay, there's the Way, my honest Friend, to live.

(Clapping his Shoulder.

There's Ninety Weight of Sterling Beaver for you,
Worth all the Rum and Trinkets in my Store;
And, would my Conscience let me do the Thing,

---

[1] In 1765, according to Alexander Henry, beaver was worth two shillings
sixpence per pound at Mackinac, or one-half pound of powder, or one pound of
shot, or one-tenth of a blanket. *Travels and Adventures*, Bain's Edition, Boston,
1901, p. 187.

I might enhance my Price, and lessen theirs,
And raise my Profits to an higher Pitch.

Murphey. I can't but thank you for your kind Instructions,
As from them I expect to reap Advantage.
But should the Dogs detect me in the Fraud,
They are malicious, and would have Revenge.

M'Dole. Can't you avoid them? Let their Vengeance light
On others Heads, no matter whose, if you
Are but secure, and have the Gain in Hand:
For they're indiff'rent where they take Revenge,
Whether on him that cheated, or his Friend,
Or on a Stranger whom they never saw,
Perhaps an honest Peasant, who ne'er dreamt
Of Fraud or Villainy in all his life;
Such let them murder, if they will a Score,
The Guilt is theirs, while we secure the Gain,
Nor shall we feel the bleeding Victims Pain.

(*Exeunt.*

SCENE II.— *A Desart.*

Enter Orsbourn *and* Honnyman, *Two* English *Hunters.*

Orsbourn.
Long have we toil'd, and rang'd the Woods in vain,
No Game, nor Track, nor Sign of any Kind
Is to be seen; I swear I am discourag'd
And weary'd out with this long fruitless Hunt.
No Life on Earth besides is half so hard,
So full of Disappointments, as a Hunter's:
Each Morn he wakes he views the destin'd Prey,
And counts the Profits of th' ensuing Day;
Each Ev'ning at his curs'd ill Fortune pines,
And till next day his Hope of Gain resigns.
By *Jove,* I'll from these Desarts hasten home,
And swear that never more I'll touch a Gun.

Honnyman. These hateful *Indians* kidnap all the Game.
Curse their black Heads! they fright the Deer and Bear,
And ev'ry Animal that haunts the Wood,
Or by their Witchcraft conjure them away.
No Englishman can get a single Shot,

While they go loaded home with Skins and Furs.
'Twere to be wish'd not one of them survived,
Thus to infest the World, and plague Mankind.
Curs'd Heathen Infidels! mere savage Beasts!
They don't deserve to breathe in Christian Air,
And should be hunted down like other Brutes.

   Orsbourn. I only wish the Laws permitted us
To hunt the savage Herd where-e'er they're found;
I'd never leave the Trade of Hunting then,
While one remain'd to tread and range the Wood.

   Honnyman. Curse on the Law, I say, that makes it **Death**
To kill an *Indian*, more than to kill a Snake.
What if 'tis Peace? these Dogs deserve no Mercy;
Cursed revengeful, cruel, faithless Devils!
They kill'd my Father and my eldest Brother.
Since which I hate their very Looks and Name.

   Orsbourn. And I, since they betray'd and kill'd my Uncle;
Hell seize their cruel, unrelenting Souls!
Tho these are not the same, 'twould ease my Heart
To cleave their painted Heads, and spill their Blood.
I abhor, detes. and hate them all,
And now cou'd an *Indian's* Heart with Pleasure.

   Honnyman. I'd join you, and soop his savage Brains for Sauce;
I lose all Patience when I think of them,
And, if you will, we'll quickly have Amends
For our long Travel and successless Hunt,
And the sweet Pleasure of Revenge to boot.

   Orsbourn. What will you do? Present, and pop one down?

   Honnyman. Yes, faith, the first we meet well fraught with Furs;
Or if there's Two, and we can make sure Work,
By *Jove*, we'll ease the Rascals of their Packs,
And send them empty home to their own Country.
But then observe, that what we do is secret,
Or the Hangman will come in for Snacks.

   Orsbourn. Trust me for that; I'll join with all my Heart;
Nor with a nicer Aim, or steadier Hand,
Would shoot a Tyger than I would an *Indian*.
There is a Couple stalking now this Way
With lusty Packs; Heav'n favour our Design.

   Hon. Silence; conceal yourself, and mind your Eye.

   Orsbourn. Are you well charg'd?

Honnyman. I am. Take you the nearest,
And mind to fire exactly when I do.
  Orsbourn. A charming Chance!
  Honnyman. Hush, let them still come nearer.
                    (*They shoot, and run to rifle the* Indians.
They're down, old Boy, a Brace of noble Bucks!
  Orsbourn. Well tallow'd, faith, and noble Hides upon 'em.
                              (*Taking up a Pack.*
We might have hunted all the Season thro'
For Half this Game, and thought ourselves well paid.
  Honnyman. By *Jove*, we might, and been at great Expence
For Lead and Powder, here's a single Shot.
  Orsbourn. I swear I've got as much as I can carry.
  Honnyman. And faith I'm not behind; this Pack is heavy.
But stop; we must conceal the tawny Dogs,
Or their blood-thirsty Countrymen will find them,
And then we're bit. There'll be the Devil to pay,
They'll murder us, and cheat the Hangman too.
  Orsbourn. Right. We'll prevent all Mischief of this Kind.
Where shall we hide their savage Carcases?
  Honnyman. There they will lie conceal'd and snug enough —
                              (*They cover them.*
But stay — perhaps ere long there'll be a War,
And then their Scalps will sell for ready Cash,
Two Hundred Crowns at least, and that's worth saving.
  Orsbourn. Well! that is true, no sooner said than done —
                              (*Drawing his Knife.*
I'll strip this Fellow's painted greasy Skull. (*Strips off the Scalp.*
  Honnyman. A damn'd tough Hide, or my Knife's devilish
      dull —   (*Takes the other Scalp.*
Now let them sleep to Night without their Caps,
And pleasant Dreams attend their long Repose.
  Orsbourn. Their Guns and Hatchets now are lawful Prize,
For they'll not need them on their present Journey.
  Honnyman. The Devil hates Arms, and dreads the smell of
      Powder;
He'll not allow such Instruments about him,
They're free from training now, they're in his Clutches.
  Orsbourn. But, *Honnyman*, d'ye think this is not Murder?
I vow I'm shock'd a little to see them scalp'd,
And fear their Ghosts will haunt us in the Dark.

Honnyman. It's no more Murder than to crack a Louse,[1]
That is, if you've the Wit to keep it private.
And as to Haunting, *Indians* have no Ghosts,
But as they live like Beasts, like Beasts they die.
I've killed a Dozen in this self-same Way,
And never yet was troubled with their Spirits.
　Orsbourn. Then I'm content; my Scruples are remov'd.
And what I've done, my Conscience justifies.
But we must have these Guns and Hatchets alter'd,
Or they'll detect th' Affair, and hang us both.
　Honnyman. That's quickly done— Let us with Speed return,
And think no more of being hang'd or haunted;
But turn our Fur to Gold, our Gold to Wine,
Thus gaily spend what we've so slily won,
And bless the first Inventor of a Gun.　　　　　*(Exeunt.*

SCENE III.— *An* English *Fort.* ·

Enter Colonel Cockum *and Captain* Frisk.

Cockum.

What shall we do with these damn'd bawling *Indians?*[2]
They're swarming every Day with their Complaints
Of Wrongs and Injuries, and God knows what—
I wish the Devil would take them to himself.
　Frisk. Your Honour's right to wish the Devil his Due.
I'd send the noisy Helhounds packing hence,
Nor spend a Moment in debating with them.

---

[1] "Twenty Indians have been murdered near here in a treacherous manner within the last six months. A young fellow executed lately for two unparalleled murders declared on the gallows that he thought it a meritorious act to kill heathen wherever they were found; and this seems to be the opinion of all the common people." Johnson in *Documentary History of New York*, VII, 852.

[2] "The officers and soldiers of the garrisons did their full part in exciting the resentment of the Indians. Formerly when the warriors came to the forts, they had been welcomed by the French with attention and respect. The inconvenience which their presence occasioned had been disregarded, and their peculiarities overlooked. But now they were received with cold looks and harsh words from the officers, and with oaths, menaces, and sometimes blows from the reckless and brutal soldiers. These marks of contempt were unspeakably galling to their haughty spirit." Parkman, *Conspiracy of Pontiac*, Chapter VII. See *Johnson Mss.*, 5, 188.

166

The more you give Attention to their Murmurs,
The more they'll plague and haunt you every Day,
Besides, their old King *Ponteach* grows damn'd saucy,
Talks of his Power, and threatens what he'll do.
Perdition to their faithless sooty Souls,
I'd let 'em know at once to keep their Distance.

Cockum. Captain, You're right; their Insolence is such
As beats my Patience; cursed Miscreants!
They are encroaching; fain would be familiar:
I'll send their painted Heads to Hell with Thunder!
I swear I'll blow 'em hence with Cannon Ball,
And give the Devil an Hundred for his supper.

Frisk. They're coming here; You see they scent your Track,
And while you'll listen, they will ne'er be silent,
But every Day improve in Insolence.

Cockum. I'll soon dispatch and storm them from my Presence.

Enter Ponteach,[1] *and other* Indian *Chiefs.*

Ponteach. Well, Mr. Colonel *Cockum*, what d' they call you?
You give no Answer yet to my Complaint;
Your Men give my Men always too much Rum,
Then trade and cheat 'em. What! d'ye think this right?

Cockum. Tush! Silence! hold your noisy cursed Nonsense;
I've heard enough of it; what is it to me?

---

[1] Pontiac was born about 1720, probably on the Maumee River. Though
his paternity is not positively established, it is most likely that his father was an
Ottawa chief and his mother a Chippewa. As early as 1746 he commanded the
Indians — mostly Ottawa — who defended Detroit against the attack of the northern tribes. It is supposed he led the Ottawa and Chippewa warriors at Braddock's defeat. He first appeared prominently in history at his meeting with
Major Rogers in 1760 (see p. 84), less than three years before the formation of
his famous conspiracy. His achievements and talents had gained him by this time
an influence over the Chippewa, Potowatomi, Huron, Shawnee, Miami, and
other Algonquin people, with the Seneca of the Six Nations, scarcely less powerful than over the Ottawa; and to the limits of the Illinois country, and through
the domain of the Creek and the Cherokee, his name was known and feared.
Physically, he was not above middle height, but his figure was remarkably sym-
metrical, well-knit, and muscular; his complexion was swarthy, his features bold
and stern, and his bearing imperious and peremptory. He was eloquent, shrewd,
energetic, and had a strong and capacious intellect, partially, but not wholly, free
from the passions, prejudices, and limitations of his race. *Pontiac Mss.* Rogers,
A Concise Account of North America. Parkman, *Conspiracy of Pontiac.* (Edition
of C. M. Burton, Detroit, 1912.)

Ponteach. What! you a Colonel, and not command your Men?
Let ev'ry one be a Rogue that has a Mind to 't.
Cockum. Why, curse your Men, I suppose they wanted Rum;
They'll rarely be content, I know, without it.
Ponteach. What then? If *Indians* are such Fools, I think
White Men like you should stop and teach them better.
Cockum. I'm not a Pedagogue to your curs'd *Indians.* (*aside.*
Ponteach. Colonel, I hope that you'll consider this.
Frisk. Why don't you see the Colonel will not hear you?
You'd better go and watch your Men yourself,
Nor plague us with your cursed endless Noise;
We've something else to do of more Importance.
Ponteach. Hah! Captain *Frisk,* what! you a great Man too?
My Bus'ness here is only with your Colonel;
And I'll be heard, or know the Reason why.
1st Chief. I thought the *English* had been better Men.
2nd Chief. *Frenchmen* would always hear an *Indian* speak,
And answer fair, and make good Promises.
Cockum. You may be d—d, and all your *Frenchmen* too.
Ponteach. Be d—d! what's that? I do not understand.
Cockum. The Devil teach you; he'll do it without a Fee.
Ponteach. The Devil teach! I Think you one great Fool.
Did your King tell you thus to treat the *Indians?*
Had he been such a Dunce he ne'er had conquer'd,
And made the running *French* for Quarter cry.
I always mind that such proud Fools are Cowards,
And never do aught that is great or good.
Cockum. Forbear your Impudence, you curs'd old Thief;
This Moment leave my Fort, and to your Country.
Let me hear no more of your hellish Clamour,
Or to D——n I will blow you all,
And feast the Devil with one hearty Meal.
Ponteach. So ho! Know you whose Country you are in?[1]
Think you, because you have subdu'd the *French,*

---

[1] "Pontiac assured me that he was inclined to live peaceably with the English
while they used him as he deserved but intimated that if they treated him with
neglect he would shut up the way and exclude them from his country; in short,
his whole conversation indicated that he was far from considering himself a conquered Prince, and he expected to be treated with the respect and honor due a
King by all who came into his country." Rogers, *A Concise Account of North
America,* p. 243.

That *Indians* too are now become your Slaves?
This Country's mine, and here I reign as King;
I value not your Threats, nor Forts, nor Guns;
I have got Warriors, Courage, Strength, and Skill.
Colonel, take care; the Wound is very deep,
Consider well, for it is hard to cure.   (*Exeunt* Indians.

 Frisk. Vile Infidels! observe their Insolence;
Old *Ponteach* puts on a mighty Air.
 Cockum. They'll always be a Torment till destroy'd,
And sent all headlong to the Devil's Kitchen.
This curs'd old Thief, no doubt, will give us Trouble,
Provok'd and madded at his cool Reception.
 Frisk. Oh! Colonel, they are never worth our minding,
What can they do against our Bombs and Cannon?
True, they may skulk, and kill and scalp a few,
But, Heav'n be thank'd, we're safe within these Walls:
Besides, I think the Governors are coming,
To make them Presents, and stablish Peace.
 Cockum. That may perhaps appease their bloody Minds,
And keep them quiet for some little Term.
God send the Day that puts them all to sleep,
Come, will you crack a Bottle at my Tent?
 Frisk. With all my Heart, and drink D——n to them.
 Cockum. I can in nothing more sincerely join.
            (*Exeunt.*

SCENE IV.— *An Apartment in the Fort.*

Enter Governors Sharp, Gripe, *and* Catchum.

     Sharp.
Here are we met to represent our King,
And by his royal Bounties to conciliate
These Indians minds to Friendship, Peace and Love,
But he that would an honest Living get
In Times so hard and difficult as these,
Must mind that good old Rule, Take care of One.
 Gripe. Ay, Christian Charity begins at home;
I think it's in the Bible, I know I've read it.
 Catchum. I join with *Paul*, that he's an Infidel
Who does not for himself and Friends provide.

Sharp. Yes, *Paul* in fact was no bad Politician,
And understood himself as well as most.
All good and wise Men certainly take care
To help themselves and Families the first;
Thus dictates Nature, Instinct, and Religion,
Whose easy Precepts ought to be obey'd.
    Gripe. But how does this affect our present Purpose?
We've heard the Doctrine; what's the Application?
    Sharp. We are intrusted with these *Indian* presents.
A Thousand Pound was granted by the King,
To satisfy them of his Royal Goodness,
His constant Disposition to their Welfare,
And reconcile their savage Minds to Peace.
Five hundred's gone; you know our late Division,
Our great Expence, *Et cetera*, no Matter:
The other Half was laid out for these Goods,
To be distributed as we think proper;
And whether Half (I only put the Question)
Of these said Goods, won't answer every End,
And bring about as long a lasting Peace
As tho' the Whole were lavishly bestow'd?[1]
    Catchum. I'm clear upon't they will, if we affirm
That Half's the Whole was sent them by the King.
    Gripe. There is no doubt but that One Third wou'd answer,
For they, poor Souls! are ignorant of the Worth
Of single things, nor know they how to add
Or calculate, and cast the whole Amount.
    Sharp. Ay, Want of Learning is a great Misfortune.
How thankful should we be that we have Schools,
And better taught and bred than these poor Heathen.
    Catchum. Yes, only these Two simple easy Rules,
Addition and Subtraction, are great Helps,
And much contribute to our Happiness.
    Sharp. 'Tis these I mean to put in Practice now;
Subtraction from these Royal Presents makes
Addition to our Gains without a Fraction.

[1] "In the zeal for retrenchment which prevailed soon after the close of hostilities, the presents which it had always been customary to give the Indians, at stated intervals, were either withheld altogether or doled out with a niggardly and reluctant hand; while, to make matters worse, the agents and officers of government often appropriated the presents to themselves, and afterwards sold them at an exorbitant price to the Indians." Parkman, *Conspiracy of Pontiac*, Chapter VII.

But let us overhawl and take the best,
Things may be given that won't do to sell.

(They overhawl the Goods, &c.

Catchum. Lay these aside; They'll fetch a noble Price.
Gripe. And these are very saleable, I think.
Sharp. The *Indians* will be very fond of these.
Is there the Half, think you?
Gripe. It's thereabouts.
Catchum. This bag of Wampum may be added yet.
Sharp. Here, Lads, convey these goods to our Apartment.
Servant. The *Indians*, Sir, are waiting at the Gate.
Gripe. Conduct them in when you've disposed of these.
Catchum. This should have been new-drawn before they
       enter'd.   *(pulling out an Inventory of the whole Goods.*
Gripe. What matters that? They cannot read, you know,
And you can read to them in gen'ral Terms.

Enter Ponteach, with several of his Chieftains.

Sharp. Welcome, my Brothers, we are glad to meet you,
And hope that you will not repent our coming.
Ponteach. We're glad to see our Brothers here the *English.*
If honourable Peace be your Desire,
We'd always have the Hatchet buried deep,
While Sun and Moon, Rivers and Lakes endure,
And Trees and Herbs within our Country grow.
But then you must not cheat and wrong the *Indians,*
Or treat us with Reproach, Contempt, and Scorn;
Else we will raise the Hatchet to the Sky,
And let it never touch the Earth again,
Sharpen its Edge, and keep it bright as Silver,
Or stain it red with Murder and with Blood.
Mind what I say, I do not tell you Lies.
Sharp. We hope you have no Reason to complain
That *Englishmen* conduct to you amiss;
We're griev'd if they have given you Offence,
And fain would heal the Wound while it is fresh,
Lest it should spread, grow painful, and severe.
Ponteach. Your Men make *Indians* drunk, and then they
       cheat 'em.
Your Officers, your Colonels, and your Captains
Are proud, morose, ill-natur'd, churlish Men,

171

Treat us with Disrespect, Contempt, and Scorn.
I tell you plainly this will never do,
We never thus were treated by the *French*,
Them we thought bad enough, but think you worse.

    Sharp. There's good and bad, you know, in every Nation;
There's some good *Indians*, some are the reverse,
Whom you can't govern, and restrain from ill;
So there's some *Englishmen* that will be bad. .
You must not mind the Conduct of a few,
Nor judge the rest by what you see of them.

    Ponteach. If you've some good, why don't you send them here?
These every one are Rogues, and Knaves, and Fools,
And think no more of *Indians* than of Dogs.
Your King had better send his good Men hither,
And keep his bad ones in some other Country;
Then you would find that Indians would do well,
Be peaceable, and honest in their Trade;
We'd love you, treat you, as our Friends and Brothers,
And Raise the Hatchet only in your Cause.

    Sharp. Our King is very anxious for your Welfare,
And greatly wishes for your Love and Friendship;
He would not have the Hatchet ever raised,
But buried deep, stamp'd down and cover'd o'er,
As with a mountain that can never move:
For this he sent us to your distant Country,
Bid us deliver you these friendly Belts,

                    (*holding out Belts of Wampum.*
All cover'd over with his Love and Kindness.
He like a Father loves you as his Children;
And like a Brother wishes you all Good;
We'll let him know the Wounds that you complain of,
And he'll be speedy to apply the Cure,
And clear the Path to Friendship, Peace and Trade.

    Ponteach. Your King, I hear's a good and upright Man,
True to his word, and friendly in his Heart;
Not proud and insolent, morose and sour,
Like these his petty Officers and Servants:
I want to see your King,[1] and let him know

    [1] "Pontiac was curious and expressed a great desire to see England, and offered me a part of his country if I would conduct him there." Rogers, *A Concise Account of North America*, p. 242.

172

What must be done to keep the Hatchet dull,
And how the Path of Friendship, Peace and Trade
May be kept clean and solid as a Rock.

  Sharp. Our King is distant over the great Lake,
But we can quickly send him your Requests;
To which he'll listen with attentive Ear,
And act as tho' you told him with your Tongue.

  Ponteach. Let him know then his People here are Rogues,
And cheat and wrong and use the *Indians* ill.
Tell him to send good Officers, and call
These proud ill natur'd Fellows from my Country,
And keep his Hunters from my Hunting Ground.
He must do this, and do it quickly too,
Or he will find the Path between us bloody.

  Sharp. Of this we will acquaint our gracious King,
And hope you and your Chiefs will now confirm
A solid Peace as if our King was present;
We're his Ambassadors, and represent him,
And bring these Tokens of his Royal Friendship
To you, your Captains, Chiefs, and valiant Men.
Read Mr. *Catchum*, you've the Inventory.

  Catchum. The *British* King, of his great Bounty, sends
To *Ponteach*, King upon the Lakes, and his Chiefs,
Two hundred, No (*aside*) a Number of fine Blankets,
Six hundred (*aside*) Yes, and several Dozen Hatchets,
Twenty thousand (*aside*) and a Bag of Wampum,
A Parcel too of Pans, and Knives, and Kettles.

  Sharp. This rich and royal Bounty you'll accept,
And as you please distribute to your Chiefs,
And let them know they come from *England's* King,
As Tokens to them of his Love and Favour.
We've taken this long Journey at great Charge,
To see and hold with you this friendly Talk;
We hope your Minds are all disposed to Peace,
And that you like our Sovereign Bounty well.

  1st Chief. We think it very small, we heard of more.[1]
Most of our Chiefs and Warriors are not here,
They all expect to share a part with us.

[1] "The government of Virginia has treated the Six Nations, Cherokees, and others with an ill-timed frugality which greatly disgusted them." Johnson's letter, (August, 1757,) *Documentary History of New York*, VII, 852.

2nd Chief. These won't reach round to more than half our
    Tribes,
Few of our Chiefs will have a single Token
Of your King's Bounty, that you speak so much of.
    3rd Chief. And those who have'nt will be dissatisfied, .
Think themselves slighted, think your King is stingy,
Or else that you his Governors are Rogues,
And keep your Master's Bounty for yourselves.
    4th Chief. We hear such Tricks are sometimes play'd with
    Indians,
King *Astenaco,* the great Southern Chief,[1]
Who's been in *England,* and has seen your King,
Told me that he was generous, kind, and true,
But that his Officers were Rogues and Knaves,
And cheated *Indians* out of what he gave.
    Gripe. The Devil's in't, I fear that we're detected (*aside.*
    Ponteach. Indians a'n't Fools, if White Men think us so;
We see, we hear, we think as well as you;
We know they're Lies, and Mischiefs in the World;
We don't know whom to trust, nor when to fear;
Men are uncertain, changing as the Wind,
Inconstant as the Waters of the Lakes,
Some smooth and fair, and pleasant as the Sun,
Some rough and boist'rous, like the Winter Storm;
Some are Insidious as the subtle Snake,
Some innocent, and harmless as the Dove;
Some like the Tyger raging, cruel, fierce,
Some like the Lamb, humble, submissive, mild,
And scarcely one is every Day the same;
But I call no Man bad, till such he's found,
Then I condemn and cast him from my Sight;
And no more trust him as a Friend and Brother.
I hope to find you honest Men and true.

[1] Astinaco was one of the three Cherokee chiefs who visited England, June—
August, 1762. They were brought on the frigate *Epreuve,* given English clothes
and a house in Suffolk street, and entertained by such men as the Earl of March,
Lord Bruce, and Mr. Montagu, by whom they were also taken to military re-
views and the navy-yard at Portsmouth. Magnificent specimens of their race,
they were a two-months' wonder in London, and a popular print was sold of
Astinaco. Nothing is known of his connection with Pontiac. See *Gentleman's
Magazine,* 1762, *passim.*

Sharp. Indeed you may depend upon our Honours,
We're faithful Servants of the best of Kings;
We scorn an Imposition on your Ignorance,
Abhor the Arts of Falshood and Deceit.
These are the Presents our great Monarch sent,
He's of a bounteous, noble, princely Mind
And had he known the Numbers of your Chiefs,
Each would have largely shar'd his Royal Goodness;
But these are rich and worthy your Acceptance,
Few Kings on Earth can such as these bestow,
For Goodness, Beauty, Excellence, and Worth.
  Ponteach. The Presents from your Sovereign I accept,
His friendly Belts to us shall be preserved,
And in Return convey you those to him.

(Belts and Furs.

Which let him know our Mind, and what we wish,
That we dislike his crusty Officers,
And wish the Path of Peace was made more plain,
The Calumet I do not chuse to smoak,
Till I see further, and my other Chiefs
Have been consulted. Tell your King from me,
That first or last a Rogue will be detected,
That I have Warriors, am myself a King,
And will be honour'd and obey'd as such;
Tell him my Subjects shall not be oppress'd,
But I will seek Redress and take Revenge;
Tell your King this; I have no more to say.
  Sharp. To our great King your Gifts we will convey,
And let him know the Talk we've had with you;
We're griev'd we cannot smoak the Pipe of Peace,
And part with stronger Proofs of Love and Friendship;
Mean time we hope you'll so consider Matters,
As still to keep the Hatchet dull and buried,
And open wide the shining Path of Peace,
That you and we may walk without a Blunder.

(Exeunt Indians.

  Gripe. Th' appear not fully satisfied, I think.
  Catchum. I do not like old Ponteach's Talk and Air,
He seems suspicious, and inclin'd to War.
  Sharp. They're always jealous, bloody, and revengeful,
You see that they distrust our Word and Honour;

No wonder then if they suspect the Traders,
And often charge them with downright Injustice.

Gripe. True, when even we that come to make them Presents,
Cannot escape their Fears and Jealousies.

Catchum. Well, we have this, at least, to comfort us;
Their good Opinion is no Commendation,
Nor their foul Slanders any Stain to Honour.
I think we've done whatever Men could do
To reconcile their savage Minds to Peace.
If they're displeas'd, our Honour is acquitted,
And we have not been wanting in our Duty
To them, our King, our Country, and our Friends.

Gripe. But what Returns are these they've left behind?
These Belts are valuable, and neatly wrought.

Catchum. This Pack of Furs is very weighty too;
The Skins are pick'd, and of the choicest Kind.

Sharp. By *Jove*, They're worth more Money than their
Presents.

Gripe. Indeed they are; the King will be no Loser.

Sharp. The King! who ever sent such Trumpery to him?

Catchum. What would the King of *England* do with Wampum?
Or Beaver Skins, d'ye think? He's not a Hatter!

Gripe. Then it's a Perquisite belongs to us?

Sharp. Yes, they're become our lawful Goods and Chattels,
By all the Rules and Laws of *Indian* Treaties.
The King would scorn to take a Gift from *Indians*,
And think us Madmen, should we send them to him.

Catchum. I understand we make a fair Division,
And have no Words nor Fraud among ourselves.

Sharp. We throw the whole into one common Stock,
And go Copartners in the Loss and Gain.
Thus most who handle Money for the Crown
Find means to make the better Half their own;
And, to your better Judgments with Submission,
The self Neglecter's a poor Politician.
These Gifts, you see, will all Expences pay;
Heav'n send an *Indian* Treaty every Day;
We dearly love to serve our King this Way.

The End of the First ACT.

ACT II.

Scene I.—*An* Indian *House.*

Enter Philip *and* Chekitan *from hunting, loaded with Venison.*

Philip.

The Day's Toil's ended, and the Ev'ning smiles
With all the Joy and Pleasantness of Plenty.
Our good Success and Fortune in the Chace
Will make us Mirth and Pastime for the Night.
How will the old King and his Hunters smile
To see us loaded with the fatt'ning Prey,
And joyously relate their own Adventures?
Not the brave Victor's Shout, or Spoils of War,
Would give such Pleasure to their gladden'd Hearts.

Chekitan. These, *Philip*, are the unstain'd Fruits of Peace,
Effected by the conqu'ring *British* Troops.
Now may we hunt the Wilds secure from Foes,
And seek our Food and Cloathing by the Chace,
While Ease and Plenty thro' our Country reign.

Philip. Happy Effects indeed! long may they last!
But I suspect the Term will be but short,
Ere this our happy Realm is curs'd afresh
With all the Noise and Miseries of War,
And Blood and Murder stain our Land again.

Chekitan. What hast thou heard that seems to threaten this,
Or is it idle Fancy and Conjectures?

Philip. Our Father's late Behaviour and Discourse
Unite to raise Suspicions in my Mind
Of his Designs? Hast thou not yet observ'd,
That tho' at first he favour'd *England's* Troops,
When they late landed on our fertile Shore,
Proclaim'd his Approbation of their March,
Convoy'd their Stores, protected them from Harm,
Nay, put them in Possession of *Detroit;*

And join'd to fill the Air with loud Huzza's
When *England's* Flag was planted on its Walls?
Yet, since, he seems displeas'd at their Success,
Thinks himself injured, treated with Neglect
By their Commanders, as of no Account,
As one subdu'd and conquer'd with the *French*,
As one, whose Right to Empire now is lost,
And he become a Vassal of their Power,
Instead of an Ally. At this he's mov'd,
And in his Royal Bosom glows Revenge,
Which I suspect will sudden burst and spread
Like Lightning from the Summer's burning Cloud,
That instant sets whole Forests in a Blaze.'

    Chekitan. Something like this I have indeed perceiv'd;
And this explains what I but now beheld,
Returning from the Chace, myself concealed,
Our Royal Father basking in the Shade,
His Looks severe, Revenge was in his Eyes,
All his great Soul seem'd mounted in his Face,
And bent on something hazardous and great.
With pensive Air he view'd the Forest round;
Smote on his Breast as if oppress'd with Wrongs,
With Indignation stamp'd upon the Ground;
Extended then and shook his mighty Arm,
As in Defiance of a coming Foe;
Then like the hunted Elk he forward sprung,
As tho' to trample his Assailants down.
The broken accents murmur'd from his Tongue,
As rumbling Thunder from a distant Cloud,
Distinct I heard, "Tis fix'd, I'll be reveng'd;
"I will make War; I'll drown this Land in Blood."
He disappear'd like the fresh-started Roe
Pursu'd by Hounds o'er rocky Hills and Dales,
That instant leaves the anxious Hunter's Eye;
Such was his Speed towards the other Chiefs.

    Philip. He's gone to sound their Minds to Peace and War,
And learn who'll join the Hazards in his Cause.
The Fox, the Bear, the Eagle, Otter, Wolf,

    ' "He puts on an air of majesty and princely grandeur, and is greatly hon-
ored and revered by all his subjects." Rogers, *A Concise Account of North
America*, p. 240.

And other valiant Princes of the Empire,
Have late resorted hither for some End
Of common Import. Time will soon reveal
Their secret Counsels and their fix'd Decrees.
Peace has its charms for those who love their Ease,
But active Souls like mine delight in Blood.
    Chekitan. Should War be wag'd, what Discords may we fear
Among ourselves? The powerful *Mohawk* King
Will ne'er consent to fight against the *English*,
Nay more, will join them as a firm Ally,
And influence other Chiefs by his Example,
To muster all their Strength against our Father.
Fathers perhaps will fight against their Sons,
And nearest Friends pursue each other's Lives;
Blood, Murder, Death, and Horror will be rife,
Where Peace and Love, and Friendship triumph now.
    Philip. Such stale Conjectures smell of Cowardice.
Our Father's Temper shews us the Reverse:
All Danger he defies, and, once resolv'd,
No Arguments will move him to relent,
No Motives change his Purpose of Revenge,
No Prayers prevail upon him to delay
The Execution of his fix'd Design:
Like the starv'd Tyger in Pursuit of Prey,
No Opposition will retard his Course;
Like the wing'd Eagle that looks down on Clouds,
All Hindrances are little in his Eye,
And his great Mind knows not the Pain of Fear.
    Chekitan. Such Hurricanes of Courage often lead
To Shame and Disappointment in the End,
And tumble blindfold on their own Disgrace.
True Valour's slow, deliberate, and cool,
Considers well the End, the Way, the Means,
And weighs each Circumstance attending them.
Imaginary Dangers it detects,
And guards itself against all real Evils.
But here *Tenesco* comes with Speed important;
His Looks and Face presage us something new.
    Tenesco. Hail, noble Youth! The News of your Return
And great Success has reach'd your Father's Ears.
Great is his Joy; but something more important

Seems to rest heavy on his anxious Mind,
And he commands your Presence at his Cabbin.

    Philip. We will attend his Call with utmost Speed,
Nor wait Refreshment after our Day's Toil.   *(Exeunt.*

Scene II.—Ponteach's *Cabbin.*

Ponteach, Philip, Chekitan, *and* Tenesco.

Ponteach.

My Sons, and trusty Counsellor *Tenesco,*
As the sweet smelling Rose, when yet a Bud,
Lies close conceal'd, till Time and the Sun's Warmth
Hath swell'd, matur'd, and brought it forth to View,
So these my Purposes I now reveal
Are to be kept with You, on pain of Death,
Till Time hath ripen'd my aspiring Plan,
And Fortune's Sunshine shall disclose the Whole;
Or should we fail, and Fortune prove perverse,
Let it be never known how far we fail'd,
Lest Fools shou'd triumph, or our Foes rejoice.

    Tenesco. The Life of great Designs is Secrecy,
And in Affairs of State 'tis Honour's Guard;
For Wisdom cannot form a Scheme so well,
But Fools will laugh if it should prove abortive;
And our Designs once known, our Honour's made
Dependent on the Fickleness of Fortune.

    Philip. What may your great and secret Purpose be,
That thus requires Concealment in its Birth?

    Ponteach. To raise the Hatchet from its short Repose,
Brighten its Edge, and stain it deep with Blood;
To scourge my proud, insulting, haughty Foes,
To enlarge my Empire, which will soon be yours:
Your Interest, Glory, Grandeur, I consult,
And therefore hope with Vigour you'll pursue
And execute whatever I command.

    Chekitan. When we refuse Obedience to your Will,
We are not worthy to be call'd your Sons.

    Philip. If we inherit not our Father's Valour,
We never can deserve to share his Empire.

Tenesco. Spoke like yourselves, the Sons of *Ponteach;*
Strength, Courage, and Obedience form the Soldier,
And the firm Base of all true Greatness lay.

  Ponteach. Our Empire now is large, our Forces strong,
Our Chiefs are wise, our Warriors valiant Men;
We are all furnish'd with the best of Arms,
And all things requisite to curb a Foe;
And now's our time, if ever, to secure
Our Country, Kindred, Empire, all that's dear,
From these Invaders of our Rights, the *English,*
And set their Bounds towards the rising Sun.
Long have I seen with a suspicious Eye
The Strength and growing Numbers of the *French;*
Their Forts and Settlements I've view'd as Snakes
Of mortal Bite, bound by the Winter Frost,
Which in some future warm reviving Day
Would stir and hiss, and spit their Poison forth,
And spread Destruction through our happy Land.
Where are we now? The *French* are all subdued,
But who are in their Stead become our Lords?
A proud, imperious, churlish, haughty Band.
The *French* familiarized themselves with us,
Studied our Tongue, and Manners, wore our Dress,
Married our Daughters, and our Sons their Maids,
Dealt honestly, and well supplied our Wants,
Used no One ill, and treated with Respect
Our Kings, our Captains, and our aged Men;
Call'd us their Friends, nay, what is more, their Children,
And seem'd like Fathers anxious for our Welfare.
Whom see we now? their haughty Conquerors
Possess'd of every Fort, and Lake, and Pass,
Big with their Victories so often gained;
On us they look with deep Contempt and Scorn,
Are false, deceitful, knavish, insolent;
Nay think us conquered, and our Country theirs,
Without a Purchase, or ev'n asking for it.
With Pleasure I wou'd call their King my Friend,
Yea, honour and obey him as my Father;
I'd be content, would he keep his own Sea,
And leave these distant Lakes and Streams to us;
Nay I would pay him Homage, if requested,

And furnish Warriors to support his Cause.
But thus to lose my Country and my Empire,
To be a Vassal to his low Commanders,
Treated with Disrespect and public Scorn
By Knaves, by Miscreants, Creatures of his Power;
Can this become a King like *Ponteach*,
Whose Empire's measured only by the Sun?
No, I'll assert my Right, the Hatchet raise,
And drive these *Britons* hence like frighted Deer,
Destroy their Forts, and make them rue the Day
That to our fertile Land they found the Way.
   Tenesco. No Contradiction to your great Design;
But will not such Proceeding injure us?
Where is our Trade and Commerce to be carry'd?
For they're possess'd of all the Country round,
Or whence Supplies of Implements for War?
     Ponteach. Whence? Take them from our conquered **running**
     Foes.
Their Fortresses are Magazines of Death,
Which we can quickly turn against themselves;
And when they're driven to their destin'd Bounds,
Their Love of Gain will soon renew their Trade.
The heartless *French*, whene'er they see us conquer,
Will join their little Force to help us on.
Nay many of their own brave trusty Soldiers,
In Hope of Gain, will give us their Assistance;
For Gain's their great Commander, and will lead them
Where their brave Generals cannot force their March:
Some have engag'd, when they see hope of Plunder,
In sly Disguise to kill their Countrymen.
   Chekitan. These Things indeed are promising and fair,
And seem a Prelude to our full Success.
But will not many *Indian* Chiefs refuse
To join the Lists, and hold themselves oblig'd
T' assist the Foe when hardly press'd by us?
   Ponteach. I've sounded all their Minds; there's but a few
That are not warm and hearty in our Cause,
And those faint Hearts we'll punish at our Leisure:
For hither tends my Purpose; to subdue
The Tribes who now their annual Homage pay
To the Imperious haughty *Mohawk* Chief,

Whose Pride and Insolence 'tis Time to curb.
He ever boasts the Greatness of his Empire,
The Swiftness, Skill and Valour of his Warriors,
His former Conquests, and his fresh Exploits,
The Terror of his Arms in distant Lands,
And on a Footing puts himself with me,
For Wisdom to contrive, and Power to do.
Such a proud Rival must not breath the Air;
I'll die in fighting, or I'll reign alone
O'er every *Indian* Nation, Tribe, and Chief.
But this in solemn Silence we conceal,
Till they're drawn in to fight the common Foe,
Then from my Face, the sly Disguise I'll cast,
And shew them *Ponteach* to their Surprize.

Tenesco. Thy Plan is wise, and may Success attend it;
May all the warlike numerous Tribes unite,
Nor cease to conquer while thou hast a Foe!
Then may they join and own thee for their Sovereign,
Pay full Submission to thy scepter'd Arm,
And universal Empire be thy own!

Chekitan. Would you the *Mohawk* Emperor displease,
And wage a bloody War, by which you made
Him and his num'rous Tribes your certain Foes?

Ponteach. Most of his Tribes will welcome the Proposal;
For long their galled Necks have felt the Yoke,
Long wish'd for Freedom from his partial Sway,
In favour of the proud incroaching *Britons*.
Nay, they have oft, in spite of his Displeasure,
Rush'd forth like Wolves upon their naked Borders,
And now, like Tygers broken from their Chains,
They'll glut themselves, and revel in their Blood.

Philip. Myself will undertake to make even *Hendrick*[1]
Our zealous Friend against the common Foe;
His strong Attachment to them I'll dissolve,
And make him rage, and thirst for Vengeance on them.

---

[1] Hendrick was a Mohawk chief, son of a Mohegan father and a Mohawk
mother. With many of his men he participated in the campaign against the French
in 1755, and at the request of General Johnson joined the English army, which
met two thousand French under Dieskau near Lake George. At the battle which
there took place, September 8, 1755, Hendrick with many of his followers was
killed. He was then less than seventy years of age.

Ponteach. This would be doing Honour to thyself,
And make thee worthy of thy Father's Crown.
The secret Means I will not now inquire, ·
Nor doubt but thus engag'd you will perform.
The Chiefs in part are knowing to my Purpose,
And think of nought but War, and Blood, and Plunder,
Till in full Council we declare our Pleasure.
But first my last Night's Dream I will relate,
Which much disturb'd my weary anxious Mind,
And must portend some signal grand Event
Of good or Evil both to me or mine.
On yonder Plain I saw the lordly Elk[1]
Snuffing the empty Air in seeming Sport,
Tossing his Head aloft, as if in Pride
Of his great Bulk and nervous active Limbs,
And Scorn of every Beast that haunts the Wood.
With mighty Stride he travelled to and fro,
And as he mov'd his Size was still increas'd,
Till his wide Branches reached above the Trees,
And his extended Trunk across the Plain.
The other Beasts beheld with wild Amaze,
Stood trembling round, nor dare they to approach
Till the fierce Tyger yell'd the loud Alarm,
When Bears, Cats, Wolves, Panthers, and Porcupines,
And other Beasts of Prey, with Force united
And savage Rage. attack'd the common Foe.
But as the busking Bull, when Summer Flies,
With keenest Sting disturb the grazing Herd,
Stands careless in some shady cool Retreat,
And from his Sides sweeps the invenom'd Mites;
Or shakes them with a Stamp into the Dust;
So he unmov'd amidst their Clamours stood,
Trampled and spurn'd them with his Hoofs and Horns,
Till all dispers'd in wild Disorder fled,
And left him Master of th' extended Plain.
    Tenesco. This Dream no doubt is full of some great Meaning,

---

[1] "The Indians have a great veneration for the elk, and imagine that to dream of it portends good fortune and long life." Rogers, *A Concise Account of North America*, p. 260. "The Indians depend much upon their dreams, and really believe the dream the whole history of their future life, . . . for which reason they make dreaming a kind of religious ceremony . . ." *Idem*, p. 215.

184

And in it bears the Fate of your Design,
But whether good or ill, to me's a Secret.
   Philip. It ne'er was counted ill to dream of Elks,
But always thought portentous of Success,
Of happy Life, and Victories in War,
Or Fortune good when we attempt the Chace.
   Chekitan. Such is the common Say; But here the Size
And all the Circumstances are uncommon,
And therefore can contain no common Meaning:
I fear these Things portend no Good to us,
That Mischiefs lurk like Serpents in the Grass,
Whose pois'nous deadly Bite precedes all Warning,
That this Design will end in mighty Ruin
To us and ours, Discord among our Friends,
And Triumph to our Foes.
   Philip. A valiant Hero!
Thou always wast a Coward, and hated War,
And lov'st to loll on the soft Lap of Peace.
Thou art a very Woman in thy Heart,
And talk'st of Snakes and Bugbears in the Dark,
Till all is Horror and Amaze about thee,
And even thy own Shadow makes thee tremble.
   Chekitan. Is there no Courage in delib'rate Wisdom?
Is all rank Cowardice but Fire and Fury?
Is it all womanish to re-consider
And weigh the Consequences of our Actions,
Before we desperately rush upon them?
Let me then be the Coward, a mere Woman,
Mine be the Praise of Coolness, yours of Rage.
   Ponteach. Peace, Peace, my Sons, nor let this casual Strife
Divide your Hearts; both mean the common Good;
Go Hand in Hand to conquer and promote it.
I'll to our worthy Doctor and the Priest,
Who for our Souls Salvation come from *France;*
They sure can solve the Mysteries of Fate,
And all the Secrets of a Dream explain;
Mean while, *Tenesco,* warn the other Chiefs
That they attend my Call within an Hour.
                             (*Exeunt* Pont. & Tenesco.
   Philip. My Warmth perhaps has carried me too far,
But it's not in me to be cool and backward

To act or speak when Kingdoms are the Prize.
My Blood runs high at the sweet Sound of Empire,·
Such as our Father's Plan ensures to us,
And I'm impatient of the least Delay.

    Chekitan. Thy Fire thou hast a Right to stile a Virtue;
Heat is our Friend when kept within due Bounds,
But if unbridled and allowed to rage,
It burns and blisters, torments and consumes,
And, Torrent-like, sweeps every Comfort by.
Think if our Father's Plan should prove abortive,
Our Troops repuls'd, or in th' Encounter slain,
Where are our conquer'd Kingdoms then to share, '
Where are our Vict'ries, Trophies, Triumphs, Crowns,
That dazzle in thy Eye, and swell thy Heart;
That nerve thy Arm, and wing thy Feet to War
With this impetuous Violence and Speed?
Crest-fallen then, our native Empire lost,
In captive Chains we drag a wretched Life,
Or fly inglorious from the conquering Foe
To barren Mountains from this fertile Land,
There to repent our Folly when too late,
In Anguish mourn, and curse our wretched Fate.

    Philip. But why so much of Mischiefs that may happen?
These are mere possibilities at most;
Creatures of Thought, which ne'er can be Objections,
In valiant Minds, to any great Attempt;
They're empty Echoes of a tim'rous Soul,
Like Bubbles driv'n by the tempestuous Storm,
The Breath of Resolution sweeps them off.
Nor dost thou judge them solid from thy Heart.
I know the secret Motive in thy Breast,
Thus to oppose our Father's great Design,
And from an Undertaking to dissuade,
In which thou'lt share the Profit and the Glory.
Hendrick, the King of *Mohawks*, hath a Daughter,
With whom I saw you dallying in the Shade,
And thought you then a Captive to her Charms.
The bright *Monelia* hangs upon thy Heart,
And softens all the Passions of thy Soul;
Her thou think'st lost should we proclaim a War,
In which the King her Father will not join.

Chekitan. What if I have a Value for *Monelia*,
Is it a Crime? Does she not merit Love
From all who see her move, or hear her speak?
　　Philip. True, she is engaging, has a charming Air;
And if thy Love is fix'd, I will assist it,
And put thee in Possession of the Joy
That thou desirest more than Crowns and Empire.
　　Chekitan. As how, dear *Philip?* Should we wage **a War**
Which *Hendrick* disapproves, the Prize is lost.
Not Empires then could make *Monelia* mine;
All Hopes are dash'd upon that fatal Rock;
Nor Gold, nor Prayers, nor Tears, nor Promises,
Nor all the Engin'ry of Love at Work,
Could save a single Moment of my Joy.
　　Philip. Yes, I will save it all, and make her thine,
Act but thy Part, and do as I prescribe,
In Peace or War thou shalt possess the Prize.
　　Chekitan. Thy Words revive my half-despairing **Heart.**
What must I act? or which Way must I turn?
I'll brave all Dangers, every Ill defy,
Risque Life itself, to call *Monelia* mine.
Help me, my *Philip*, and I'll be thy Slave,
Resign my Share of Empire to thy Hand,
And lay a Claim to nothing but *Monelia.*
　　Philip. Rewards I do not ask; I am thy Brother,
And hold my Kindness to thee as a Debt.
Thou know'st I have engag'd to bring King *Hendrick*
To join the Lists, and fight against our Foes,
To rouse him to Revenge, and Rage, and War,
And make him zealous in the common Cause.
Nay, with uncommon Fury he shall rave,
And urge his Warriors on to Blood and Murder.
When this is done, *Monelia* may be thine,
Hendrick will court Alliance to our Tribe,
And joy to call great *Ponteach's* Son his own.
　　Chekitan. But should you fail in these Attempts, **and he**
Prove obstinately fix'd against the War,
Where's then *Monelia?* where is *Chekitan?*
My Hopes are blasted, all my Joys are fled,
Like the vain Phantoms of a Midnight Dream,
Are scattered like the Dust before a Whirlwind,

And all my Soul is left a Void for Pain,
Vexation, Madness, Phrensy, and Despair,
And all the Pains of disappointed Love.
Better I ne'er had flattered my fond Heart,
Nor sooth'd my Mind with Prospects of my Joy,
Than thus to perish on the Point of Hope.

Philip. Leave all to me; I've so concerted Matters,
That I defy ev'n Fate to disappoint me.
Exert thyself, and to *Monelia* go,
Before th' assembled Chiefs in Council meet;
Urge it to her, and to her Brother *Torax*,
That should their Father prove refractory,
Withdraw himself, and order his Domesticks
To hasten home at News of our Design;
Urge it, I say, to them; *Torax* loves War;
To linger here in Hopes of his Return,
Which tell them I'll effect ere twice the Sun
Has run the Circuit of his daily Race.
Here they may loiter careless, range the Woods,
As tho' the Noise of War had not been heard.
This will give full Success to both our Wishes:
Thoul't gain the Prize of Love, and I of Wrath,
In favour to our Family and State.
Thoul't tame the Turtle, I shall rouse the Tyger;
The one will soothe thy Soul to soft Repose,
The other prove a Terror to our Foes.

Chekitan. I see the subtle Argument thou'lt use,
And how thou'lt work upon the old King's Weakness.
Thou'lt set his strong Affection for his Children
At War against his Kindness for our Foes,
By urging their Attachment to our Cause,
That they'll endure ev'n Banishment and Death,
Rather than cease to be our stedfast Friends.

Philip. All this I'll urge, nay more, I will convince him,
These Foes to us can be no Friends to him;
I'll thunder in his Ears their growing Power,
Their Villainies and Cheats upon his Subjects:
That their fair Shew of Love is foul Disguise;
That in their Hearts they hate the name of *Indians*,
And court his Friendship only for their Profit;

That when no longer he subserves their Ends,
He may go whistle up some other Friends.
  Chekitan. This must alarm and bring him to our Mind.
I'll hasten to my Charge with utmost Speed,
Strain every Nerve, and every Power exert;
Plead, promise, swear like any Christian Trader;
But I'll detain them till our Ends are answer'd,
And you have won their Father to our Purpose.   (*Exit.*

Philip, solus.
Oh! what a wretched Thing is a Man in Love!
All Fear — all Hope — all Diffidence — all Faith —
Distrusts the greatest Strength, depends on Straws —
Soften'd, unprovident, disarm'd, unman'd,
Led blindfold; every Power denies its Aid,
And every Passion's but a Slave to this;
Honour, Revenge, Ambition, Interest, all
Upon its Altar bleed — Kingdoms and Crowns
Are slighted and contemn'd, and all the Ties
Of Nature are dissolv'd by this poor Passion:
Once have I felt its Poison in my Heart,
When this same *Chekitan* a Captive led
The fair *Donanta* from the *Illinois;*
I saw, admir'd, and lov'd the charming Maid,
And as a Favour ask'd her from his Hands,
But he refus'd and sold her for a Slave.
My Love is Dead, but my Resentment lives,
And now's my Time to let the Flame break forth,
For while I pay this antient Debt of Vengeance,
I'll serve my Country, and advance myself.
He loves *Monelia* — *Hendrick* must be won —
Monelia and her Brother both must bleed —
This is my Vengeance on her Lover's Head —
Then I'll affirm, 'twas done by *Englishmen* —
And to gain Credit both with Friends and Foes,
I'll wound myself, and say that I receiv'd it
By striving to assist them in the Combat.
This will rouse *Hendrick's* Wrath, and arm his **Troops**
To Blood and Vengeance on the common Foe.
And further still my Profit may extend;

My Brother's Rage will lead him into Danger,
And, he cut off, the Empire's all my own.
Thus am I fix'd; my Scheme of Goodness laid,
And I'll effect it, tho' thro' Blood I wade,
To desperate Wounds apply a Desperate Cure,
And to tall Structures lay Foundations sure;
To Fame and Empire hence my Course I bend,
And every Step I take shall thither tend.

End of the Second ACT.

ACT III.

SCENE I.—*A Forest.*

Chekitan *seeing* Torax *and* Monelia *coming towards them.*

As the young Hunter, anxious in the Chace,
With beating Heart and quivering Hand espies
The wish'd for Game, and trembles for th' Event,
So I behold the bright *Monelia's* Steps,
Whom anxiously I've sought, approach this way —
What shall I say? or how shall I accost her?
It is a fatal Minute to mistake in.
The Joy or Grief of Life depends upon 't;
It is the important Crisis of my Fate.
I've thought a thousand things to say and do,
But know not which to say or do the first.
Shall I begin with my old Tale of Love?
Or shall I shock her with the News of War?
Must I put on the Face of Joy or Grief?
Seem unconcern'd or full of Doubts and Fears?
How unprepar'd I am for the Encounter!
I'd rather stand against an Host of Foes—
But she draws near, and Fate must guide me now.

Enter Torax *and* Monelia.

Where tend your Steps with such an Air of Joy?
  Torax. To view the Beauties of th' extended **Lake**,
And on its mossy Bank recline at Ease,
While we behold the Sports of Fish and Fowl,
Which in this Calm no doubt will be diverting.
And these are new Amusements to *Monelia*,
She never saw the Sea or Lakes before.
  Chekitan. I'm glad our Country's aught to give such **Pleasure**
To one deservedly so welcome in it.
  Monelia. That I am welcome you have oft assur'd me,

That I deserve it you may be mistaken,
The outside Shew, the Form, the Dress, the Air,
That please at first Acquaintance, oft deceive us,
And prove more Mimickers of true Desert,
Which always brightens by a further Trial,
Appears more lovely as we know it better,
At least can never suffer by Acquaintance.
Perhaps then you To-morrow will despise
What you esteem to-Day, and call deserving.
   Chekitan. My Love to you, *Monelia*, cannot change.
Your Beauty, like the Sun, for ever pleases,
And like the Earth, my Love can never move.
   Monelia. The Earth itself is sometimes known to shake,
And the bright Sun by Clouds is oft conceal'd,
And gloomy Night succeeds the Smiles of Day —
So Beauty oft by foulest Faults is veil'd,
And after one short Blaze admir'd no more,
Loses its Lustre, drops its sparkling Charms,
The Lover sickens, and his Passion dies.
Nay worse, he hates what he so doted on.
Time only proves the Truth of Worth and Love,
The one may be a Cheat, the other change,
And Fears, and Jealousies, and mortal Hate,
Succeed the Sunshine of the warmest Passion.
   Chekitan. Have I not vow'd my Love to you, *Monelia*,
And open'd all the Weakness of my Heart?
You cannot think me false and insincere,
When I repeat my Vows to love you still;
Each time I see you move, or hear you speak,
It adds fresh Fuel to the growing Flame.
You're like the rising Sun, whose Beams increase
As he advances upward to our View;
We gaze with growing Wonder till we're blind,
And every Beauty fades and dies but his.
Thus shall I always view your growing Charm,
And every Day and Hour with fresh Delight.
Witness thou Sun and Moon, and Stars above,
Witness ye purling Streams and quivering Lakes,
Witness ye Groves and Hills, and Springs and Plains,
Witness ye Shades, and the cool Fountain, where
I first espied the Image of her Charms,

And starting saw her on th' adjacent Bank,
If I to my *Monelia* prove untrue.
  Monelia. Hoh! now your Talk is so much like a Christian's,
That I must be excus'd if I distrust you,
And think your fair Pretenses all designing.
I once was courted by a spruce young Blade,
A lac'd Coat Captain, warlike, active, gay,
Cockaded Hat and Medal on his Breast,
And everything was clever but his Tongue;
He swore he lov'd, O! how he swore he lov'd,
Call'd on his God and Stars to witness for him,
Wish'd he might die, be blown to Hell and damn'd,
If ever he lov'd woman so before:
Call'd me his Princess, Charmer, Angel, Goddess,
Swore nothing else was ever half so pretty,
So dear, so sweet, so much to please his Taste,
He kiss'd, he squeez'd, and press'd me to his Bosom,
Vow'd nothing could abate his ardent Passion,
Swore he should die, should drown, or hang himself,
Could not exist if I denied his Suit,
And said a thousand Things I cannot name:
My simple Heart, made soft by so much Heat,
Half gave Consent, meaning to be his Bride.
The Moment thus unguarded, he embrac'd,
And impudently ask'd to stain my Virtue.
With just Disdain I push'd him from my Arms,
And let him know he'd kindled my Resentment;
The Scene was chang'd from Sunshine to a Storm,
O! then he curs'd, and swore, and damn'd, and sunk,
Call'd me proud Bitch, pray'd Heav'n to blast my Soul,
Wish'd Furies, Hell, and Devils had my Body,
To say no more; bid me begone in Haste
Without the smallest Mark of his Affection.
This was an *Englishman*, a Christian Lover.
  Chekitan. Would you compare an Indian Prince to those
Whose Trade it is to cheat, deceive, and flatter?
Who rarely speak the Meaning of their Hearts?
Whose Tongues are full of Promises and Vows?
Whose very Language is a downright Lie?
Who swear and call on Gods when they mean nothing?
Who call it complaisant, polite good Breeding,

To say Ten thousand things they don't intend,
And tell their nearest Friends the basest Falsehoods?
I know you cannot think me so perverse,
Such Baseness dwells not in an *Indian's* Heart,
And I'll convince you that I am no Christian.

    Monelia. Then do not swear, nor vow, nor promise much,
An honest Heart needs none of this Parade;
Its Sense steals softly to the listning Ear,
And Love, like a rich Jewel we most value,
When we ourselves by Chance espy its Blaze
And none proclaims where we may find the Prize.
Mistake me not, I don't impeach your Honour,
Nor think you undeserving my Esteem;
When our Hands join you may repeat your Love,
But save these Repetitions from the Tongue.

    Chekitan. Forgive me, if my Fondness is too pressing,
'Tis Fear, 'tis anxious Fear, that makes it so.

    Monelia. What do you fear? have I not said enough?
Or would you have me swear some Christian Oath?

    Chekitan. No, but I fear our Love will be oppos'd,
Your Father will forbid our Hands to join.

    Monelia. I cannot think it; you are *Ponteach's* Son,
Heir to an Empire large and rich as his.

    Chekitan. True; but your Father is a Friend to *Britons*,
And mine a Foe, and now is fix'd on War,
Immediate War: This Day the Chiefs assemble,
To raise the Hatchet, and to arm the Troops.

    Monelia. Then I must leave your Realm, and bid Adieu,
In spite of your fond Passion, or my own;
For I can never disoblige my Father,
Though by it I were sure to gain an Empire.

    Chekitan. Then *Chekitan's* undone, undone forever.
Unless your Father by kind Fate is mov'd
To be our Friend, and join the Lists with mine.

    Torax. Nothing would please me better; I love War,
And think it time to curb the *English* Pride,
And give a check to their increasing Power.
The Land is ravag'd by their numerous Bands,
And every Day they're growing more our Lords.

    Chekitan. Are you sincere, or do you feign this Speech?

    Torax. Indeed my Tongue does not bely my Heart;

And but my Father's wrong-turn'd Policy
Forbids, I'd instant join in War with you,
And help to set new Limits to their Power.

    Chekitan. 'Tis plain, if they proceed, nor you nor I
Shall rule an Empire, or possess a Crown,
Our Countries all will soon become a Prey
To Strangers; we perhaps shall be their Slaves.
But will your Father be convinc'd of this?

    Torax. I doubt he'll not. The good old Man esteems
And dotes upon them as most worthy Friends;
I've told him often that he cherish'd Serpents
To bite his Children, and destroy his Friends.
But this he calls the Folly of my Youth,
Bids me be silent, shew Respect to Age,
Nor sow Sedition in my Father's Empire.

    Chekitan. Stiff as he is, he yet may be subdued;
And I've a Power prepar'd that will attack him.
Should he refuse his Aid to our Design,
Retire himself, and bid his Troops to follow,
Yet *Philip* stands engag'd for his Return,
Ere twice the Sun hath ris'n and blest the Earth.
Philip is eloquent, and so prepar'd,
He cannot fail to bend him to our Purpose.
You and *Monelia* have a Part to act;
To linger here, should he in Haste retreat
Till *Philip* follows and employs his Force.
Your Stay will add new Life to the Design,
And be of mighty Weight to gain Success.

    Monelia. How shall we tarry midst the Noise of War,
In Danger of our Lives from Friends and Foes;
This will be deem'd a Madness by our Father,
And will deserve his most severe Rebuke.

    Chekitan. Myself will be a Sponsor for your Safety;
And should your Father baffle our Attempts,
Conduct you home from all the Noise of War,
Where may you long in Peace and Plenty smile,
While I return to mourn my hapless Fate.
But should Success attend on *Philip's* Purpose,
Your Father will not discommend your Stay,
But smiling give new Vigour to the War;
Which being ended, and our Foes subdu'd,

The happy Fruits of Peace succeed to all,
But we shall taste the greater Sweets of Love.
    Torax. The Purport of our Stay is hid from me;
But Philip's subtle, crafty as the Fox,
We'll give full Scope to his inticing Art,
And help him what we can to take the Prey.
    Monelia. In your Protection then I trust myself,
Nor will delay beyond th' appointed Term,
Lest anxious Fears pssess our Father's Heart,
Or Mischiefs happen that incur his Anger.
    Torax. It is agreed; we now pursue our Walk;
Mean time consult what else may be of Use,
You're pain'd with Love, and I'm in Pain for War.   (*Exeunt.*
    Chekitan solus. The Game is sure—Her Brother's on my
      Side—
Her Brother and my own—My Force is strong—
But could her Father now be rous'd to War,
How should I triumph and defy even Fate?
But Fortune favours all advent'rous Souls:
I'll now to *Philip;* tell him my Success,
And rouse up every Spark of Vigour in him:
He will conceive fresh Hopes, and be more zealous.

SCENE II.—Ponteach's *Cabbin.*

Ponteach, *an* Indian *Conjurer, and* French *Priest.*

Ponteach.

Well! have you found the Secret of my Dream,
By all your Cries, and Howls, and Sweats, and Prayers?
Or is the Meaning still conceal'd from Man,
And only known to Genii and the Gods?
    Conjurer. Two Hours I've lain within the sultry Stove,[1]

---

   [1] "Among the tribes to the southward you will find a conjurer in almost every village, who pretends to great things, both in politics and physic, undertaking to reveal the most hidden secrets, and to tell what passes in the most secret cabinets, and cause the most difficult negotiations to succeed, to procure good fortune to their warriors and hunters, etc.; the conjurer, to prepare himself for these exploits, takes a sound sweat in a stove and directly after it plunges into a river or lake, be it ever so cold." Rogers, *A Concise Account of North America,* p. 247.

While Floods of Sweat run trickling from my Skin;
With Howls and Cries and all the Force of Sound
Have I invok'd your Genius and my own,
Smote on my Breast, and beat against my Head,
To move an Answer and the Secret learn.
But all in Vain, no Answer can I have,
Till I first learn what secret Purposes
And great Designs are brooding in your Mind.

    Priest. At our pure Virgin's Shrine I've bowed my **Knees,**
And there in fervent Prayer pour'd out my Soul;
Call'd on Saint *Peter,* call'd on all the Saints
That know the Secrets both of Heaven and Earth,
And can reveal what Gods themselves can do:
I've us'd the Arts of our most holy Mother,
Which I receiv'd when I forsook the World,
And gave myself to Holiness and Heaven;
But can't obtain the Secret of your Dream,
Till I first know the Secrets of your Heart,
Or what you hope or wish to be effected.
'Tis on these Terms we learn the Will of God,
What Good or Ill awaits on Kings or Kingdoms;
And without this, St. *Peter's* Self can't tell,
But at a Dream like yours would be confounded.

    Ponteach. You're well agreed — Our Gods are much **alike—**
And I suspect both Rogues — What! wont they tell!
Should they betray my Scheme, the whole is blown.
And yet I fain would know. I'll charge them first.   *(aside.*
Look here; if I disclose a Secret to you,
·Tell it to none but silent honest Gods;
Death to you both, if you reveal to Men.

    Both. We will, we will, the Gods alone shall know.

    Ponteach. Know then that I have fix'd on speedy **War,**
To drive these new Encroachers from my Country.
For this I mean t'engage our several Tribes,
And when our Foes are driven to their Bounds,
That we may stand and hold our Rights secure,
Unite our Strength under one common Head,
Whom all these petty Kings must own their Lord,
Not even *Hendrick's* self shall be excused.
This is my purpose.   Learn if it shall prosper,
Or will it end in Infamy and Shame?

Conjurer.　*Smiting on his Breast, groaning, and muttering in*
his Cloak or Blanket, falls down upon the Ground,
beats his Head against it, and pretends to listen;
then rises, and says with a rumbling hideous Voice,

Success and Victory shall attend your Arms;
You are the mighty Elk that none can conquer,
And all the Tribes shall own you for their King.
Thus, say the Genii, does your Dream intend.

　　Priest. (*looking up to Heaven in a praying Posture for a small*
Space, says)

Had I but known you was resolv'd on War,
And War against those Hereticks the *English*,
I need not to have ask'd a God or Saint
To signify the Import of your Dream.
Your great Design shall have a prosperous End,
'Tis by the Gods approv'd, and must succeed.
Angels and Saints are dancing now in Heaven:
Your enemies are theirs, are hated by them,
And they'll protect and help you as their Champion,
That fights their Battles, and defends their Cause.
Our great St. *Peter* is himself a Warrior;
He drew his Sword against such Infidels,
And now, like him, you'll gain immortal Honour,
And Gods in Heaven and Saints on Earth will praise you.

　　Ponteach. The Gods and Genii do as you have said.
I'll to the Chiefs, and hasten them to Arms.

　　　　　　　　　　　　　　(*Exeunt* Pont. *&* Conj.

　　　　　　　　　　Priest, solus.

This, by St. *Peter*, goes as I would have it.
The Conjurer agreed with me to pump him,
Or else deny to solve his dubious Vision:
But, that we've so agreed in our responses,
Is all mere Providence, and rul'd by Heaven,
To give us further Credit with this *Indian.*
Now he is fix'd — will wage immediate War —
This will be joyful News in *France* and *Rome*,
That *Ponteach* is in Arms, and won't allow
The *English* to possess their new-gain'd Empire:
That he has slain their Troops, destroy'd their Forts,
Expell'd them from the Lakes to their old Limits:
That he prefers the *French*, and will assist

To repossess them of this fertile Land.
By all the Saints, of this I'll make a Merit,
Declare myself to be the wise Projector;
This may advance me towards St. *Peter's* Chair,
And these blind Infidels by Accident
May have a Hand in making me a Pope —
But stop — Won't this defeat my other Purpose?
To gain the *Mohawk* Princess to my Wishes?
No — by the holy Virgin, I'll surprise her,
And have one hearty Revel in her Charms.
But now I'll hasten to this *Indian* Council;
I may do something there that's à-propos.   (*Exit.*

Scene III.— *An* Indian *Senate-House.*

Ponteach, Tenesco, Philip, Astinaco, Bear, Wolf, *and*
French *Priest.*

Ponteach.

Are all the Chiefs and Warriors here assembled,
That we expect to honour this Day's Council?
   Tenesco. All are conven'd except the *Mohawk* King,
Who, as we are inform'd, denies his Presence.
   Philip. I've half succeeded with the stubborn Chief,
He will not join in Council, but hath promised,
Till further Notice, not to be our Foe:
He'll see how we unite, and what Success
Attends our Arms; in short, he gives strong Hints
That he will soon befriend the common Cause.
   Ponteach. Do what he will, 'tis this explains my Meaning;
                              (*taking up the Hatchet.*
You are all well appris'd of my Design,
Which every passing Moment but confirms:
Nay, my Heart's pain'd while I with-hold my Hand
From Blood and Vengeance on our hated Foes.
Tho' I should stand alone, I'll try my Power
To punish their Encroachments, Frauds, and Pride;
Yet tho' I die, it is my Country's Cause,
'Tis better thus to die than be despis'd;
Better to die than be a Slave to Cowards,

Better to die than see my Friends abus'd;
The Aged scorn'd, the Young despis'd and spurn'd.
Better to die than see my Country ruin'd,
Myself, my Sons, my Friends reduc'd to Famine,
Expell'd from hence to barren Rocks and Mountains,
To curse our wretched Fate and pine in Want;
Our pleasant Lakes and Fertile Lands usurp'd
By Strangers, Ravagers, rapacious Christians.
Who is it don't prefer a Death in War
To this impending Wretchedness and Shame?
Who is it loves his Country, Friends or Self,
And does not feel Resentment in his Soul?
Who is it sees their growing Strength and Power,
And how we waste and fail by swift Degrees,
That does not think it Time to rouse and arm,
And kill the Serpent ere we feel it sting,
And fall the Victims of its painful Poison?
Oh! could our Fathers from their Country see
Their antient Rights encroach'd upon and ravag'd,
And we their Children slow, supine, and careless
To keep the Liberty and Land they left us,
And tamely fall a Sacrifice to Knaves!
How would their Bosoms glow with patriot Shame,
To see their Offspring so unlike themselves?
They dared all Dangers to defend their Rights,
Nor tamely bore an Insult from a Foe.
Their plain rough Souls were brave and full of Fire,
Lovers of War, nor knew the Pain of Fear.
Rouse, then, ye Sons of antient Heroes, rouse,
Put on your Arms, and let us act a Part
Worthy the Sons of such renowned Chiefs.
Nor urge I you to Dangers that I shun,
Or mean to act my Part by words alone;
This Hand shall wield the Hatchet in the Cause,
These Feet pursue the frighted running Foe,
This Body rush into the hottest Battle;
There should I fall, I shall secure my Honour,
And, dying, urge my Countrymen to Vengeance
With more Success than all the Force of Words.
Should I survive, I'll shed the foremost Tear
O'er my brave Countrymen that chance to fall;

I'll be the foremost to revenge their Blood,
And, while I live, honour both them and theirs.
I add no more, but wait to hear your Minds.

    Tenesco. Tho' I'm a Warrior, and delight in Arms,
Have oft with Pleasure heard the Sound of Battle,
And oft return'd with Victory and Triumph;
Yet I'm not fond to fight without just Cause,
Or shed the Blood of Men for my Diversion:
But I have seen, with my own Eyes I've seen,
High Provocations from our present Foes,
Their Pride and Insults, Knavery and Frauds,
Their large Encroachments on our common Rights,
Which every Day increase, are seen by all,
And grown so common, they are disregarded.
What calls on us more loudly for Revenge,
Is their Contempt and Breach of public Faith.
When we complain, they sometimes promise fair;
When we grow restless, Treaties are propos'd,
And Promises are gilded then with Presents.
What is the End? Still the old Trade goes on;
Their Colonels, Governors, and mighty Men,
Cheat, lye, and break their solemn Promises,
And take no Care to have our Wrongs redress'd.
Their King is distant, would he hear our Prayers:
Still we've no other Way to come at Justice,
But by our Arms to punish Wrongs like these,
And Wrongs like these are national and public,
Concern us all, and call for public Vengeance.
And Wrongs like these are recent in our Minds.

    Philip. Public or private Wrongs, no matter which.
I think our Hunters ought to be reveng'd;
Their Bodies are found torn by rav'nous Beasts,
But who doubts they were kill'd by *Englishmen?*
Their Heads are scalp'd, their Arms and Jewels gone,
And Beasts of Prey can have no Use for these.
No, they were murdered, slily, basely shot,
And who that has a Heart does not resent it?
O how I long to tear their mangled Limbs!
Yes, I could eat their Hearts, and drink their Blood,
And revel in their Torments, Pains, and Tortures;
And, though I go alone, I'll seek Revenge.

Astinaco. This is the Fire and Madness of your Youth,
And must be curb'd to do your Country Service.
Facts are not always what they seem to be,
And this perhaps may be the Fault of One
Whom their Laws punish if you once detect him.
Shall we then, to revenge your Countrymen,
To recompence a Wrong by one committed,
Rouse all to Arms, and make a general Slaughter?
'Tis higher Motives move my Mind to War,
And make me zealous in the common Cause.
But hear me — 'Tis no Trifle we're upon —
If we have Wisdom, it must now be used;
If we have Numbers, they must be united;
If we have Strength, it must be all exerted;
If we have Courage it must be inflamed,
And every Art and Stratagem be practis'd:
We've more to do than fright a Pigeon Roost,
Or start a timorous flock of running Deer;
Yes, we've a strong, a warlike stubborn Foe,
Unus'd to be repuls'd and quit the Field,
Nay, flush'd with Victories and long Success,
Their Numbers, Strength, and Courage all renown'd,
'Tis little of them that you see or know.
I've seen their Capital, their Troops and Stores,
Their Ships, their Magazines of Death and Vengeance,
And, what is more, I've seen their potent King,
Who like a God sits over all the World,
And thunders forth his Vengeance thro' the Earth,
When he is pleas'd, Smiles sit upon his Face,
And Goodness flows in Rivers at his Feet;
When he's provok'd, 'tis like a fiery Tempest,
All's Terror and Amazement in his Presence,
And frighted Heroes trembling flee his Wrath.
What then is to be done? what may we hope?
At most, by secret, sly, and subtle Means
To curb these vagrant Outcasts of his Subjects,
Secure our Countries from their further Ravage,
And make ourselves of more Importance to them,
Perhaps procure a Peace to our Advantage.
In this I'll join and head my valiant Troops,
Who will not fail to act a valiant Part.

The Bear. What is the Greatness of their King to us?
What of his Strength or Wisdom? Shall we fear
A Lion chain'd, or in another World?
Or what avails his flowing Goodness to us?
Does not the ravenous Tyger feed her Young?
And the fierce Panther fawn upon his Mate?
Do not the Wolves defend and help their Fellows
The poisonous Serpent feed her hissing Brood,
And open wide her Mouth for their Protection?
So this good King shews Kindness to his own,
And favours them, to make a Prey of others;
But at his Hands, we may expect no Favour.
Look back, my Friends, to our Forefathers' Time,
Where is their Country? where their pleasant Haunts?
The running Streams and shady Forests where?
They chas'd the flying Game, and liv'd in Plenty.
Lo, these proud Strangers now possess the Whole;
Their Cities, Towns, and Villages arise,
Forests are spoil'd, the Haunts of Game destroy'd,
And all the Sea Coasts made one general Waste.
Between the Rivers Torrent-like they sweep,
And drive our Tribes towards the setting Sun.
They who once liv'd on yon delightful Plains
Are now no more, their very Name is lost.
The Sons of potent Kings, subdu'd and murder'd,
Are Vagrants, and unknown among their Neighbours.
Where will the Ravage stop? the Ruin where?
Does not the Torrent rush with growing Speed,
And hurry us to the same wretched End?
Let us grow wise then by our Fathers Folly,
Unite our Strength, too long it's been divided,
And mutual Fears and Jealousies obtain'd:
This has encourag'd our encroaching Foes,
But we'll convince them, once, we dare oppose them.
    The Wolf. Yet we have Strength by which we may **oppose,**
But every Day this Strength declines and fails.
Our great Forefathers, ere these Strangers came,
Liv'd by the Chace, with Nature's Gifts content,
The cooling Fountain quench'd their raging Thirst.
Doctors, and Drugs, and Med'cines were unknown,
Even Age itself was free from Pain and Sickness.

Swift as the Wind, o'er Rocks and Hills they chas'd
The flying Game, the bounding Stag outwinded,
And tir'd the savage Bear, and tam'd the Tyger;
At Evening feasted on the past Day's Toil,
Nor then fatigu'd; the merry Dance and Song
Succeeded; still with every rising Sun
The Sport renew'd; or if some daring Foe
Provok'd their Wrath, they bent the hostile Bow,
Nor waited his Approach, but rush'd with Speed,
Fearless of Hunger, Thirst, Fatigue, or Death.
But we their soften'd Sons, a puny Race,
Are weak in Youth, fear Dangers where they're not;
Are weary'd with what was to them a Sport,
Panting and breathless in one short Hour's Chace;
And every Effort of our Strength is feeble.
We're poison'd with the Infection of our Foes,
Their very Looks and Actions are infectious,
And in deep Silence spread Destruction round them.
Bethink yourselves while any Strength remains;
Dare to be like your Fathers, brave and strong,
Nor further let the growing Poison spread.
And would you stop it, you must resolve to conquer,
Destroy their Forts and Bulwarks, burn their Towns,
And keep them at a greater Distance from us.
O 'tis a Day I long have wish'd to see,
And, aged as I am, my Youth returns
To act with Vigour in so good a Cause.
Yes, you shall see the old Wolf will not fail
To head his Troops, and urge them on to Battle.

 Ponteach. Your Minds are all for War, we'll not delay;
Nor doubt but others gladly will comply,
When they behold our Union and Success.

 Tenesco. This Holy Priest has something to propose
That may excite us all to greater Zeal.

 Ponteach. Let him be heard: 'Tis something from his Gods,
And may import the common Interest much.

 Priest. (*Coming from one Side, where he hath stood listening.*)
'Tis not to show my Eloquence of Speech,
Or drown your Senses with unmeaning Sound,
That I desire Admittance to your Council;
It is an Impulse from the Gods that moves me,

That what I say will be to your Advantage.
Oh! With what secret Pleasure I behold
So many wise and valiant Kings unite,
And in a Cause by Gods and Saints espous'd.
Heaven smiles on your Design, and it shall prosper.
You're going to fight the Enemies of God;
Rebels and Traitors to the King of Kings;
Nay those who once betray'd and kill'd his Son,
Who came to save you *Indians* from Damnation —
He was an *Indian*, therefore they destroy'd him;[1]
He rose again and took his flight to Heaven;   —
But when his Foes are slain he'll quick return;
And be your kind Protector, Friend, and King.
Be therefore brave and fight his Battles for him;
Spare not his Enemies, where-e'r you find 'em:
The more you murder them, the more you please him;
Kill all you captivate, both old and young,
Mothers and Children, let them feel your Tortures;
He that shall kill a *Briton*, merits Heaven.
And should you chance to fall, you'll be convey'd
By flying Angels to your King that's there
Where these your hated Foes can never come.
Doubt you the Truth of this my Declaration?
I have a Witness here that cannot lye (*pulling out a burning Glass.*
This Glass was touch'd by your great Saviour's Hand,
And after left in holy *Peter's* Care;
When I command, it brings down Fire from Heaven,
To witness for me that I tell no Lye
                              (*The* Indians *gather round and gaze.*
Behold — Great God, send Fire, convince these *Indian* Kings
That I'm their Servant, and report the Truth,
                    (*in a very Praying posture and solemn canting Tone.*
Am sent to teach them what they ought to do,

[1] Doubtful authority has it that a part of the far-western Jesuit catechism of the seventeenth century ran: "Q. Who killed Jesus Christ? A. The bloody English." In 1763 there were many godly and influential priests, Jesuits and others, who did unforgettable service in the vicinity of Detroit for the beleaguered and all but overwhelmed English. Père Pothier, chief of the Wyandot village there, tried to dissuade his flock from attack. Père Jonois, chief of the Ottawa mission at Mackinac, brought the news of the fall of that post in a letter from Captain Etherington, "who spoke in the highest terms" of its bearer. *Pontiac Mss.* Parkman, *Conspiracy of Pontiac*, pp. 214, 243.

To kill and scalp, to torture and torment
Thy murderous treacherous Foes, the hateful *English*.
    (*it takes Fire, the* Indians *are amaz'd, and retreat from it.*
    Ponteach. Who can now doubt the Justice of our Cause,
Or this Man's Mission from the King above,
And that we ought to follow his Commands?
    Astinaco. 'Tis wonderful indeed — It must be so —
    Tenesco. This cannot be a Cheat — It is from Heaven —
    All. We are convinc'd and ready to obey;
We are impatient to revenge our King.
    Ponteach. (*Takes up the bloody Hatchet and flourishes it round*)
Thus do I raise the Hatchet from the Ground,
Sharpen'd and bright may it be stain'd with Blood,
And never dull'd nor rusted till we've conquer'd,
And taught proud *Englishmen* to dread its Edge.
    All. (*Flourishing their Hatchets, and striking them upon a
    Block.*)
Thus will we hew and carve their mangled Bodies,
And give them to the Beasts and Birds for Food.
    Ponteach. And thus our Names and Honours will maintain
While Sun and Moon, Rivers and Trees remain;
Our unborn Children shall rejoice to hear
How we their Fathers made the *English* fear.

The WAR SONG.

To the Tune of Over the Hills and far away, sung by Tenesco *the head Warrior. They all join in the Chorus, and
dance while that is singing in a Circle round him; and during
the Chorus the Musick plays.*

Where-e'r the Sun displays his Light,
Or Moon is seen to shine by Night,
Where-e'r the noisy Rivers flow
Or Trees and Grass and Herbage grow.   *Chorus.*

Be't known that we this War begin
With proud insulting *Englishmen;*
The Hatchet we have lifted high,   (*holding up their Hatchets.*)
And them we'll conquer or we'll die.   *Chorus.*

The Edge is keen, the Blade is bright,
Nothing saves them but their Flight;

And then like Heroes we'll pursue,
Over the Hills and Valleys through.   *Chorus.*

They'll like frighted Women quake,
When they behold a hissing Snake;
Or like timorous Deer away,
And leave both Goods and Arms a Prey.   *Chorus.*

Pain'd with Hunger, Cold, or Heat,
In Haste they'll from our Land retreat;
While we'll employ our scalping Knives —
          (*drawing and flourishing their scalping Knives.*
Take off their Sculls, and spare their Lives.   *Chorus.*

Or in their Country they'll complain,
Nor ever dare return again;
Or if they should they'll rue the Day,
And curse the Guide that shew'd the Way.   *Chorus.*

If Fortune smiles, we'll not be long
Ere we return with Dance and Song,
But ah! if we should chance to die,
Dear Wives and Children do not cry.   *Chorus.*

Our Friends will ease your Grief and Woe,
By double Vengeance on the Foe;
Will kill, and scalp, and shed their Blood,
Where-e'er they find them thro' the Wood.   *Chorus.*

No pointing Foe shall ever say
'Twas there the vanquish'd *Indian* lay;
Or boasting to his Friends relate
The Tale of our unhappy Fate.   *Chorus.*

Let us with Courage then away
To hunt and seize the frighted Prey;
Nor think of Children, Friend or Wife,
While there's an *Englishman* alive.   *Chorus.*

In Heat and Cold, thro' Wet and Dry,
Will we pursue, and they shall fly
To Seas which they a Refuge think,
And there in wretched Crouds they'll sink.
                   Chorus.   Exeunt omnes singing.

The End of the Third ACT.

207

ACT IV.

Scene I.—*The Border of a Grove.*

Enter Tenesco *to* Philip *and* Chekitan.

Tenesco.

The Troops are all assembled, some have march'd,
Perhaps are now engag'd, and warm in Battle;
The rest have Orders where to bend their Course.
Each Tribe is headed by a valiant Chief,
Except the *Bulls* which fall to one of you;
The other stays to serve the State at home,
Or back us, should our Forces prove too weak.

    Philip. The *Bulls* are brave, had they a brave Commander,
They'd push the Battle home with sure Success.
I'd chuse of all the Troops to be their Leader;
For tho' I'd neither Courage, Skill, nor Strength,
Honour attends the Man who heads the Brave;
Many are dubb'd for Heroes in these Times,
Who owe their Fame to those whom they commanded.

    Tenesco. But we shall ne'er suspect your Title false;
Already you've confirm'd your Fame and Courage,
And prov'd your Skill and Strength as a Commander.

    Philip. Still I'll endeavor to deserve your Praise,
Nor long delay the Honour you propose.

    Chekitan. But this will interfere with your Design,
And oversets the Scheme of winning *Hendrick.*

    Philip. Ah true—and kills your Hopes—This man's in
      Love.   (*To* Tenesco.

    Tenesco. Indeed! In Love with whom? King *Hendrick's*
      Daughter?

    Philip. The same; and I've engag'd to win her Father.

    Tenesco. This may induce him to espouse our Cause.
Which likewise you engag'd should be effected.

    Philip. But then I can't command as was propos'd
I must resign that Honour to this Lover,
While I conduct and form this double Treaty.

Tenesco. I am content if you but please yourselves
By means and Ways not hurtful to the Public.
   Chekitan. Was not the Public serv'd, no private Ends
Would tempt me to detain him from the Field,
Or in his Stead propose myself a Leader;
But every Power I have shall be exerted:
And if in Strength or Wisdom I should fail,
I dare presume you'll ever find me faithful.
   Tenesco. I doubt it not—You'll not delay your Charge;
The Troops are all impatient for the Battle.
                       (*Exeunt* Tenesco *and* Philip.

               Chekitan, solus.
This is not to my Mind — But I must do it —
If Philip heads the Troops, my Hopes are blown —
I must prepare, and leave the Event to Fate
And him —'Tis fix'd — There is no other Choice;
Monelia I must leave, and think of Battles—
She will be safe — But Oh the Chance of War —
Perhaps I fall—and never see her more —
This shocks my Soul in spite of Resolution —
The bare Perhaps is more than Daggers to me —
To part for ever! I'd rather stand against
Embattled Troops than meet this single Thought;
A Thought in Poison dipp'd and pointed round;
O how it pains my doubting trembling Heart!
I must not harbour it — My Word is gone —
My Honour calls — and, what is more, my Love.
            (*Noise of* Monelia *striving behind the Scene.*
What Sound is that?— It is *Monelia's* Voice;
And in Distress — What Monster gives her Pain?
   (*Going towards the Sound, the Scene opens and discovers the*
     Priest with her.)

       Scene II.— *Monelia and Priest.*

What do I see? The holy Priest is with her.
   Monelia. (*Struggling with the Priest, and trying to disengage*
No, I would sooner die than be dishonour'd —   [*herself.*)
Cut my own Throat, or drown me in the Lake.
   Priest. Do you love *Indians* better than us white Men?

Monelia. **Nay,** should an *Indian* make the foul Attempt,
I'd murder him, or kill my wretched Self.

Priest. I must, I can, and will enjoy you now.

Monelia. You must! You shan't, you cruel, barbarous
   Christian.

Chekitan. Hold, thou mad Tyger — What Attempt is this?
                                          (seizing him.
Are you a Christian Priest? What do you here? *(pushes him.*
What was his will, *Monelia?* He is dumb.

Monelia. May he be dumb and blind, and senseless quite,
That has such brutal Baseness in his Mind.

Chekitan. Base, false Deceiver, what could you intend?
                                     (making towards him.

Monelia. Oh I am faint — You have preserv'd my Honour,
Which he, foul Christian, thirsted to destroy.
                                     (Priest attempts to go.

Chekitan. Stay; leave your Life to expiate your Crime:
Your heated Blood shall pay for your Presumption.
                         (offering to strike him with a Hatchet.

Priest. Good Prince, forbear your pious Hand from Blood;
I did not know you was this Maiden's Lover,
I took her for a Stranger, half your Foe.

Chekitan. Did you not know she was King *Hendrick's*
   Daughter?
Did you not know that she was not your Wife?
Have you not told us, holy Men like you
Are by the Gods forbid all fleshly Converse?
Have you not told us, Death, and Fire, and Hell
Await those who are incontinent,
Or dare to violate the Rites of Wedlock?
That your God's mother liv'd and died a Virgin,
And thereby set Example to her Sex?
What means all this? Say you such Things to us,
That you alone may revel in these Pleasures?

Priest. I have a Dispensation from St. *Pett.*
To quench the Fire of Love when it grows painful,
This makes it innocent like Marriage Vows;
And all our holy Priests, and she herself,
Commits no Sin in this Relief of Nature:
For, being holy, there is no Pollution
Communicated from us as from others;

Nay, Maids are holy after we've enjoy'd them,
And, should the Seed take Root, the Fruit is pure.
   Chekitan. Oh vain Pretence! Falshood and foul Deception!
None but a Christian could devise such Lies!
Did I not fear it might provoke your Gods,
Your Tongue should never frame Deceit again.
If there are Gods, and such as you have told us,
They must abhor all Baseness and Deceit,
And will not fail to punish Crimes like yours.
To them I leave you — But avoid my Presence,
Nor let me ever see your hated Head,
Or hear your lying Tongue within this Country.
   Priest. Now by St. *Peter* I must go — He's raging.   (*aside.*
   Chekitan. That Day I do, by your great dreadful God,
This Hand shall cleave your Head, and spill your Blood,
Not all your Prayers, and Lyes, and Saints shall save you.
   Priest. I've got his Father's Secret, and will use it.
Such Disappointment ought to be reveng'd.   (*aside.*
   Chekitan. Don't mutter here, and conjure up your Saints,
I value not their Curses, or your Prayers.
                    (*stepping towards the Priest to hurry him.*
   Priest. By all the Saints, young Man, thou shalt repent it.
                              (*Exit.*
   Monelia. Base, false Dissembler — Tyger, Snake, a Christian!
I hate the Sight; I fear the very Name.
O Prince, what has not your kind Presence sav'd me!
   Chekitan. It sav'd to me more than my Father's Empire;
Far more than Crowns and Worlds — It sav'd *Monelia*,
The Hope of whom is more than the Creation.
In this I feel the Triumphs of an Hero,
And glory more than if I'd conquer'd Kingdoms.
   Monelia. O I am thine, I'm more than ever thine;
I am your Captive now, your lawful Prize:
You've taken me in War, a dreadful War!
And snatch'd me from the hungry Tyger's Jaw.
More than my Life and Service is your Due,
And had I more I would devote it to you.
   Chekitan. O my *Monelia!* rich is my Reward,
Had I lost Life itself in the Encounter;
But still I fear that Fate will snatch you from me.
Where is your Brother? Why was you alone?

Enter Torax, from listening to their Discourse.

Torax. Here am I: What would you of me?
Monelia. Torax!
I've been assaulted by a barbarous Man,
And by mere Accident escap'd my Ruin.
    Torax. What Foe is here? The *English* are not come?
    Monelia. No: But a Christian lurk'd within the Grove,
And every Christian is a Foe to Virtue;
Insidious, subtle, cruel, base, and false!
Like Snakes, their very Eyes are full of Poison;
And where they are not Innocence is safe.
    Torax. The holy Priest! Is he so vile a Man?
I heard him mutter Threat'nings as I past him.
    Chekitan. I spar'd his guilty Life, but drove him hence,
On Pain of Death and Tortures, never more
To tread the Earth, or breathe the Air with me.
Be warn'd by this to better tend your Charge.
You see how Mischiefs lye conceal'd about us,
We tread on Serpents ere we hear them hiss,
And Tygers lurk to seize the incautious Prey.
I must this Hour lead forth my Troops to Battle,
They're now in Arms, and waiting my Command.
    Monelia. What Safety shall I have when you are gone?
I must not, cannot, will not longer tarry,
Lest other Christians, or some other Foe,
Attempt my Ruin.
    Chekitan. Torax will be your Guard.
My Honour suffers, should I now decline;
It is my Country's Cause; I've pawn'd my Word,
Prevented *Philip*, to make sure of you.
He stays. 'Tis all in favour to our Love:
We must at present please ourselves with Hopes.
    Monelia. Oh! my fond heart no more conceals its Flame;
I fear, my Prince, I fear our Fates are cruel:
There's something whispers in my anxious Breast,
That if you go, I ne'er shall see you more.
    Chekitan. Oh! how her Words unman and melt my Soul!
As if her Fears were Prophecies of Fate.   (*aside.*
I will not go and leave you thus in Fears;
I'll frame Excuses — *Philip* shall command —

I'll find some other Means to turn the King;
I'll venture Honour, Fortune, Life, and Love,
Rather than trust you from my Sight again.
For what avails all that the World can give?
If you're with-held, all other Gifts are Curses,
And Fame and Fortune serve to make me wretched.
   Monelia. Now you grow wild — You must not think of
     staying;
Our only Hope, you know, depends on *Philip.*
I will not fear, but hope for his Success,
And your Return with Victory and Triumph,
That Love and Honour both may crown our Joy.
   Chekitan. Now this is kind; I am myself again.
You had unman'd and soften'd all my Soul,
Disarm'd my Hand, and cowardiz'd my Heart:
But now in every Vein I feel an Hero,
Defy the thickest Tempest of the War:
Yes, like a Lion conscious of his Strength,
Fearless of Death I'll rush into the Battle;
I'll fight, I'll conquer, triumph and return;
Laurels I'll gain and lay them at your Feet.
   Monelia. May the Success attend you that you wish!
May our whole Scheme of Happiness succeed!
May our next Meeting put an End to Fear,
And Fortune shine upon us in full Blaze!
   Chekitan. May Fate preserve you as her Darling Charge!
May all the Gods and Goddesses, and Saints,
If conscious of our Love, turn your Protectors!
And the great thundering God with Lightning burn
Him that but means to interrupt your Peace.

                          (*Exeunt.*

Scene III.— Indian *Senate-House.*

Ponteach *and* Philip.

Ponteach.
Say you that *Torax* then is fond of War?
   Philip. He is, and waits impatient my Return.
   Ponteach. 'Tis friendly in you thus to help your Brother;

But I suspect his Courage in the Field;
A love-sick Boy makes but a cow'rdly Captain.
    Philip. His Love may spur him on with greater Courage;
He thinks he's fighting for a double Prize;
And but for this, and Hopes of greater Service
In forwarding the Treaty with the *Mohawk*,
I now had been in Arms and warm in Battle.
    Ponteach. I much commend the Wisdom of your Stay.
Prepare yourself, and hasten to his Quarters;
You cannot make th' Attempt with too much Speed.
Urge ev'ry Argument with Force upon him,
Urge my strong Friendship, urge your Brother's Love,
His Daughter's Happiness, the common Good;
The general Sense of all the *Indian* Chiefs,
The Baseness of our Foes, our Hope of Conquest;
The Richness of the Plunder if we speed;
That we'll divide and share it as he pleases;
That our Success is certain if he joins us.
Urge these, and what besides to you occurs;
All cannot fail, I think, to change his Purpose.
    Philip. You'd think so more if you knew all my Plan.
                                   (*aside.*

I'm all prepar'd now I've receiv'd your Orders,
But first must speak t' his Children ere I part,
I am to meet them in the further Grove.
    Ponteach. Hark! there's a shout — We've News of some
        Success;
It is the Noise of Victory and Triumph.

Enter a Messenger.

Huzza! for our brave Warriors are return'd
Loaded with Plunder and the Scalps of Christians.

Enter Warrior.

    Ponteach. What have you done? Why all this Noise and
        Shouting?
    1st Warrior. Three Forts are taken, all consum'd and
        plunder'd;
The *English* in them all destroy'd by Fire,
Except some few escap'd to die with Hunger.

2nd Warrior. We've smoak'd the Bear in spite of all his Craft,
Burnt up their Den, and made them take the Field:
The mighty Colonel *Cockum* and his Captain
Have dull'd our Tomhocks; here are both their Scalps:
(nolding out the Two Scalps.
Their Heads are split, our Dogs have eat their Brains.
   Philip. If that be all they've eat, the Hounds will starve.
   3d Warrior. These are the Scalps of those two famous Cheats
Who bought our Furs for Rum, and sold us Water.
(holding out the Scalps, which Ponteach takes.
Our Men are loaded with their Furs again,
And other Plunder from the Villains Stores.
   Ponteach. All this is brave! (*tossing up the scalps, which others*
catch, and toss and throw them about.
This Way we'll serve them all.
   Philip. We'll cover all our Cabbins with their Scalps:
   Warriors. We'll fat our Dogs upon their Brains and Blood.
   Ponteach. Ere long we'll have their Governors in Play:
   Philip. And knock their grey-wig'd Scalps about this Way.
   Ponteach. The Game is started; Warriors hunt away,
Nor let them find a Place to shun your Hatchets.
   All Warriors. We will; We will soon shew you other Scalps.
   Philip. Bring some alive; I long to see them dance
In Fire and Flames, it us'd to make them caper.
   Warriors. Such Sport enough you'll have before we've done.
(Exeunt.
   Ponteach. This still will help to move the *Mohawk* King.
Spare not to make the most of our Success.
   Philip. Trust me for that — Hark; there's another Shout;
(shouting without.
A Shout for Prisoners — Now I have my Sport.
   Ponteach. It is indeed; and there's a Number too.

Enter Warriors.

We've broke the Barrier, burnt their Magazines,
Slew Hundreds of them, and pursu'd the rest
Quite to their Settlements.
   2nd Warrior. There we took
Their famous Hunters *Honnyman* and *Orsbourn;*
The last is slain, this is his bloody Scalp.   (*tossing it up.*
With them we found the Guns of our lost Hunters,

215

And other Proofs that they're the Murderers;
Nay, *Honnyman* confesses the base Deed,
And, boasting, says, he's kill'd a Score of *Indians*.
    3d Warrior. This is the bloody Hunter: This his Wife;
                (*leading them forward, pinioned and tied together.*
With Two young Brats that will be like their Father.
We took them in their Nest, and spoil'd their Dreams.
    Philip. Oh I could eat their Hearts and drink their Blood,
Were they not Poison, and unfit for Dogs.
Here, you Blood-hunter, have you lost your feeling?
You Tygress Bitch! You Breeder up of Serpents!
       (*slapping* Honnyman *in the Face, and kicking his Wife.*
    Ponteach. Stop — We must first consult which way to torture.
And whether all shall die — We will retire.
                Philip, going.
Take care they don't escape.
    Warrior. They're bound secure.
             (*Exeunt* Indians, *manent Prisoners.*

Scene IV.

Mrs. Honnyman.

O *Honnyman*, how desperate is our Case!
There's not a single Hope of Mercy left:
How savage, cruel, bloody did they look!
Rage and Revenge appear'd in every Face.
    Honnyman. You may depend upon't, we all must die.
I've made such Havock, they'll have no Compassion;
They only wait to study out new Torments:
All that can be inflicted or endur'd,
We may expect from their relentless Hands.
Their brutal Eyes ne'er shed a pitying Tear;
Their savage Hearts ne'er had a Thought of Mercy;
Their Bosoms swell with Rancour and Revenge,
And, Devil-like, delight in others Plagues,
Love Torments, Torture, Anguish, Fire, and Pain,
The deep-fetch'd Groan, the melancholy Sigh,
And all the Terrors and Distress of Death,
These are their Musick, and enhance their Joy.
In Silence then submit yourself to Fate:

Make no Complaint, nor ask for their Compassion;
This will confound and half destroy their Mirth;
Nay, this may put a stop to many Tortures,
To which our Prayers and Tears and Plaints would move them.

Mrs. Hon. O dreadful Scene! Support me, mighty God,
To pass the Terrors of this dismal Hour,
All dark with Horrors, Torments, Pains, and Death!
O let me not despair of thy kind Help;
Give Courage to my wretched groaning Heart!

Honnyman. Tush, Silence! You'll be overheard.

Mrs. Hon. O my dear Husband! 'Tis an Hour for Prayer,
An Infidel would pray in our Distress:
An Atheist would believe there was some God
To pity Pains and Miseries so great.

Honnyman. If there's a God, he knows our secret Wishes;
This Noise can be no Sacrifice to him;
It opens all the Springs of our weak Passions.
Besides, it will be Mirth to our Tormentors;
They'll laugh, and call this Cowardice in Christians,
And say Religion makes us all mere Women.

Mrs. Hon. I will suppress my Grief in Silence then,
And secretly implore the Aid of Heaven.
Forbid to pray! O dreadful Hour indeed!   (*pausing.*
Think you they will not spare our dear sweet Babes?
Must these dear Innocents be put to Tortures,
Or dash'd to Death, and share our wretched Fate?
Must this dear Babe that hangs upon my Breast
                    (*looking upon her Infant.*
Be snatch'd by savage Hands and torn in Pieces!
O how it rends my Heart! It is too much!
Tygers would kindly soothe a Grief like mine;
Unconscious Rocks would melt, and flow in Tears
At this last Anguish of a Mother's Soul.
                    (*pauses, and views her Child again.*
Sweet Innocent! It smiles at this Distress,
And fondly draws this final Comfort from me:
Dear Babe, no more: Dear *Tommy* too must die,
                    (*looking at her other Child.*
Oh my sweet First-born! Oh I'm overpower'd.   (*pausing.*

Honnyman. I had determin'd not to shed a tear;   (*weeping.*
But you have all unmann'd my Resolution;

You've call'd up all the Father in my Soul;
Why have you nam'd my Children? O my Son!

(*looking upon him.*

My only Son — My Image — Other Self!
How have I doted on the charming Boy,
And fondly plann'd his Happiness in Life!
Now his Life ends: Oh the Soul-bursting Thought!
He falls a Victim for his Father's Folly.
Had I not kill'd their Friends, they might have spar'd
My Wife, my Children, and perhaps myself,
And this sad dreadful Scene had never happen'd,.
But 'tis too late that I perceive my Folly;
If Heaven forgive, 'tis all I dare to hope for.
   Mrs. Hon. What! have you been a Murderer indeed!
And kill'd the Indians for Revenge and Plunder?
I thought you rash to tempt their brutal Rage,
But did not dream you guilty as you said.
   Honnyman. I am indeed. I murder'd many of them,
And thought it not amiss, but now I fear.
   Mrs. Honn. O shocking Thought! Why have you let me know
Yourself thus guilty in the Eye of Heaven?
That I and my dear Babes were by you brought
To this Extreme of Wretchedness and Woe?
Why have you let me know the solemn Weight
Of horrid Guilt that lies upon us all?
To have died innocent, and seen these Babes
By savage Hands dash'd to immortal Rest,
This had been light, for this implies no Crime:
But now we die as guilty Murderers,
Not savage *Indians*, but just Heaven's Vengeance
Pursues our Lives with all these Pains and Tortures.
This is a Thought that points the keenest Sorrow,
And leaves no Room for Anguish to be heighten'd.
   Honnyman. Upbraid me not, nor lay my Guilt to Heart;
You and these Fruits of our past morning Love
Are innocent. I feel the Smart and Anguish,
The Stings of Conscience, and my Soul on Fire.
There's not a Hell more painful than my Bosom,
Nor Torments for the Damn'd more keenly pointed.
How could I think to murder was no Sin?
Oh my lost Neighbour! I seduc'd him too.

Now Death with all its Terrors disappears,
And all I fear's a dreadful Something-after;
My Mind forebodes a horrid woful Scene,
Where Guilt is chain'd and tortur'd with Despair.
   Mrs. Hon. The Mind oppress'd with Guilt may find Relief.
   Honnyman. Oh could I reach the pitying Ear of Heaven,
And all my Soul evaporate in Sound,
'Twould ask Forgiveness! but I fear too late;
And next I'd ask that you and these dear Babes
Might bear no Part in my just Punishment.
Who knows but by pathetic Prayers and Tears
Their savage Bosoms may relent towards you,
And fix their Vengeance where just Heaven points it?
I still will hope, and every Motive urge.
Should I succeed, and melt their rocky Hearts,
I'd take it as a Presage of my Pardon,
And die with Comfort when I see you live.
                        (Death Halloo is heard without.
   Mrs. Hon. Hark! they are coming — Hear that dreadful
   Halloo.
   Honnyman. It is Death's solemn Sentence to us all;
They are resolv'd, and all Intreaty's vain.
O horrid Scene! how shall I act my Part?
Was it but simple Death to me alone!
But all your Deaths are mine, and mine the Guilt.

   Enter Indians, *with Stakes, Hatchets, and Firebrands.*

O horrid Preparation, more than Death!
   Ponteach. Plant down the Stakes, and let them be confin'd.
                      (they loose them from each other.
First kill the Tygers, then destroy their Whelps.
   Philip. This Brat is in our Way, I will dispatch it.
                (offering to snatch the sucking Infant.
   Mrs. Hon. No, my dear Babe shall in my Bosom die;
There is its Nourishment, and there its End.
   Philip. Die both together then, 'twill mend the Sport;
Tie the other to his Father, make a Pair;
Then each will have a Consort in their Pains;
Their sweet Brats with them, to increase the Dance.
         *(they are tied down facing each other upon their
             Knees, and their Backs to the Stakes.*

Warrior. All now is ready; they are bound secure.
Philip. Whene'er you please, their jovial Dance begins.

(*to* Ponteach

Mrs. Hon. O my dear Husband! What a Sight is this!
Could ever fabling Poet draw Distress
To such Perfection! Sad Catastrophe!
There are not Colours for such deep-dyed Woe,
Nor Words expressive of such heighten'd Anguish.
Ourselves, our Babes, O cruel, cruel Fate!
This, this is Death indeed with all its Terrors.

Honnyman. Is there no secret Pity in your Minds?
Can you not feel some tender Passion move,
When you behold the Innocent distress'd?
True, I am guilty, and will bear your Tortures:
Take your Revenge by all the Arts of Torment;
Invent new Torments, lengthen out my Woe,
And let me feel the keenest Edge of Pain:
But spare this innocent afflicted Woman,
Those smiling Babes who never yet thought Ill,
They never did nor ever will offend you.

Philip. It cannot be: They are akin to you,
Well learnt to hunt and murder, kill and rob.

Ponteach. Who ever spar'd a Serpent in the Egg?
Or left young Tygers quiet in their Den?

Warrior. Or cherishes young Vipers in his Bosom?

Philip. Begin, begin; I'll lead the merry Dance.

(*offering at the Woman with a Firebrand.*

Ponteach. Stop: Are we not unwise to kill this Woman?
Or sacrifice her Children to our Vengeance?
They have not wrong'd us; can't do present Mischief.
I know her Friends; they're rich and powerful,
And in their Turn will take severe Revenge:
But if we spare, they'll hold themselves oblig'd,
And purchase their Redemption with rich Presents.
Is not this better than an Hour's Diversion,
To hear their Groans, and Plaints, and piteous Cries?

Warriors. You Counsel's wise, and much deserves our Praise;
They shall be spar'd.

Ponteach. Untie, and take them hence;

(*they untie the Woman and the oldest Child from* Honnyman,
and retire a little to consult his Death.

When the War ends her Friends shall pay us for it.

 Philip. I'd rather have the Sport than all the Pay.

 Honnyman. O now, kind Heaven, thou hast heard my Prayer,
And what's to follow I can meet with Patience.

 Mrs. Hon. O my dear Husband, could you too be freed!

               (*weeping.*

Yet must I stay and suffer Torments with you.
This seeming Mercy is but Cruelty!
I cannot leave you in this Scene of Woe,
'Tis easier far to stay and die together!

 Honnyman. Ah! but regard our Childrens Preservation;
Conduct their Youth, and form their Minds to Virtue;
Nor let them know their Father's wretched End,
Lest lawless Vengeance should betray them too.

 Mrs. Hon. If I must live, I must retire from hence,
Nor see your fearful Agonies in Death;
This would be more than all the Train of Torments.
The horrid Sight would sink me to the Dust;
These helpless Infants would become a Prey
To worse than Beasts, to savage, bloody Men.

 Honnyman. Leave me—They are prepar'd, and coming on[1]—
Heav'n save you all! O 'tis the last dear Sight!

 Mrs. Hon. Oh may we meet where Fear and Grief are
  banish'd!
Dearest of Men, adieu — Adieu till then.

      (*Exit, weeping with her Children.*

 Philip. Bring Fire and Knives, and Clubs, and Hatchets all;

---

[1] "If the sentence of a prisoner be death, the whole village sets up the death-hollo or cry, and the execution is no longer deferred than till they can make the necessary preparations for it. They first strip the person who is to suffer naked and fixing two posts in the ground, they fasten to them two pieces crossways, one about two feet from the ground, the other about five or six feet higher; they then oblige the unhappy victim to mount upon the lower crosspiece; and in this posture they burn him all over the body, sometimes first daubing him all over with pitch. The whole village, men, women, and children, assemble around him, and everyone has a right to torture him in whatever manner they please. If none of his bystanders are inclined to lengthen out his torments, he is not long kept in pain, but is either shot to death with arrows or inclosed with dry bark, to which they set fire; they then leave him on the frame, and in the evening run from cabin to cabin and strike with small twigs their furniture, the walls and roof of their cabins, to prevent his spirit from remaining there to take vengeance for the evils committed on the body." Rogers, *A Concise Account of North America,*
p. 235.

Let the old Hunter feel the Smart of Pain.

(*they fall upon* Honnyman *with various Instruments of Torture.*

Honnyman. Oh! this is exquisite! (*groaning and struggling.*

1st Warrior. Hah! Does this make you dance?

2d Warrior. This is fine fat Game!

Philip. Make him caper.

(*striking him with a Club, kicking, &c.*

Honnyman. O ye eternal powers, that rule on high,

If in your Minds be Sense of human Woe,

Hear my Complaints, and pity my Distress!

Philip. Ah call upon your Gods, you faint-heart Coward!

Honnyman. Oh dreadful Racks! When will this Torment end?

Oh for a Respite from all Sense of Pain!

'Tis come — I go — You can — no more torment   (*dies.*

Philip. He's dead; he'll hunt no more; h' as done with
     Game.   (*striking the dead Body, and spitting in the Face.*

Ponteach. Drive hence his wretched Spirit, lest it plague us;

Let him go hunt the Woods; he's now disarm'd.

(*They run round brushing the Walls, &c. to dislodge the Spirit.*

All. Out, Hunters, out, your Business here is done.

Out to the Wilds, but do not take your Gun.

Ponteach, (*to the Spirit*)

Go, tell our Countrymen, whose Blood you shed,

That the great Hunter *Honnyman* is dead:

That we're alive, we'll make the *English* know,

Whene'er they dare to serve us *Indians* so:

This will be joyful News to Friends from *France*,

We'll join the Chorus then, and have a Dance.

(*Exeunt omnes, dancing, and singing the two last Lines.*

End of the Fourth ACT.

ACT V.

SCENE I.—*The Border of a Grove, in which* Monelia *and* Torax *are asleep.*

Enter Philip, *speaking to himself.*

As a dark Tempest brewing in the Air,
For many Days hides Sun and Moon, and Stars,
At length grown ripe, bursts forth and forms a Flood
That frights both Men and Beasts, and drowns the Land;
So my dark Purpose now must have its Birth,
Long nourish'd in my Bosom, 'tis matur'd,
And ready to astonish and embroil
Kings and their Kingdoms, and decide their Fates.
Are they not here? Have I delay'd too long?

(he espies them asleep.

Yes, in a Posture too beyond my Hopes,
Asleep! This is the Providence of Fate,
And proves she patronizes my Design,
And I'll shew her that Philip is no Coward.

(taking up his Hatchet in one Hand, and Scalping Knife in the other, towards them.

A Moment now is more than Years to come:
Intrepid as I am, the Work is shocking.

(he retreats from them.

Is it their Innocence that shakes my Purpose?
No; I can tear the Suckling from the Breast,
And drink their Blood who never knew a Crime.
Is it because my Brother's Charmer dies?
That cannot be, for that is my Revenge.
Is it because *Monelia* is a woman?
I've long been blind and deaf to their Enchantments.
Is it because I take them thus unguarded?
No; though I act the Coward, it's a Secret.
What is it that shakes my firm and fix'd Resolve?

'Tis childish Weakness: I'll not be unman'd.

(approaches and retreats again.

There's something awful in the Face of Princes,
And he that sheds their Blood, assaults the Gods:
But I'm a Prince, and 'tis by me they die;

(advances arm'd as before.

Each Hand contains the Fate of future Kings,
And, were they Gods, I would not balk my Purpose.

(stabs Monelia with the Knife.

    Torax. Hah, *Philip*, are you come? What can you mean?

(Torax starts and cries out.

    Philip. Go learn my Meaning in the World of Spirits;

(knocks him down with his Hatchet, &c.

'Tis now too late to make a Question of it.
The Play is ended *(looking upon the Bodies)* now succeeds the
    Farce.
Hullo! Help! Haste! the Enemy is here.

(calling at one of the Doors, and returning.

Help is at Hand—But I must first be wounded:

(wounds himself.

Now let the Gods themselves detect the Fraud.

Enter an Indian.

What means your Cry? Is any Mischief here?
    Philip. Behold this flowing Blood; a desperate Wound!

(shewing his Wound.

And there's a Deed that shakes the Root of Empires.

(pointing to the Bodies.

    2d Ind. O fatal Sight! the *Mohawk* Prince is murder'd.
    3d Ind. The Princess too is weltering in her Blood.
    Philip. Both, both are gone; 'tis well that I escap'd. .

Enter Ponteach.

What means this Outcry, Noise, and Tumult here?
    Philip. O see, my Father! see the Blood of Princes,
A Sight that might provoke the Gods to weep,
And drown the Country in a Flood of Tears.
Great was my Haste, but could not stop the Deed;
I rush'd among their Numbers for Revenge,
They frighted fled; there I receiv'd this Wound.

(shewing his Wound to Ponteach.

224

Ponteach. Who, what were they? or where did they escape?
Philip. A Band of *English* Warriors, bloody Dogs!
This Way they ran from my vindictive Arm,   *(pointing, &c.*
Which but for this base Wound would sure have stopp'd them.
     Ponteach. Pursue, pursue, with utmost Speed pursue,
                              (to the Warriors present.
Outfly the Wind till you revenge this Blood;
'Tis royal Blood, we hold it as our own.
                    (Exeunt Warriors in haste.
This Scene is dark, and doubtful the Event;
Some great Decree of Fate depends upon it,
And mighty Good or Ill awaits Mankind.
The Blood of Princes cannot flow in vain,
The Gods must be in Council to permit it:
It is the Harbinger of their Designs,
To change, new-mould, and alter Things on Earth:
And much I fear, 'tis ominous of Ill
To me and mine; it happen'd in my Kingdom.
Their Father's Rage will swell into a Torrent—
They were my Guests— His Wrath will centre here;
Our guilty Land hath drunk his Children's Blood.
     Philip. Had I not seen the flying Murderers,
Myself been wounded to revenge their Crime,
Had you not hasten'd to pursue the Assassins,
He might have thought us treacherous and false,
Or wanting in our hospitable Care:
But now it cannot but engage his Friendship,
Rouse him to Arms, and with a Father's Rage
He'll point his Vengeance where it ought to fall;
And thus this Deed, though vile and dark as Night,
In its Events will open Day upon us,
And prove of great Advantage to our State.
     Ponteach. Haste then; declare our Innocence and **Grief;**
Tell the old King we mourn as for our own,   ·
And are determin'd to revenge his Wrongs;
Assure him that our Enemies are his,
And rouse him like a Tyger to the Prey.
     Philip. I will with Speed; but first this bleeding **Wound**
Demands my Care, lest you lament me too.
                    (Exit, to have his Wound dress'd.

Ponteach, solus.

Pale breathless Youths! Your Dignity still lives:

(*viewing the Bodies.*

Your Murderers were blind, or they'd have trembled,
Nor dar'd to wound such Majesty and Worth;
It would have tam'd the savage running Bear,
And made the raging Tyger fondly fawn;
But your more savage Murderers were Christians.
Oh the distress'd good King! I feel for him,
And wish to comfort his desponding Heart;
But your last Rites require my present Care.   .   (*Exit.*

SCENE II.— *The Senate-House.*

Ponteach, Tenesco, *and others.*

Ponteach.

Let all be worthy of the royal Dead;
Spare no Expence to grace th' unhappy Scene,
And aggrandize the solemn gloomy Pomp
With all our mournful melancholy Rites.

  Tenesco. It shall be done; all Things are now preparing.
  Ponteach. Never were Funeral Rites bestow'd more just;
Who knew them living, must lament them dead;
Who sees them dead, must wish to grace their Tombs
With all the sad Respect of Grief and Tears.

  Tenesco. The Mourning is as general as the News;
Grief sits on every Face, in every Eye,
And gloomy Melancholy in Silence reigns:
Nothing is heard but Sighs and sad Complaints,
As if the First-born of the Realm were slain.

  Ponteach. Thus would I have it; let no Eye be dry,
No Heart unmov'd, let every Bosom swell
With Sighs and Groans. What Shouting do I hear?

(*a Shouting without, repeated several Times.*

  Tenesco. It is the Shout of Warriors from the Battle;
The Sound of Victory and great Success.

(*he goes to listen to it.*

  Ponteach. Such is the State of Men and human Things;
We weep, we smile, we mourn, and laugh thro' Life,

226

Here falls a Blessing, there alights a Curse,
As the good Genius or the evil reigns.
It's right it should be so. Should either conquer,
The World would cease, and Mankind be undone
By constant Frowns or Flatteries from Fate;
This constant Mixture makes the Potion safe,
And keeps the sickly Mind of Man in health.

Enter Chekitan.

It is my Son. What has been your Success?
  Chekitan. We've fought the Enemy, broke thro' their **Ranks**,
Slain many on the Spot, pursu'd the rest
Till Night conceal'd and sav'd them from our Arms.
  Ponteach. 'Tis bravely done, and shall be duely **honor'd**
With all the Signs and Marks of public Joy.
  Chekitan. What means this Gloom I see in every **Face?**
These smother'd Groans and stifled half-drawn Sighs;
Does it offend that I've return'd in Triumph?
  Ponteach. I fear to name — And yet it must be known.
                              (*aside.*

Be not alarm'd, my Son, the Laws of Fate
Must be obey'd: She will not hear our Dictates.
I'm not a Stranger to your youthful Passion,
And fear the Disapointment will confound you.
  Chekitan. Has he not sped? Has Ill befel my Brother?
  Ponteach. Yes, he is wounded but — *Monelia's* slain,
And *Torax* both. Slain by the cowardly *English*,
Who 'scap'd your Brother's wounded threatning Arm,
But are pursued by such as will revenge it —
  Chekitan. Oh wretched, wretched, wretched *Chekitan!*
                              (*aside.*
  Ponteach. I know your're shock'd —The Scene hath shock'd
    us all,
And what we could, we've done to wipe the Stain
From us, our Family, our Land and State;
And now prepare due Honours for the Dead,
With all the solemn Pomp of public Grief,
To shew Respect as if they were our own.
  Chekitan. Is this my Triumph after Victory?
A solemn dreadful pompous Shew:
Why have I scap'd their Swords and liv'd to see it?   (*aside.*

Monelia dead! aught else I cou'd have borne:
I'm stupify'd: I can't believe it true;
Shew me the Dead; I will believe my Eyes,
But cannot mourn or drop a Tear till then.

    Tenesco. I will conduct you to them — Follow me —
                      (*Exeunt* Tenesco *and* Chekitan.

    Ponteach. This is a sad Reception from a Conquest,
And puts an awful Gloom upon our Joy;
I fear his Grief will over-top his Reason;
A Lover weeps with more than common Pain.
Nor flows his greatest Sorrow at his Eyes:
His Grief is inward, and his Heart sheds Tears,
And in his Soul he feels the pointed Woe,
When he beholds the lovely Object lost.
The deep-felt Wound admits no sudden Cure;
The festering Humor will not be dispers'd,
It gathers on the Mind, and Time alone,
That buries all Things, puts an End to this.

                                (*Exeunt omnes.*

Scene III.— *The Grove, with the dead Bodies;*
Tenesco *pointing* Chekitan *to them.*

Tenesco.
There lie the Bodies, Prince, a wretched Sight!
Breathless and pale.

    Chekitan. A wretched Sight indeed;   (*going towards them.*
O my *Monelia;* has thy Spirit fled?
Art thou no more? a bloody breathless Corpse!
Am I return'd full flush'd with Hopes of Joy,
With all the Honours Victory can give,
To see thee thus? Is this, is this my Welcome?
Is this our Wedding? Wilt thou not return?
O charming Princess, art thou gone for ever?
Is this the fatal Period of our Love?
O! had I never seen thy Beauty bloom,
I had not now been griev'd to see it pale:
Had I not known such Excellence had liv'd,
I shou'd not now be curs'd to see it dead:

228

Had not my Heart been melted by thy Charms,
It would not now have bled to see them lost.
O wherefore, wherefore, wherefore do I live:
Monelia is not—What's the World to me?
All dark and gloomy, horrid, waste, and void:
The Light of the Creation is put out!—
The Blessings of the Gods are all withdrawn!
Nothing remains but Wretchedness and Woe;
Monelia's gone: *Monelia* is no more.
The Heavens are veil'd because she don't behold them;
The Earth is curs'd, for it hath drunk her Blood;
The Air is Poison, for she breathes no more:
Why fell I not by the base *Briton's* Sword?
Why press'd I not upon the fatal Point?
Then had I never seen this worse than Death,
But dying said, 'tis well—*Monelia* lives.

   Tenesco. Comfort, my Prince, nor let your Passion swell
To such a Torrent, it o'erwhelms your Reason,
And preys upon the Vitals of your Soul.
You do but feed the Viper by this View;
Retire, and drive the Image from your Thought,
And Time will soon replace you every Joy.

   Chekitan. O my *Tenesco*, had you ever felt
The gilded Sweets, or pointed Pains of Love,
You'd not attempt to sooth a Grief like mine.
Why did you point me to the painful Sight?
Why have you shewn this Shipwreck of my Hopes,
And plac'd me in this beating Storm of Woe.
Why was I told of my *Monelia's* Fate?
Why wa'n't the wretched Ruin all conceal'd
Under some fair Pretence—That she had fled—
Was made a Captive, or had chang'd her Love—
Why wa'n't I left to guess her wretched End?
Or have some slender Hope that she still liv'd?
You've all been cruel; she died to torment me;
To raise my Pain, and blot out every Joy.—

   Tenesco. I fear'd as much: His Passion makes him wild—

                                 (*aside.*

I wish it may not end in perfect Phrensy.

   Chekitan. Who were the Murderers? Where did they fly?
Where was my Brother, not to take Revenge?

Shew me their Tracks, I'll trace them round the Globe:
I'll fly like lightning, ravage the whole Earth—
Kill every thing I meet, or hear, or see.
Depopulate the World of Men and Beasts,
'Tis all too little for that single Death. ·

(*pointing to* Monelia's *corpse.*

I'll tear the Earth that dar'd to drink her Blood;
Kill Trees, and Plants, and every springing Flower:
Nothing shall grow, nothing shall be alive,
Nothing shall move; I'll try to stop the Sun,
And make all dark and barren, dead and sad;
From his tall Sphere down to the lowest Centre,
There I'll descend, and hide my wretched Self,
And reign sole Monarch in a World of Ruin.

Tenesco. This is deep Madness, it hath seiz'd his Brain.

(*aside.*

Chekitan. But first I'll snatch a parting last Embrace.

(*he touches and goes to embrace the Corpse.*

Thou dear cold Clay! forgive the daring Touch;
It is thy *Chekitan*, thy wounded Lover.
'Tis; and he hastens to revenge thy Death.

(Torax *groans and attempts to speak.*

Torax. Oh, oh, I did not—Philip—Philip—Oh.

(Chekitan *starts.*

Chekitan. What—did I not hear a Groan? and *Philip* call'd?
Tenesco. It was, it was, and there is Motion too.

(*approaches* Torax, *who groans and speaks again.*

Torax. Oh! Oh! Oh! Oh! Oh! *Philip*—help. Oh! Oh!
Tenesco. He is alive—We'll raise him from the Ground.

(*they lift him up and speak to him.*

Torie, are you alive? or are our Ears deceiv'd?
Torax. Oh Philip, do not—do not—be so cruel.
Chekitan. He is bewilder'd, and not yet himself.
Pour this into his Lips—it will revive him.

(*they give him something.*

Tenesco. This is a Joy unhop'd for in Distress.

(Torax *revives more.*

Torax. Oh! *Philip, Philip!*—Where is *Philip* gone?
Tenesco. The Murderers are pursued—He will go soon.
And now can carry Tidings of your Life.
Torax. He carry Tidings! he's the Murderer.

Tenesco. He is not murder'd; he was slightly wounded,
And hastens now to see the King your Father.

 Torax. He is a false, a barbarous bloody Man,
A Murderer, a base disguis'd Assassin.

 Chekitan. He still is maz'd, and knows not whom he's with.

 Torax. Yes, you are *Chekitan*, and that's *Monelia*,
(pointing to the Corpse.
This is *Tenesco* — *Philip* stabb'd my Sister,
And struck at me; here was the stunning Blow:
(pointing to his Head.
He took us sleeping in this silent Grove;
There by Appointment from himself we waited.
I saw him draw the bloody Knife from her,
And, starting, ask'd him, Why, or what he meant?
He answered with the Hatchet on my Skull,
And doubtless thought me dead and bound in Silence.
I am myself, and what I say is Fact.

 Tenesco. The *English* 'twas beset you; *Philip* ran
For your Assistance, and himself is wounded.

 Torax. He may be wounded, but he wounded me;
No Englishman was there, he was alone.
I dare confront him with his Villainy:
Depend upon't, he's treacherous, false, and bloody.

 Chekitan. May we believe, or is this all a Dream?
Are we awake? Is *Torax* yet alive?
Or is it Juggling, Fascination all?

 Tenesco. 'Tis most surprising! What to judge I know not.
I'll lead him hence; perhaps he's still confus'd.

 Torax. I gladly will go hence for some Relief,
But shall not change, from what I've now aver'd.

 Tenesco. Then this sad Storm of Ruin's but begun. (*aside.*
Philip must fly, or next it lights on him.
(Exeunt Tenesco and Torax led by him.
 Chekitan. And can this be — Can *Philip* be so false?
Dwells there such Baseness in a Brother's Heart?
So much Dissimulation in the Earth?
Is there such Perfidy among Mankind?
It shocks my Faith — But yet it must be so —
Yes, it was he, *Monelia*, shed thy Blood.
This made him forward to commence our Friend,
And with unusual Warmth engage to help us;

It was for this so chearful he resign'd
To me the Honour of Command in War;
The *English* Troops would never come so near;
The Wounds were not inflicted by their Arms.
All, all confirms the Guilt on *Philip's* Head,
You died, *Monelia*, by my Brother's Hand;
A Brother too intrusted with our Love.
I'm stupify'd and senseless at the Thought;
My Head, my very Heart is petrify'd.
This adds a Mountain to my Weight of Woe.
It now is swell'd too high to be lamented;
Complaints, and Sighs, and Tears are thrown away,
Revenge is all the Remedy that's left;
But what Revenge is equal to the Crime?
His life for her's! An Atom for the Earth —
A single Fly — a Mite for the Creation:
Turn where I will I find myself confounded:
But I must seek and study out new Means.
Help me, ye Powers of Vengeance! grant your Aid,
Ye that delight in Blood, and Death, and Pain!
Teach me the Arts of Cruelty and Wrath,
Till I have Vengeance equal to my Love,
And my *Monelia's* Shade is satisfied.   (*Exit.*

SCENE IV.

Philip, solus.
His Grief no Doubt will rise into a Rage,
To see his Charmer rolling in her Blood,
I chuse to see him not till my Return;
By then the Fierceness of the Flame may cease;
Nay, he'll grow cool, and quite forget his Love,
When I report her Father's kindled Wrath,
And all the Vengeance he intends to take.
                    (Chekitan *comes in sight.*
But this he, I cannot now avoid him;
How shall I sooth his Grief — He looks distracted —
I'm such a Stranger grown to Tears and Pity,
I fear he will not think I sympathize.

232

Enter Chekitan.

Chekitan.   Have I then found thee, thou false hearted
   Traitor?
Thou Tyger, Viper, Snake, thou worse than Christian;
Blood thirsty Butcher, more than Murderer!
Thou every Thing but what Men ought to love!
Do you still live to breathe and see the Sun?
And face me with your savage guilty Eye?
   Philip.   I fear'd, alas, you would run mad and rave.
Why do you blame me that I am not dead?
I risk'd my Life, was wounded for your Sake,
Did all I could for your *Monelia's* Safety,
And to revenge you on her Murderers.
Your Grief distracts you, or you'd thank me for 't.
   Chekitan.   Would you still tempt my Rage, and fire my Soul,
Already bent to spill your treacherous Blood?
You base Dissembler! know you are detected,
Torax still lives, and has discover'd all.
                              (Philip *starts and trembles.*
   Philip.   *Torax* alive!— It cannot— must not be   (*aside.*
   Chekitan.   Well may you shake— You cannot mend your
   Blow.
He lived to see, what none but you could think of,
The bloody Knife drawn from *Monelia's* Breast.
Had you a thousand Lives, they'd be too few;
Had you a Sea of Blood, 'twould be too small
To wash away your deep-dy'd Stain of Guilt.
Now you shall die; and O if there be Powers
That after Death take Vengeance on such Crimes,
May they pursue you with their Flames of Wrath,
Till all their Magazines of Pain are spent.
                        (*he attacks* Philip *with his Hatchet.*
   Philip.   I must defend myself (*drawing his Hatchet*) the Case
   is desperate.   (*Fights,* Philip *falls.*
Fate is too hard; and I'm oblig'd to yield.
'Twas well begun — but has a wretched End —
Yet I'm reveng'd — She cannot live again.
You cannot boast to've shed more Blood than I —
Oh had I — had I — struck but one Blow more!   (*dies.*
   Chekitan.   What have I done! this is my Brother's Blood!

233

A guilty Murderer's Blood! He was no Brother.
All Nature's Laws and Ties are hence dissolv'd;
There is no Kindred, Friendship, Faith, or Love
Among Mankind — *Monelia's* dead — The World
Is all unhing'd — There's universal War —
She was the Tie, the Centre of the Whole;
And she remov'd, all is one general Jar.
Where next, *Monelia*, shall I bend my Arm
To heal this Discord, this Disorder still,
And bring the Chaos Universe to Form?
Blood still must flow and float the scatter'd Limbs
Till thy much injur'd love in Peace subsides.
Then every jarring Discord once will cease,
And a new World from these rude Ruins rise.   (*pauses.*
Here then I point the Edge, from hence shall flow
                           (*pointing his knife to his Heart.*
The raging crimson Flood, this is the Fountain
Whose swift Day's Stream shall waft me to thy Arms,
Lest *Philip's* Ghost should injure thy Repose.   (*stabs himself.*
I come, I come, *Monelia*, now I come —
Philip — away — She's mine in spite of Death.   (*dies.*

Enter Tenesco.

Oh! I'm too late, the fatal Work is done.
Unhappy Princes; this your wretched End;
Your Country's Hopes and your fond Father's Joy;
Are you no more? Slain by each other's Hands,
Or what is worse; or by the Air you breath'd?
For all is Murder, Death, and Blood about us:
Nothing safe; it is contagious all:
The Earth, and Air, and Skies are full of Treason!
The Evil Genius rules the Universe,
And on Mankind rains Tempests of Destruction.
Where will the Slaughter of the Species end?
When it begins with Kings and with their Sons,
A general Ruin threatens all below.
How will the good King hear the sad Report.
I fear th' Event; but as it can't be hid,
I'll bear it to him in the softest Terms,
And summon every Power to sooth his Grief,
And slack the Torrent of his royal Passion.   (*Exit.*

234

Ponteach, solus.

The Torrent rises, and the Tempest blows;
Where will this rough rude Storm of Ruin end?
What crimson Floods are yet to drench the Earth?
What new-form'd Mischiefs hover in the Air,
And point their Stings at this devoted Head?
Has Fate exhausted all her Stores of Wrath,
Or has she other Vengeance in Reserve?
What can she more? My Sons, my Name is gone;
My Hopes all blasted, my Delights all fled;
Nothing remains but an afflicted King,
That might be pitied by Earth's greatest Wretch.
My Friends; my Sons, ignobly, basely slain,
Are more than murder'd, more than lost by Death.
Had they died fighting in their Country's Cause,
I should have smil'd and gloried in their Fall;
Yes, boasting that I had such Sons to lose,
I would have rode in Triumph o'er their Tombs.
But thus to die, the Martyrs of their Folly,
Involv'd in all the complicated Guilt
Of Treason, Murder, Falshood, and Deceit,
Unbridled Passion, Cowardice, Revenge,
And every Thing that can debase the Man,
And render him the just Contempt of all,
And fix the foulest Stain of Infamy,
Beyond the Power of Time to blot it out;
This is too much; and my griev'd Spirit sinks
Beneath the Weight of such gigantic Woe.
Ye that would see a piteous wretched King,
Look on a Father griev'd and curs'd like me;
Look on a King whose Sons have died like mine!
Then you'll confess that these are dangerous Names,
And put it in the Power of Fate to curse us;
It is on such she shews her highest Spite.
But I'm too far — 'Tis not a Time to grieve
For private Losses, when the Public calls.

Enter Tenesco, *looking sorrowful.*

What are your Tidings? — I have no more Sons.

Tenesco. But you have Subjects, and regard their Safety.
The treacherous Priest, intrusted with your Councils,
Has publish'd all, and added his own Falshoods;
The Chiefs have all revolted from your Cause,
Patch'd up a Peace, and lend their Help no more.
    Ponteach. And is this all? we must defend ourselves,
Supply the place of Numbers with our Courage,
And learn to conquer with our very Looks:
This is a Time that tries the Truth of Valour;
He shews his Courage that dares stem the Storm,
And live in spite of Violence and Fate.
Shall holy Perfidy and seeming Lyes .
Destroy our Purpose, sink us into Cowards?
    Tenesco. May your Hopes prosper! I'll excite the Troops
By your Example still to keep the Field.   *Exit.*
    Ponteach. 'Tis coming on. Thus Wave succeeds to Wave,
Till the Storm's spent, then all subsides again —
The Chiefs revolted: — My Design betray'd: —
May he that trusts a Christian meet the same!
They have no Faith, no Honesty, no God,
And cannot merit Confidence from Men.
Were I alone the boist'rous Tempest's Sport,
I'd quickly move my shatter'd trembling Bark,
And follow my departed Sons to Rest.
But my brave Countrymen, my Friends, my Subjects,
Demand my Care; I'll not desert the Helm,
Nor leave a dang'rous station in Distress;
Yes, I will live, in spite of Fate I'll live;
Was I not *Ponteach*, was I not a King,
Such Giant Mischiefs would not gather round me.
And since I'm *Ponteach*, since I am a King,
I'll shew myself Superior to them all;
I'll rise above this Hurricane of Fate,
And shew my Courage to the Gods themselves.

Enter Tenesco, *surprised and pausing.*

I am prepar'd, be not afraid to tell;
You cannot speak what *Ponteach* dare not hear.
    Tenesco. Our bravest Troops are slain, the rest pursu'd;
All is Disorder, Tumult, and Rebellion.
Those that remain insist on speedy Flight;

You must attend them, or be left alone
Unto the Fury of a conquering Foe,
Nor will they long expect your royal Pleasure.
    Ponteach. Will they desert their King in such an Hour,
When Pity might induce them to protect him?
Kings like the Gods are valued and ador'd,
When Men expect their Bounties in Return,
Place them in Want, destroy the giving Power,
All Sacrifices and Regards will cease.
Go, tell my Friends that I'll attend their Call.
                                (rising. Exit Tenesco.
I will not fear—but must obey my Stars: *(looking round.*
Ye fertile Fields and glad'ning Streams adieu;
Ye Fountains that have quench'd my scorching Thirst,
Ye Shades that hid the Sun-beams from my Head,
Ye Groves and Hills that yielded me the Chace,
Ye flow'ry Meads, and Banks, and bending Trees,
And thou proud Earth, made drunk with Royal Blood,
I am no more your Owner and your King.
But witness for me to your new base Lords,
That my unconquer'd Mind defies them still;
And though I fly, 'tis on the Wings of Hope.
Yes, I will hence where there's no *British* Foe,
And wait a Respite from this Storm of Woe;
Beget more Sons, fresh Troops collect and arm,
And other Schemes of future Greatness form;
Britons may boast, the Gods may have their Will,
Ponteach I am, and shall be *Ponteach* still.'   *(Exit.*

FINIS.

¹ The most severe blow to Pontiac's hopes was, of course, the successful defence of Detroit and Fort Pitt. His hopes were finally crushed by the receipt of a letter from M. Neyon, the French commander at Fort des Chartres, advising him to desist from further warfare, as peace had been concluded between France and Great Britain. However, unwilling to abandon entirely his project, he made an attempt to incite the tribes along the Mississippi to join in another effort. Being unsuccessful in this attempt, he finally made peace at Detroit, August 17, 1765. In 1769 he attended a drinking carousal at Cahokia, Illinois, where he was murdered by a Kaskaskia Indian. *Handbook of American Indians.*

ALSO FROM LEONAUR

AVAILABLE IN SOFTCOVER OR HARDCOVER WITH DUST JACKET

AFGHANISTAN: THE BELEAGUERED BRIGADE *by G. R. Gleig*—An Account of Sale's Brigade During the First Afghan War.

IN THE RANKS OF THE C. I. V *by Erskine Childers*—With the City Imperial Volunteer Battery (Honourable Artillery Company) in the Second Boer War.

THE BENGAL NATIVE ARMY *by F. G. Cardew*—An Invaluable Reference Resource.

THE 7TH (QUEEN'S OWN) HUSSARS: Volume 4—1688-1914 *by C. R. B. Barrett*—Uniforms, Equipment, Weapons, Traditions, the Services of Notable Officers and Men & the Appendices to All Volumes—Volume 4: 1688-1914.

THE SWORD OF THE CROWN *by Eric W. Sheppard*—A History of the British Army to 1914.

THE 7TH (QUEEN'S OWN) HUSSARS: Volume 3—1818-1914 *by C. R. B. Barrett*—On Campaign During the Canadian Rebellion, the Indian Mutiny, the Sudan, Matabeleland, Mashonaland and the Boer War Volume 3: 1818-1914.

THE KHARTOUM CAMPAIGN *by Bennet Burleigh*—A Special Correspondent's View of the Reconquest of the Sudan by British and Egyptian Forces under Kitchener—1898.

EL PUCHERO *by Richard McSherry*—The Letters of a Surgeon of Volunteers During Scott's Campaign of the American-Mexican War 1847-1848.

RIFLEMAN SAHIB *by E. Maude*—The Recollections of an Officer of the Bombay Rifles During the Southern Mahratta Campaign, Second Sikh War, Persian Campaign and Indian Mutiny.

THE KING'S HUSSAR *by Edwin Mole*—The Recollections of a 14th (King's) Hussar During the Victorian Era.

JOHN COMPANY'S CAVALRYMAN *by William Johnson*—The Experiences of a British Soldier in the Crimea, the Persian Campaign and the Indian Mutiny.

COLENSO & DURNFORD'S ZULU WAR *by Frances E. Colenso & Edward Durnford*—The first and possibly the most important history of the Zulu War.

U. S. DRAGOON *by Samuel E. Chamberlain*—Experiences in the Mexican War 1846-48 and on the South Western Frontier.

LEONAUR

ALSO FROM LEONAUR
AVAILABLE IN SOFTCOVER OR HARDCOVER WITH DUST JACKET

THE 2ND MAORI WAR: 1860-1861 *by Robert Carey*—The Second Maori War, or First Taranaki War, one more bloody instalment of the conflicts between European settlers and the indigenous Maori people.

A JOURNAL OF THE SECOND SIKH WAR *by Daniel A. Sandford*—The Experiences of an Ensign of the 2nd Bengal European Regiment During the Campaign in the Punjab, India, 1848-49.

THE LIGHT INFANTRY OFFICER *by John H. Cooke*—The Experiences of an Officer of the 43rd Light Infantry in America During the War of 1812.

BUSHVELDT CARBINEERS *by George Witton*—The War Against the Boers in South Africa and the 'Breaker' Morant Incident.

LAKE'S CAMPAIGNS IN INDIA *by Hugh Pearse*—The Second Anglo Maratha War, 1803-1807.

BRITAIN IN AFGHANISTAN 1: THE FIRST AFGHAN WAR 1839-42 *by Archibald Forbes*—From invasion to destruction-a British military disaster.

BRITAIN IN AFGHANISTAN 2: THE SECOND AFGHAN WAR 1878-80 *by Archibald Forbes*—This is the history of the Second Afghan War-another episode of British military history typified by savagery, massacre, siege and battles.

UP AMONG THE PANDIES *by Vivian Dering Majendie*—Experiences of a British Officer on Campaign During the Indian Mutiny, 1857-1858.

MUTINY: 1857 *by James Humphries*—Authentic Voices from the Indian Mutiny-First Hand Accounts of Battles, Sieges and Personal Hardships.

BLOW THE BUGLE, DRAW THE SWORD *by W. H. G. Kingston*—The Wars, Campaigns, Regiments and Soldiers of the British & Indian Armies During the Victorian Era, 1839-1898.

WAR BEYOND THE DRAGON PAGODA *by Major J. J. Snodgrass*—A Personal Narrative of the First Anglo-Burmese War 1824 - 1826.

THE HERO OF ALIWAL *by James Humphries*—The Campaigns of Sir Harry Smith in India, 1843-1846, During the Gwalior War & the First Sikh War.

ALL FOR A SHILLING A DAY *by Donald F. Featherstone*—The story of H.M. 16th, the Queen's Lancers During the first Sikh War 1845-1846.

LEONAUR

ALSO FROM LEONAUR
AVAILABLE IN SOFTCOVER OR HARDCOVER WITH DUST JACKET

AT THEM WITH THE BAYONET *by Donald F. Featherstone*—The first Anglo-Sikh War 1845-1846.

STEPHEN CRANE'S BATTLES *by Stephen Crane*—Nine Decisive Battles Recounted by the Author of 'The Red Badge of Courage'.

THE GURKHA WAR *by H. T. Prinsep*—The Anglo-Nepalese Conflict in North East India 1814-1816.

FIRE & BLOOD *by G. R. Gleig*—The burning of Washington & the battle of New Orleans, 1814, through the eyes of a young British soldier.

SOUND ADVANCE! *by Joseph Anderson*—Experiences of an officer of HM 50th regiment in Australia, Burma & the Gwalior war.

THE CAMPAIGN OF THE INDUS *by Thomas Holdsworth*—Experiences of a British Officer of the 2nd (Queen's Royal) Regiment in the Campaign to Place Shah Shuja on the Throne of Afghanistan 1838 - 1840.

WITH THE MADRAS EUROPEAN REGIMENT IN BURMA *by John Butler*—The Experiences of an Officer of the Honourable East India Company's Army During the First Anglo-Burmese War 1824 - 1826.

IN ZULULAND WITH THE BRITISH ARMY *by Charles L. Norris-Newman*—The Anglo-Zulu war of 1879 through the first-hand experiences of a special correspondent.

BESIEGED IN LUCKNOW *by Martin Richard Gubbins*—The first Anglo-Sikh War 1845-1846.

A TIGER ON HORSEBACK *by L. March Phillips*—The Experiences of a Trooper & Officer of Rimington's Guides - The Tigers - during the Anglo-Boer war 1899 - 1902.

SEPOYS, SIEGE & STORM *by Charles John Griffiths*—The Experiences of a young officer of H.M.'s 61st Regiment at Ferozepore, Delhi ridge and at the fall of Delhi during the Indian mutiny 1857.

CAMPAIGNING IN ZULULAND *by W. E. Montague*—Experiences on campaign during the Zulu war of 1879 with the 94th Regiment.

THE STORY OF THE GUIDES *by G.J. Younghusband*—The Exploits of the Soldiers of the famous Indian Army Regiment from the northwest frontier 1847 - 1900.

ALSO FROM LEONAUR

ALSO FROM LEONAUR

AVAILABLE IN SOFTCOVER OR HARDCOVER WITH DUST JACKET

COLBORNE: A SINGULAR TALENT FOR WAR *by John Colborne*—The Napoleonic Wars Career of One of Wellington's Most Highly Valued Officers in Egypt, Holland, Italy, the Peninsula and at Waterloo.

NAPOLEON'S RUSSIAN CAMPAIGN *by Philippe Henri de Segur*—The Invasion, Battles and Retreat by an Aide-de-Camp on the Emperor's Staff.

WITH THE LIGHT DIVISION *by John H. Cooke*—The Experiences of an Officer of the 43rd Light Infantry in the Peninsula and South of France During the Napoleonic Wars.

WELLINGTON AND THE PYRENEES CAMPAIGN VOLUME I: FROM VITORIA TO THE BIDASSOA *by F. C. Beatson*—The final phase of the campaign in the Iberian Peninsula.

WELLINGTON AND THE INVASION OF FRANCE VOLUME II: THE BIDASSOA TO THE BATTLE OF THE NIVELLE *by F. C. Beatson*—The final phase of the campaign in the Iberian Peninsula.

WELLINGTON AND THE FALL OF FRANCE VOLUME III: THE GAVES AND THE BATTLE OF ORTHEZ *by F. C. Beatson*—The final phase of the campaign in the Iberian Peninsula.

NAPOLEON'S IMPERIAL GUARD: FROM MARENGO TO WATERLOO *by J. T. Headley*—The story of Napoleon's Imperial Guard and the men who commanded them.

BATTLES & SIEGES OF THE PENINSULAR WAR *by W. H. Fitchett*—Corunna, Busaco, Albuera, Ciudad Rodrigo, Badajos, Salamanca, San Sebastian & Others.

SERGEANT GUILLEMARD: THE MAN WHO SHOT NELSON? *by Robert Guillemard*—A Soldier of the Infantry of the French Army of Napoleon on Campaign Throughout Europe.

WITH THE GUARDS ACROSS THE PYRENEES *by Robert Batty*—The Experiences of a British Officer of Wellington's Army During the Battles for the Fall of Napoleonic France, 1813 .

A STAFF OFFICER IN THE PENINSULA *by E. W. Buckham*—An Officer of the British Staff Corps Cavalry During the Peninsula Campaign of the Napoleonic Wars.

THE LEIPZIG CAMPAIGN: 1813—NAPOLEON AND THE "BATTLE OF THE NATIONS" *by F. N. Maude*—Colonel Maude's analysis of Napoleon's campaign of 1813 around Leipzig.

LEONAUR

ALSO FROM LEONAUR
AVAILABLE IN SOFTCOVER OR HARDCOVER WITH DUST JACKET

BUGEAUD: A PACK WITH A BATON *by Thomas Robert Bugeaud*—The Early Campaigns of a Soldier of Napoleon's Army Who Would Become a Marshal of France.

WATERLOO RECOLLECTIONS *by Frederick Llewellyn*—Rare First Hand Accounts, Letters, Reports and Retellings from the Campaign of 1815.

SERGEANT NICOL *by Daniel Nicol*—The Experiences of a Gordon Highlander During the Napoleonic Wars in Egypt, the Peninsula and France.

THE JENA CAMPAIGN: 1806 *by F. N. Maude*—The Twin Battles of Jena & Auerstadt Between Napoleon's French and the Prussian Army.

PRIVATE O'NEIL *by Charles O'Neil*—The recollections of an Irish Rogue of H. M. 28th Regt.—The Slashers—during the Peninsula & Waterloo campaigns of the Napoleonic war.

ROYAL HIGHLANDER *by James Anton*—A soldier of H.M 42nd (Royal) Highlanders during the Peninsular, South of France & Waterloo Campaigns of the Napoleonic Wars.

CAPTAIN BLAZE *by Elzéar Blaze*—Life in Napoleons Army.

LEJEUNE VOLUME 1 *by Louis-François Lejeune*—The Napoleonic Wars through the Experiences of an Officer on Berthier's Staff.

LEJEUNE VOLUME 2 *by Louis-François Lejeune*—The Napoleonic Wars through the Experiences of an Officer on Berthier's Staff.

CAPTAIN COIGNET *by Jean-Roch Coignet*—A Soldier of Napoleon's Imperial Guard from the Italian Campaign to Russia and Waterloo.

FUSILIER COOPER *by John S. Cooper*—Experiences in the 7th (Royal) Fusiliers During the Peninsular Campaign of the Napoleonic Wars and the American Campaign to New Orleans.

FIGHTING NAPOLEON'S EMPIRE *by Joseph Anderson*—The Campaigns of a British Infantryman in Italy, Egypt, the Peninsular & the West Indies During the Napoleonic Wars.

CHASSEUR BARRES *by Jean-Baptiste Barres*—The experiences of a French Infantryman of the Imperial Guard at Austerlitz, Jena, Eylau, Friedland, in the Peninsular, Lutzen, Bautzen, Zinnwald and Hanau during the Napoleonic Wars.

LEONAUR

ALSO FROM LEONAUR
AVAILABLE IN SOFTCOVER OR HARDCOVER WITH DUST JACKET

CAPTAIN COIGNET *by Jean-Roch Coignet*—A Soldier of Napoleon's Imperial Guard from the Italian Campaign to Russia and Waterloo.

HUSSAR ROCCA *by Albert Jean Michel de Rocca*—A French cavalry officer's experiences of the Napoleonic Wars and his views on the Peninsular Campaigns against the Spanish, British And Guerilla Armies.

MARINES TO 95TH (RIFLES) *by Thomas Fernyhough*—The military experiences of Robert Fernyhough during the Napoleonic Wars.

LIGHT BOB *by Robert Blakeney*—The experiences of a young officer in H.M 28th & 36th regiments of the British Infantry during the Peninsular Campaign of the Napoleonic Wars 1804 - 1814.

WITH WELLINGTON'S LIGHT CAVALRY *by William Tomkinson*—The Experiences of an officer of the 16th Light Dragoons in the Peninsular and Waterloo campaigns of the Napoleonic Wars.

SERGEANT BOURGOGNE *by Adrien Bourgogne*—With Napoleon's Imperial Guard in the Russian Campaign and on the Retreat from Moscow 1812 - 13.

SURTEES OF THE 95TH (RIFLES) *by William Surtees*—A Soldier of the 95th (Rifles) in the Peninsular campaign of the Napoleonic Wars.

SWORDS OF HONOUR *by Henry Newbolt & Stanley L. Wood*—The Careers of Six Outstanding Officers from the Napoleonic Wars, the Wars for India and the American Civil War.

ENSIGN BELL IN THE PENINSULAR WAR *by George Bell*—The Experiences of a young British Soldier of the 34th Regiment 'The Cumberland Gentlemen' in the Napoleonic wars.

HUSSAR IN WINTER *by Alexander Gordon*—A British Cavalry Officer during the retreat to Corunna in the Peninsular campaign of the Napoleonic Wars.

THE COMPLEAT RIFLEMAN HARRIS *by Benjamin Harris as told to and transcribed by Captain Henry Curling, 52nd Regt. of Foot*—The adventures of a soldier of the 95th (Rifles) during the Peninsular Campaign of the Napoleonic Wars.

THE ADVENTURES OF A LIGHT DRAGOON *by George Farmer & G.R. Gleig*—A cavalryman during the Peninsular & Waterloo Campaigns, in captivity & at the siege of Bhurtpore, India.

LEONAUR

ALSO FROM LEONAUR

AVAILABLE IN SOFTCOVER OR HARDCOVER WITH DUST JACKET

THE LIFE OF THE REAL BRIGADIER GERARD VOLUME 1—THE YOUNG HUSSAR 1782-1807 *by Jean-Baptiste De Marbot*—A French Cavalryman Of the Napoleonic Wars at Marengo, Austerlitz, Jena, Eylau & Friedland.

THE LIFE OF THE REAL BRIGADIER GERARD VOLUME 2—IMPERIAL AIDE-DE-CAMP 1807-1811 *by Jean-Baptiste De Marbot*—A French Cavalryman of the Napoleonic Wars at Saragossa, Landshut, Eckmuhl, Ratisbon, Aspern-Essling, Wagram, Busaco & Torres Vedras.

THE LIFE OF THE REAL BRIGADIER GERARD VOLUME 3—COLONEL OF CHASSEURS 1811-1815 *by Jean-Baptiste De Marbot*—A French Cavalryman in the retreat from Moscow, Lutzen, Bautzen, Katzbach, Leipzig, Hanau & Waterloo.

THE INDIAN WAR OF 1864 *by Eugene Ware*—The Experiences of a Young Officer of the 7th Iowa Cavalry on the Western Frontier During the Civil War.

THE MARCH OF DESTINY *by Charles E. Young & V. Devinny*—Dangers of the Trail in 1865 by Charles E. Young & The Story of a Pioneer by V. Devinny, two Accounts of Early Emigrants to Colorado.

CROSSING THE PLAINS *by William Audley Maxwell*—A First Hand Narrative of the Early Pioneer Trail to California in 1857.

CHIEF OF SCOUTS *by William F. Drannan*—A Pilot to Emigrant and Government Trains, Across the Plains of the Western Frontier.

THIRTY-ONE YEARS ON THE PLAINS AND IN THE MOUNTAINS *by William F. Drannan*—William Drannan was born to be a pioneer, hunter, trapper and wagon train guide during the momentous days of the Great American West.

THE INDIAN WARS VOLUNTEER *by William Thompson*—Recollections of the Conflict Against the Snakes, Shoshone, Bannocks, Modocs and Other Native Tribes of the American North West.

THE 4TH TENNESSEE CAVALRY *by George B. Guild*—The Services of Smith's Regiment of Confederate Cavalry by One of its Officers.

COLONEL WORTHINGTON'S SHILOH *by T. Worthington*—The Tennessee Campaign, 1862, by an Officer of the Ohio Volunteers.

FOUR YEARS IN THE SADDLE *by W. L. Curry*—The History of the First Regiment Ohio Volunteer Cavalry in the American Civil War.

www.ingramcontent.com/pod-product-compliance
Lightning Source LLC
Chambersburg PA
CBHW032042080426
42733CB00006B/164